AF412215

7,100 ISLANDS   THE PHILIPPINES

BY THE SAME AUTHOR

*Travel and Fiction*

Tropical Quest (8th impression); Foyles Book
    Club choice; Adventurers Book Club
    choice
Eastern Quest (Foyles Book Club choice)
Wild Africa's Silent Call (Foreword by
    Peter Scott); Foyles Book Club choice
Let's Visit Kenya, Tanzania, Uganda
    (for the nine-to-eleven-year-old reader)
Safari with a Camera
Safari
The Motorist's Holiday Guide to Europe
The Photographer's Holiday Guide to Europe
A Guide to Germany (4th impression).
    American edition titled *Germany*
A Guide to Switzerland
Continental Autocamping
Townsend's Caribbean Guide (Foreword
    by His Excellency Donald C. Granado)
Townsend's Guide to East Africa and its
    National Parks
A Night in Trinidad (B.B.C. Radio)
A Question of Psychology (B.B.C. Radio)
Tag Along Tiger (B.B.C. Radio)
The Long Road
The Green Drum
80,000 Mile Safari
Capricious Circles
Islands of the World (A.B.C. Television)

*Photographic*

Underwater Photography (2nd impression,
    completely revised and reset
Your A-Z Guide to Better Movies
    (also in paperback)
The Practical Guide to Holiday and
    Family Movies
How to Use 16 mm (also in paperback)
Filming in Colour (also in paperback)
Cine Photography (3rd impression)
Film in Research (5th impression)
Photographic Processing (2nd impression)
Guide to Movie Making
Sporting Photography
A Complete Guide to Home Movies
Glossary of Terms in Photography and
    Cinematography (four languages)
Glossary of Terms in Advertising and
    Public Relations (four languages)
Holiday Photography in Colour
Better Homes and Gardens—Photography
    for your Family (editor); American edition
Photography in Colour (B.B.C. Radio and
    Television)
Industrial Photography
Advertising Photography

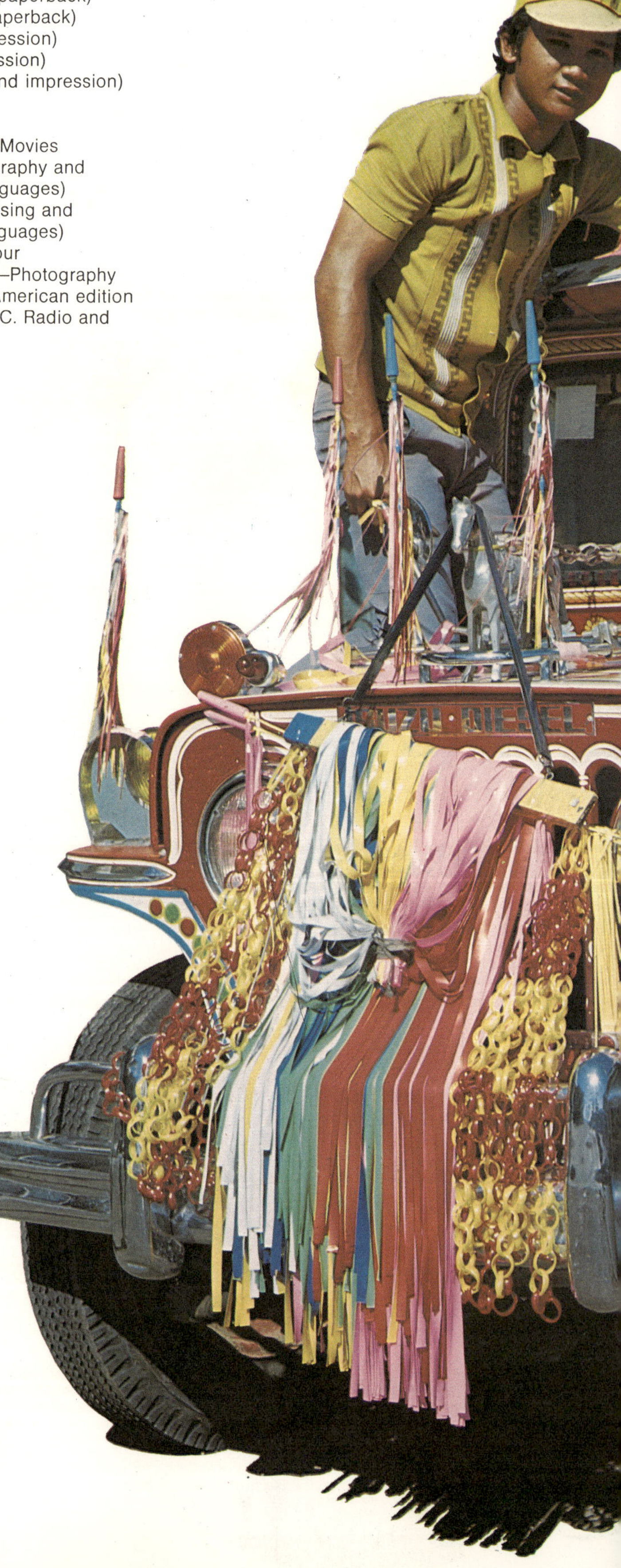

# 7,100 ISLANDS
# THE PHILIPPINES

## DEREK TOWNSEND

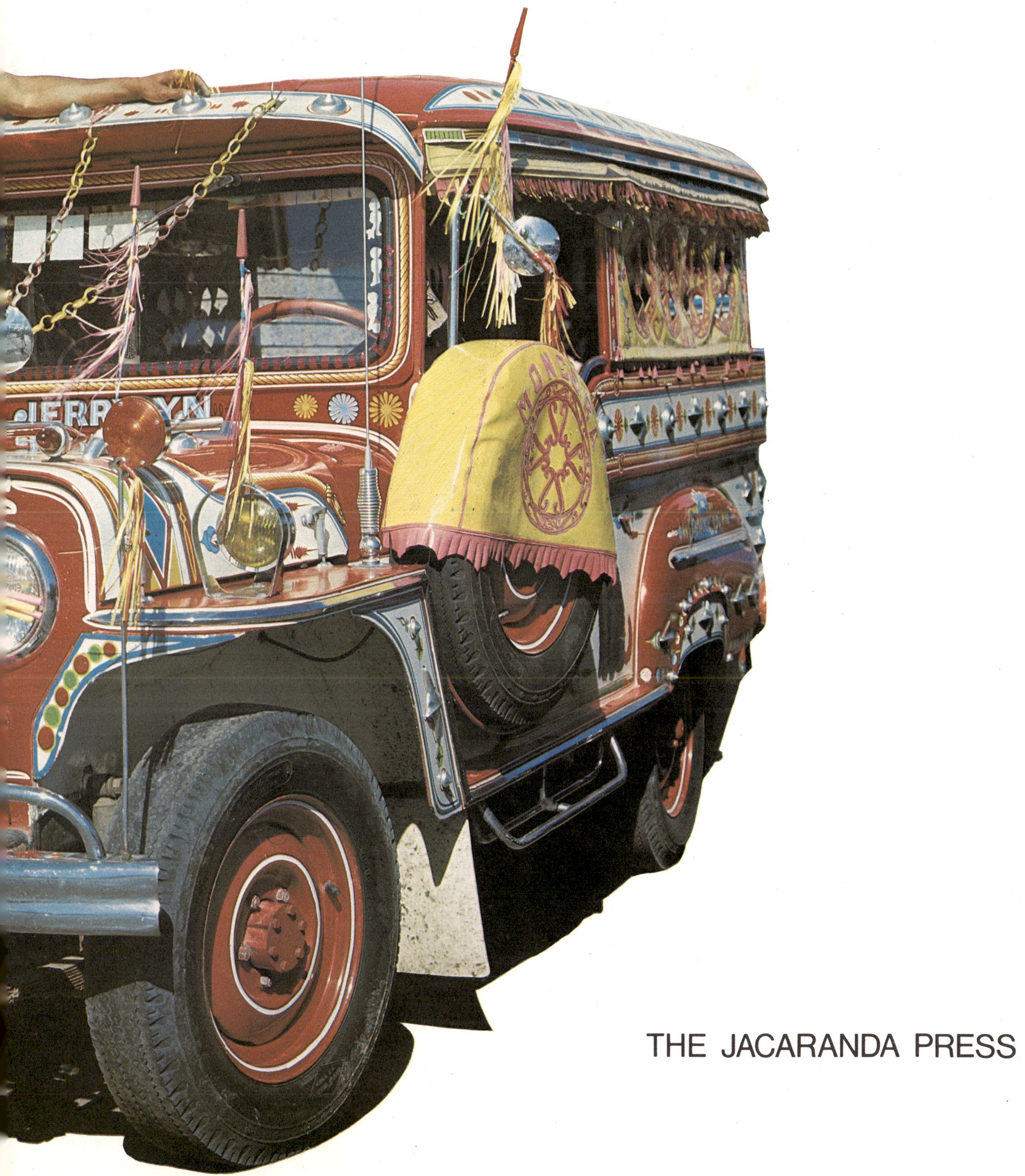

THE JACARANDA PRESS

First published 1973 by
JACARANDA PRESS PTY LTD
46 Douglas Street, Milton, Q.
32 Church Street, Ryde, N.S.W.
37 Little Bourke Street, Melbourne, Vic.
142 Colin Street, West Perth, W.A.
154 Marion Road, West Richmond, S.A.
57 France Street, Auckland, N.Z.
P.O. Box 3395, Port Moresby, P.N.G.
122 Regents Park Road, London NW1
70A Greenleaf Road, Singapore 10
P.O. Box 239, Makati, Rizal, Philippines

Typesetting by Savage & Co. Pty Ltd

Printed in Singapore

© Derek Townsend 1973

National Library of Australia
Card Number and ISBN 0 7016 0608 8

All rights reserved. No part of this publication
may be reproduced, stored in a retrieval system,
or transmitted in any form or by any means,
electronic, mechanical, photocopying, recording,
or otherwise, without the prior permission of
the publisher.

Text and photographs by Derek Townsend
Designed by Stuart Harrison

*Front Jacket:* A ''psychedelic'' jeepney—
it is the cheapest form of transport and
unique to the Philippines.

*Back Jacket:* Nelia Sancho, a beautiful
Filipino who was crowned Queen of the
Pacific.

A souvenir and handicraft shop that is ▷
typical of the mountain provinces.

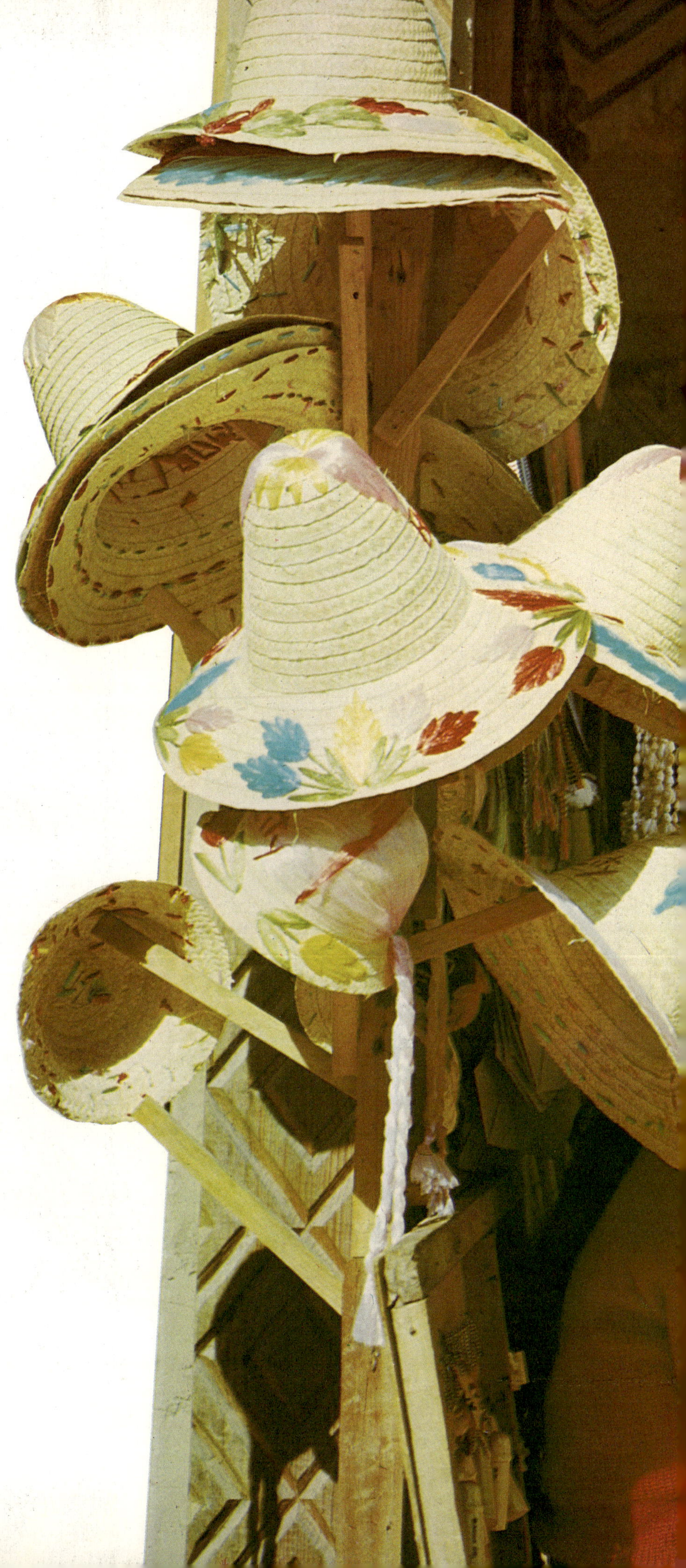

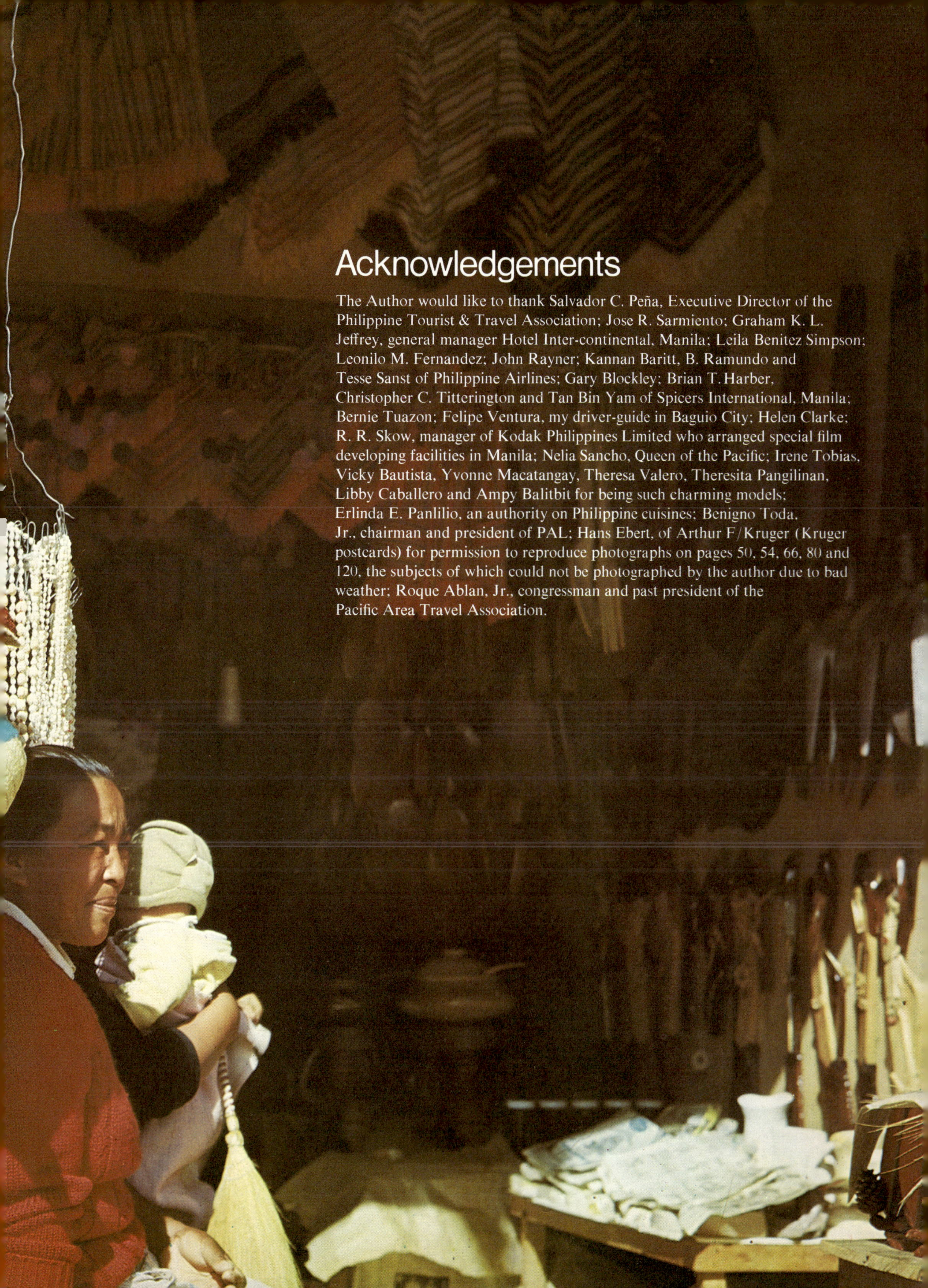

# Acknowledgements

The Author would like to thank Salvador C. Peña, Executive Director of the Philippine Tourist & Travel Association; Jose R. Sarmiento; Graham K. L. Jeffrey, general manager Hotel Inter-continental, Manila; Leila Benitez Simpson; Leonilo M. Fernandez; John Rayner; Kannan Baritt, B. Ramundo and Tesse Sanst of Philippine Airlines; Gary Blockley; Brian T. Harber, Christopher C. Titterington and Tan Bin Yam of Spicers International, Manila; Bernie Tuazon; Felipe Ventura, my driver-guide in Baguio City; Helen Clarke; R. R. Skow, manager of Kodak Philippines Limited who arranged special film developing facilities in Manila; Nelia Sancho, Queen of the Pacific; Irene Tobias, Vicky Bautista, Yvonne Macatangay, Theresa Valero, Theresita Pangilinan, Libby Caballero and Ampy Balitbit for being such charming models; Erlinda E. Panlilio, an authority on Philippine cuisines; Benigno Toda, Jr., chairman and president of PAL; Hans Ebert, of Arthur F/Kruger (Kruger postcards) for permission to reproduce photographs on pages 50, 54, 66, 80 and 120, the subjects of which could not be photographed by the author due to bad weather; Roque Ablan, Jr., congressman and past president of the Pacific Area Travel Association.

# Author's Note

Many countries and their peoples have been depicted in books that are mainly
composed of photographs.  Yet, for me, even the best of these publications
seem to lack complete communication.  One page might feature a well
composed long shot of Hong Kong's Aberdeen harbour tightly packed with
fishing junks—but, who are those figures on the left?  Children?  What are they
doing on deck?  The next page shows neon signs in close-up, and the one after
an aerial view of Kowloon on a sunny day.  Aberdeen harbour has gone, neon
signs blaze in some obscure street or alley, and abruptly we are 3,000 feet above
Hong Kong.  These pictures have no continuity and simply flash by, doing
little to involve the reader/viewer.

In this book, by utilizing my experience of movie production and still
photography, I have tried to capture the best of both worlds.  Wherever
possible, I have taken sequence pictures that "open-up" a scene, each picture
being an extension of the preceding shot.  I have employed movie film
techniques—first a long shot to establish the location, then a medium or
medium close shot to show the main subject(s) in detail; then a close-up, or the
occasional big close-up, to explore one special aspect or feature.  (In the film
world, these categories or "types of shot" are referred to by the initials
LS, MS, MCS, CU and BCU.)  Finally, the scene is further explored by shots
taken from different angles and points-of-view.

Using this technique in a book, I have found the involvement to be much
greater.  Through such photographs, readers "travel" around a particular
country with an ever-increasing appreciation of its peoples and culture . . .
I hope you will do the same.

To facilitate this process, the captions, generally, are more informative
than usual.

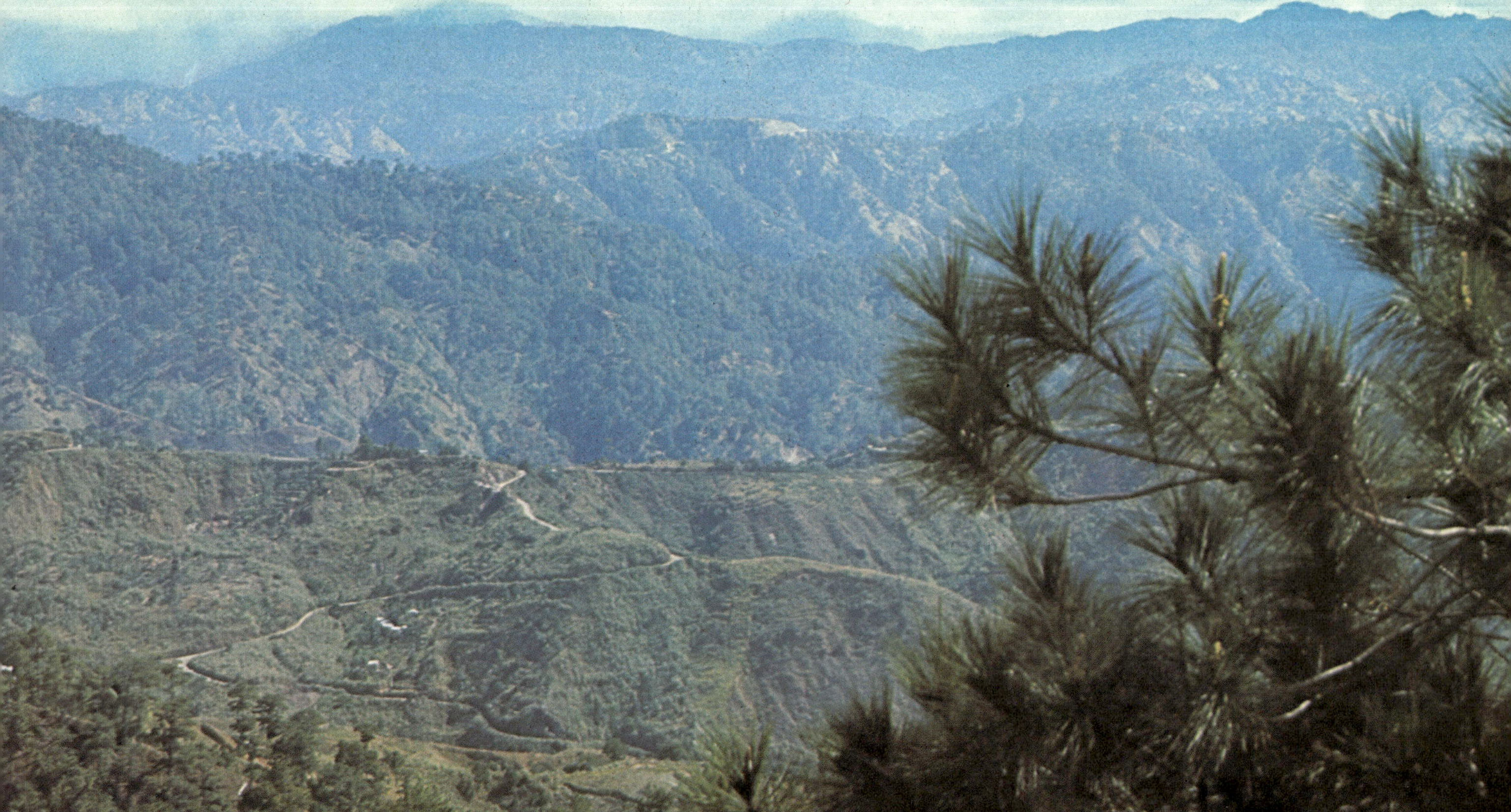

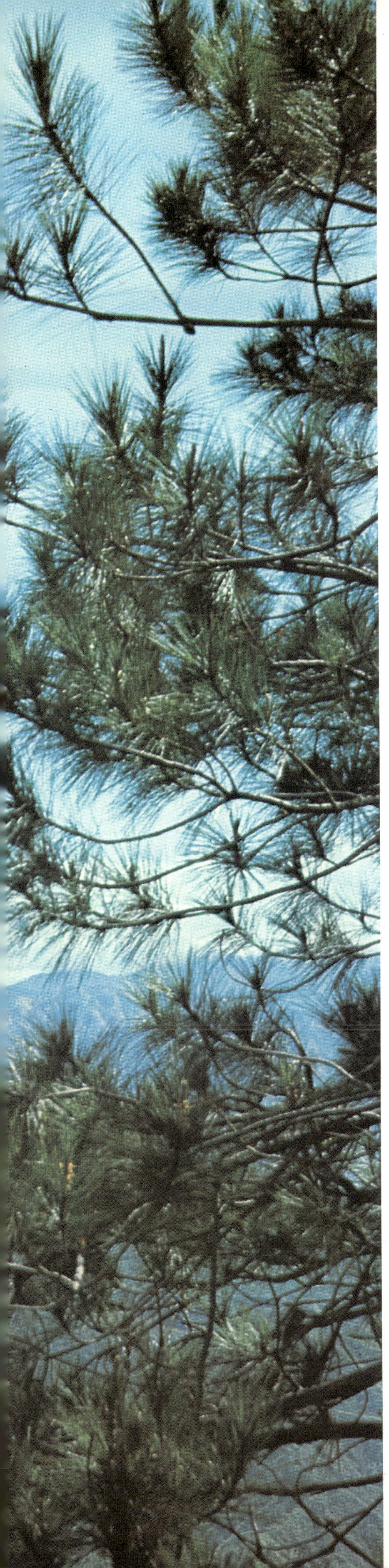

# Contents


Introduction   15

More Than 7,100 Islands   23

*The Gateway   23*
*The Ravages of War   39*
*Risen from the Ashes   39*
*Houses for the Rich and the Poor   43*
*Heritage from the War—a lingua franca   44*
*A Culture before Christ   44*
*Spanish Rule   51*
*The Filipinos   53*
*Nights Alive   69*
*Gourmet's Potpourri   79*
*To Pagsanjan Falls   83*

Corregidor Island   93

To Baguio and Banaue   103

Round and About   105

*Further Afield   121*

National Parks   132

Golf Courses   134

Notes on Photographic Equipment   136

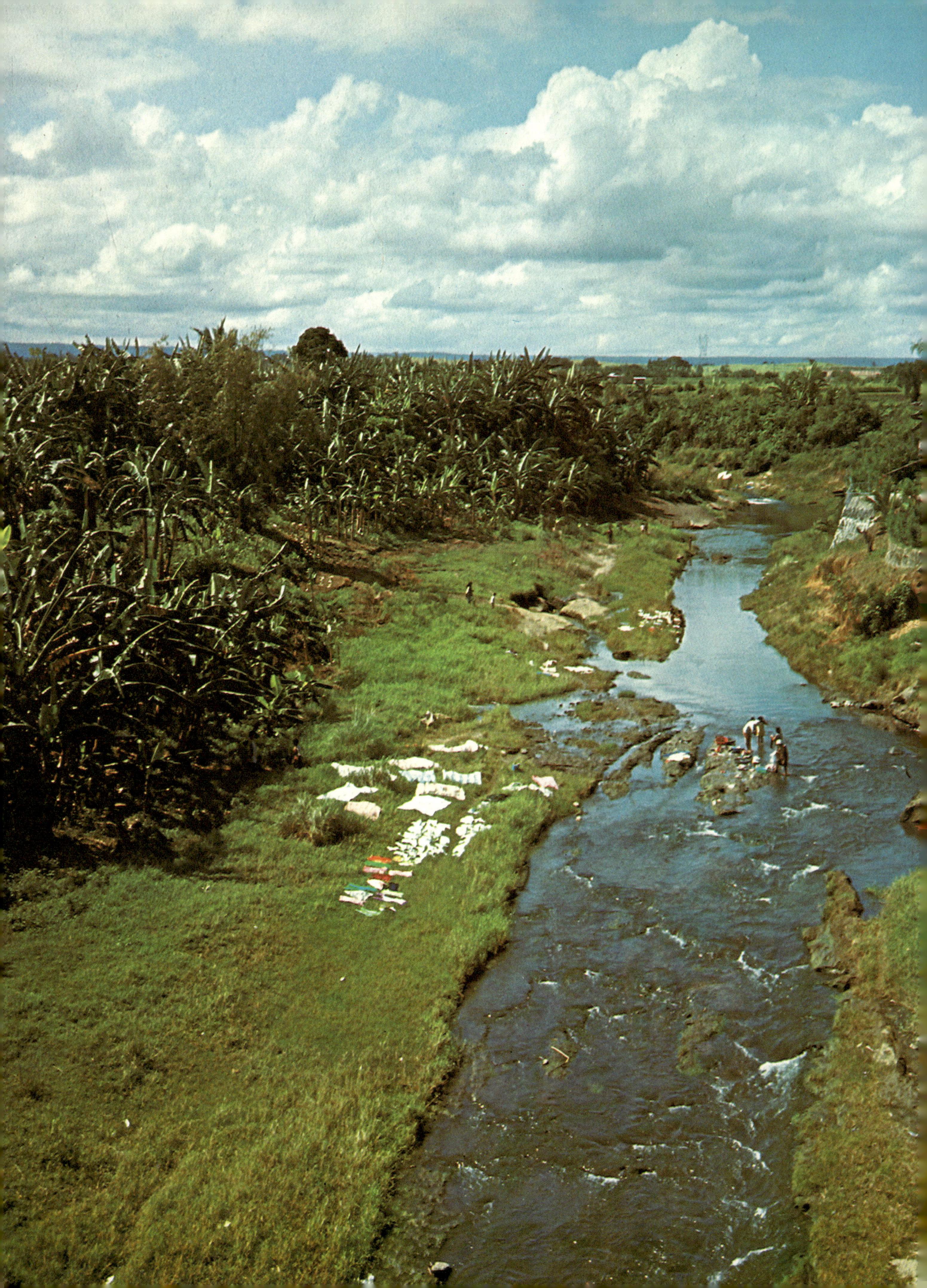

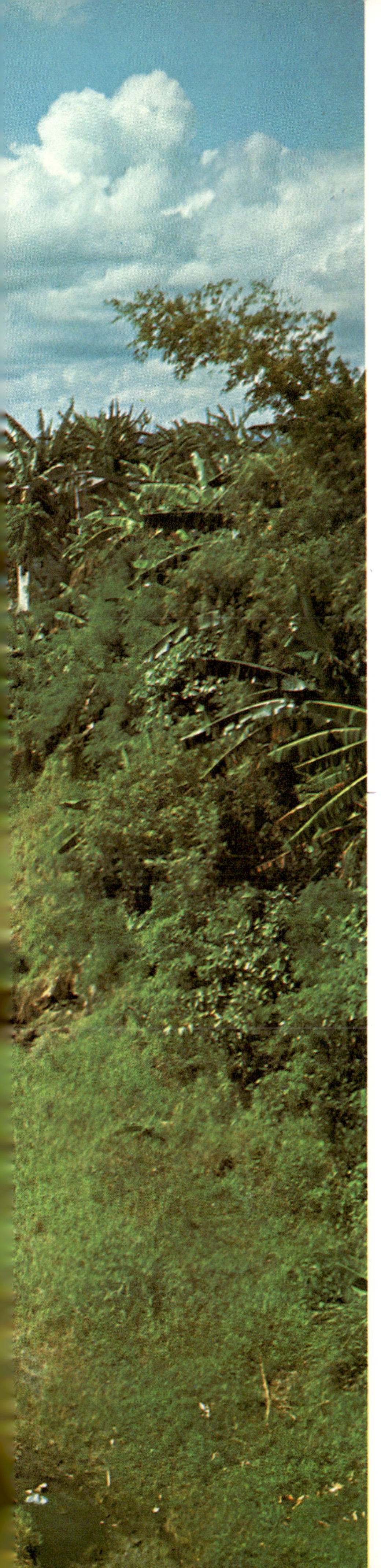

The Philippines is a picturesque land of
many rivers—some more than 200 miles
long. For the village folk, the waterways
are the hub of their lives. While the men
work in the fields, the women and children
flock to the river to talk, to play, and to
wash. Poverty and wealth flourish side by
side along the river banks: lissom young
women in silk dresses—others in clothes
rotted by the sun. But all these river
bankers are gay and friendly, enjoying the
leisurely rhythm of their outdoor existence.

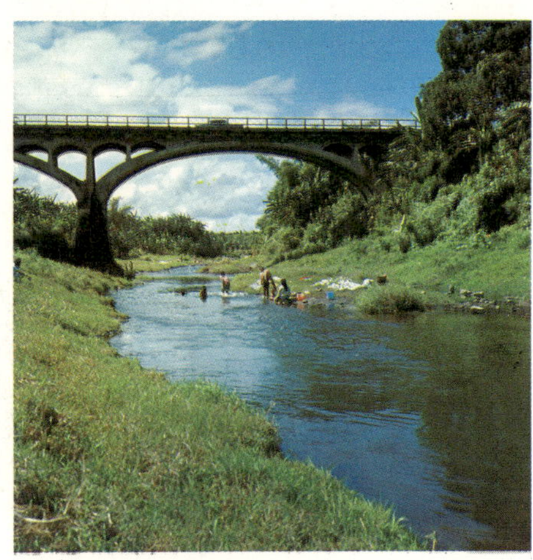

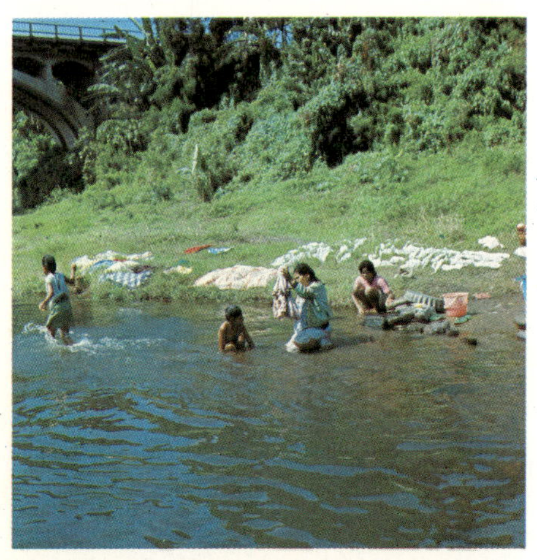

Naked children, looking cheerful and healthy, tumble about in the water. Even though the population grows yearly by four per cent, Filipinos have all the living space they need. These youngsters will never experience overcrowded conditions like those in Hong Kong where each child has less than 20 square feet of space for playing and growing-up.

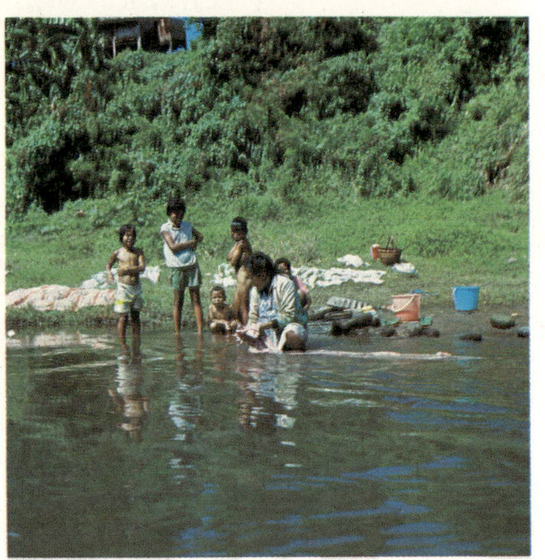

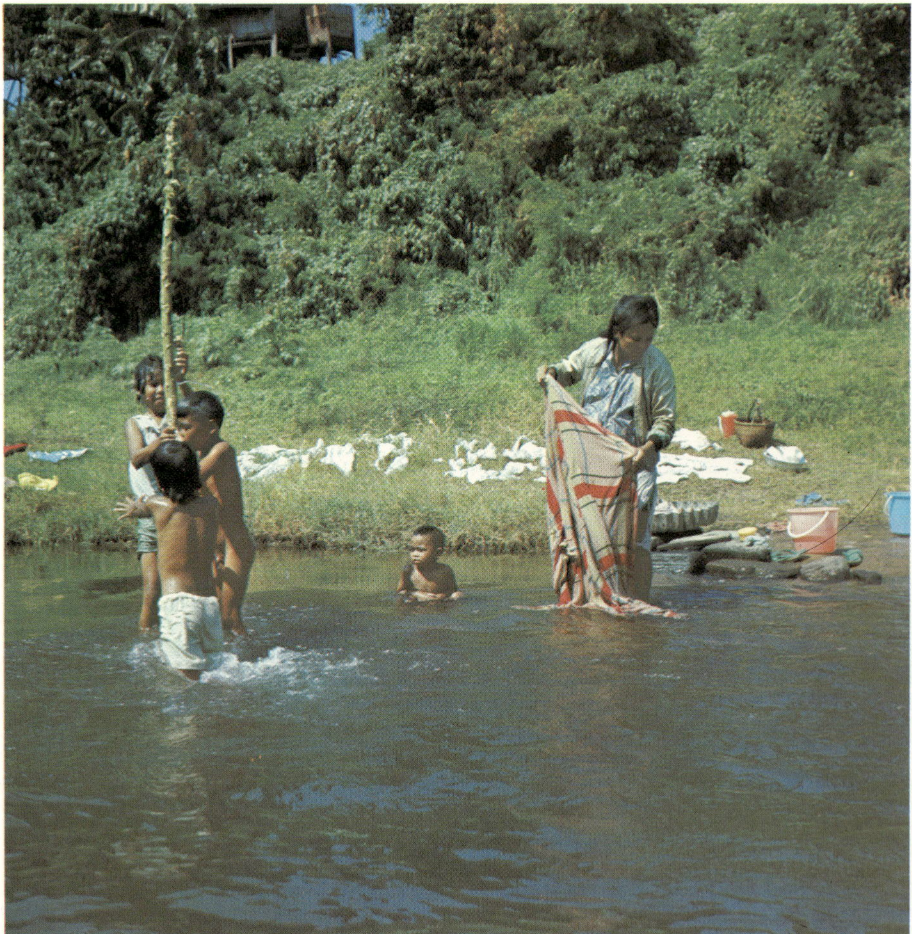

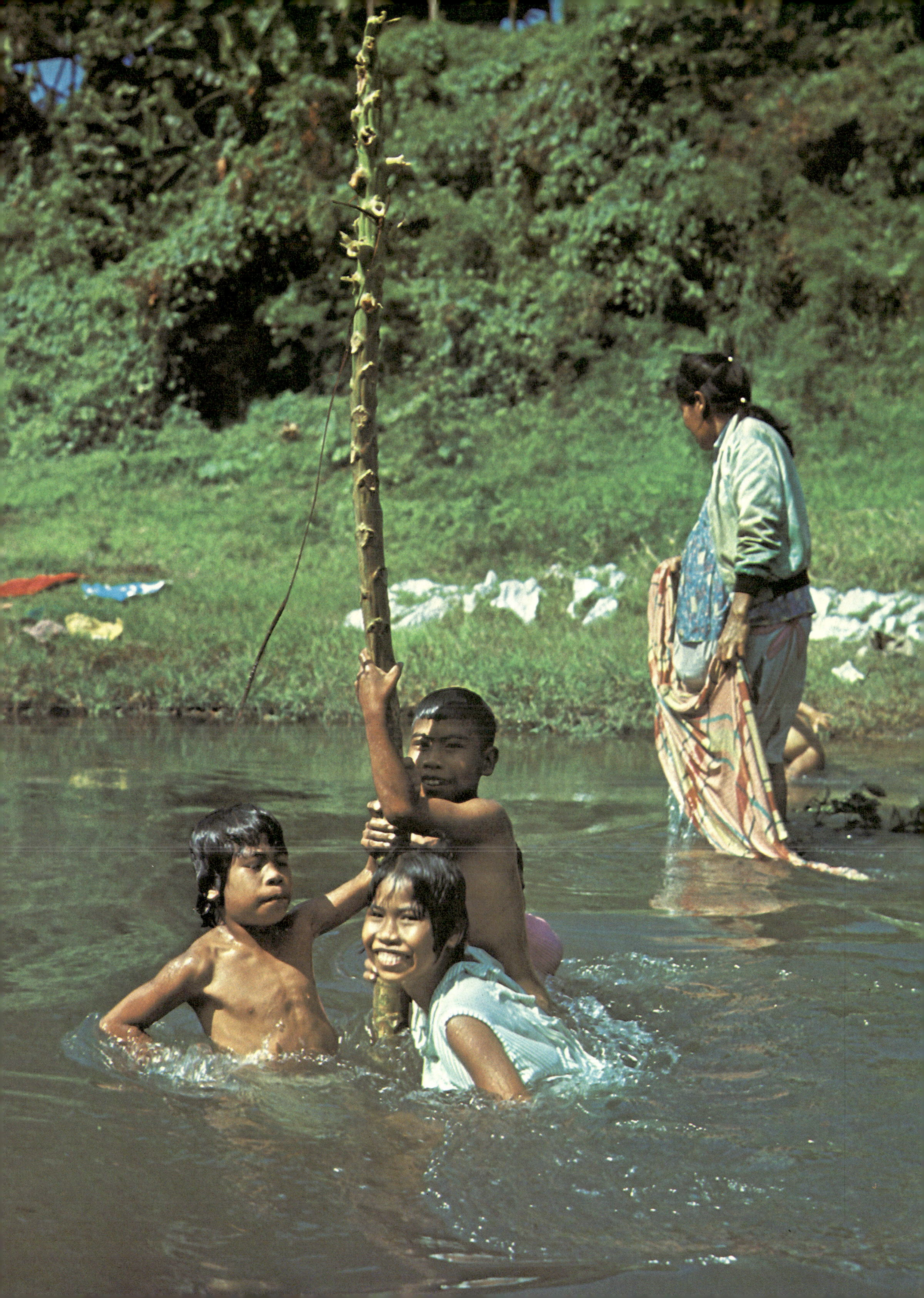

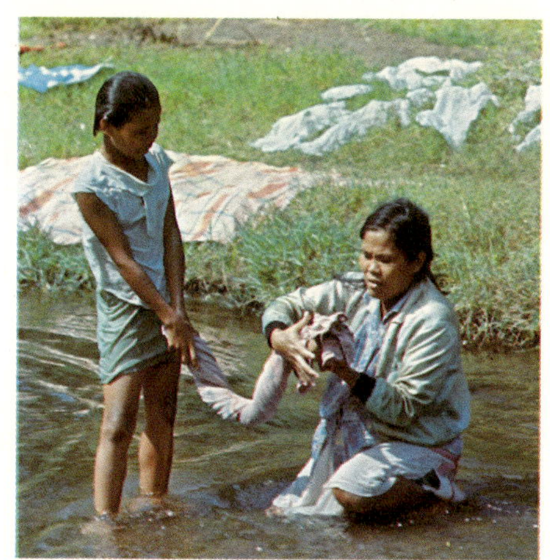

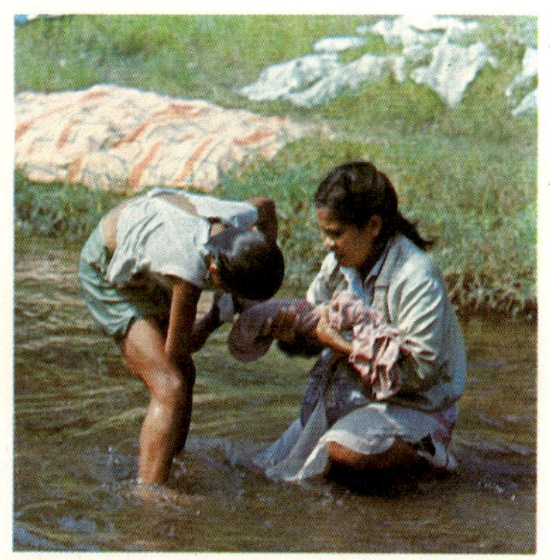

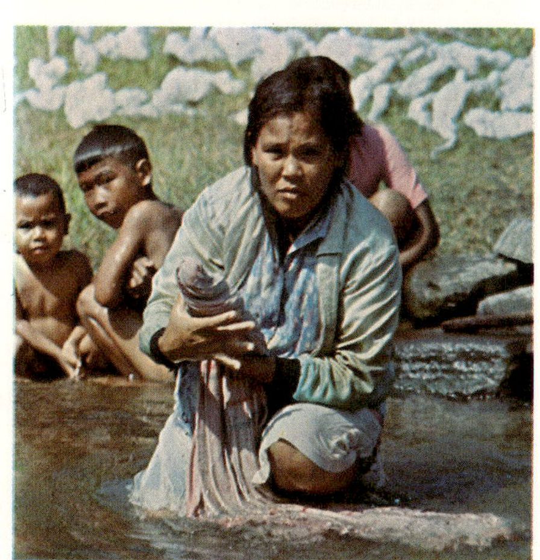

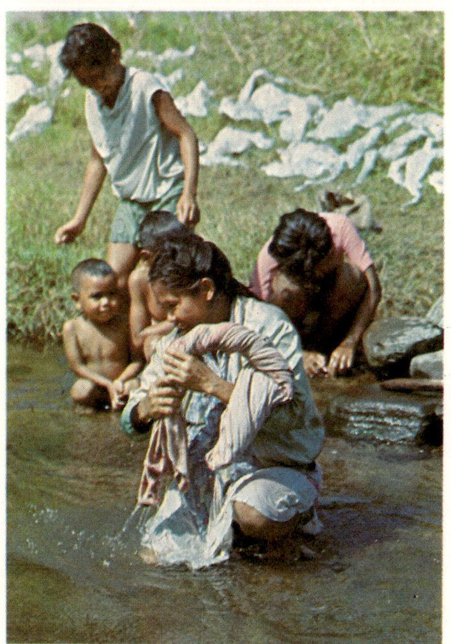

Laundry is done in the traditional manner.
Clothes are either beaten with a piece of
wood or sloshed against rocks, the impact
producing a sharp note like the crack of a
rifle.  After this drastic treatment they are
finally wrung-out by vigorous twisting that
often causes disintegration!

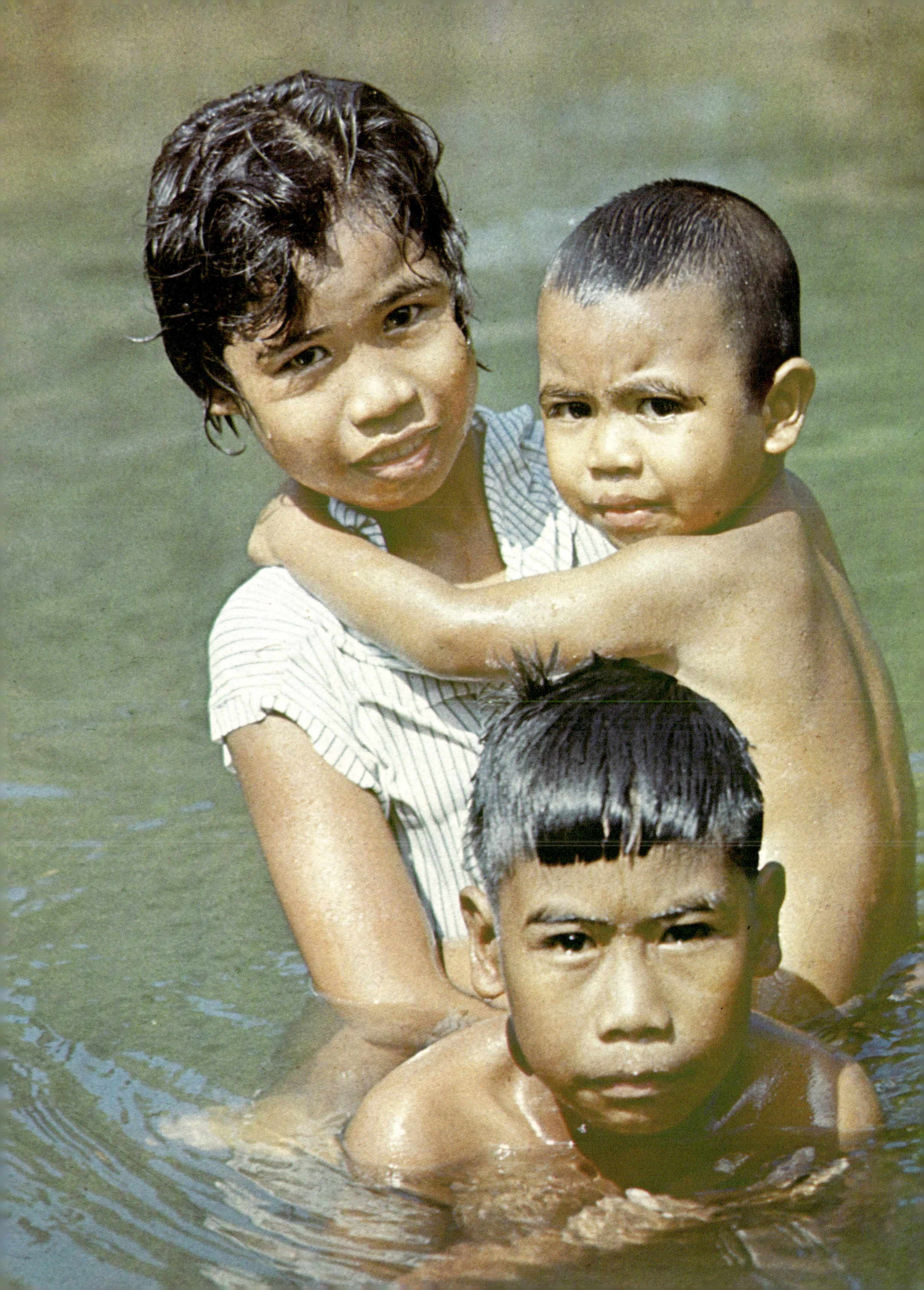

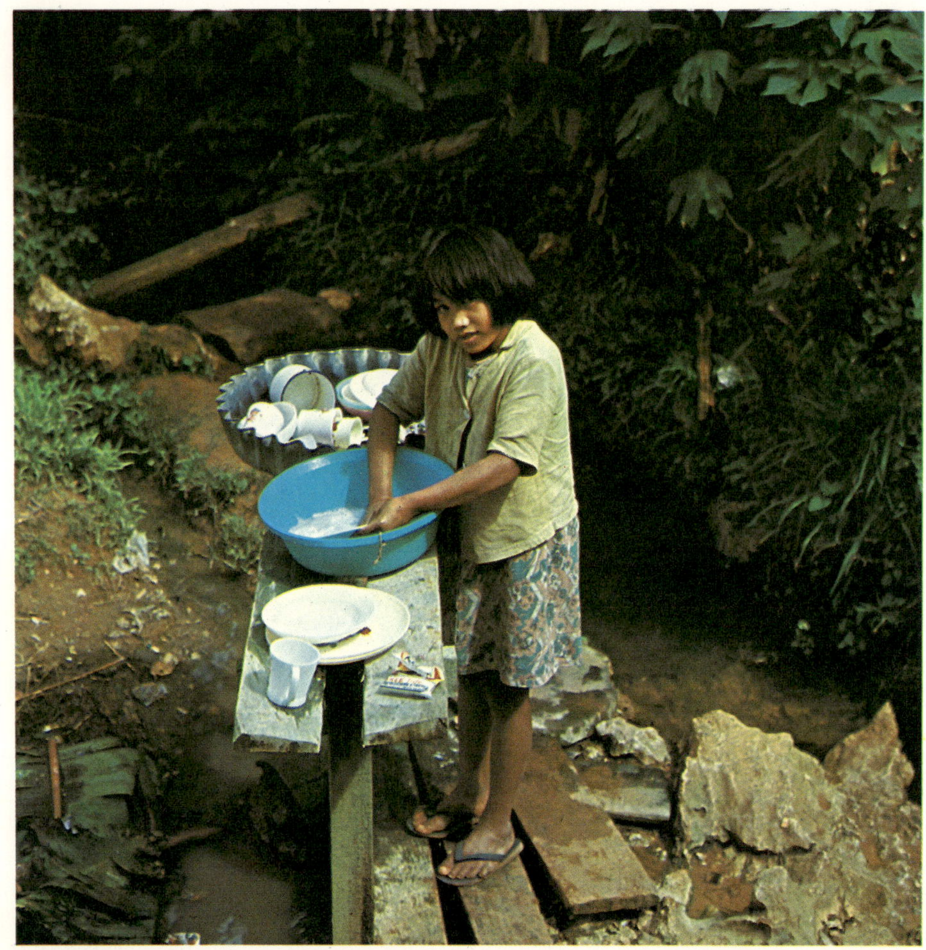

Mother and father work on the land. The older children go to school, the younger children take care of the babies and attend to household duties. Generally, daughters spend their time in the kitchen which, in this family, is outside and conveniently located by a stream which means constant running water.

*Below:* Those who are *not* within easy access of a river have to wash in a more conventional and less companionable manner.

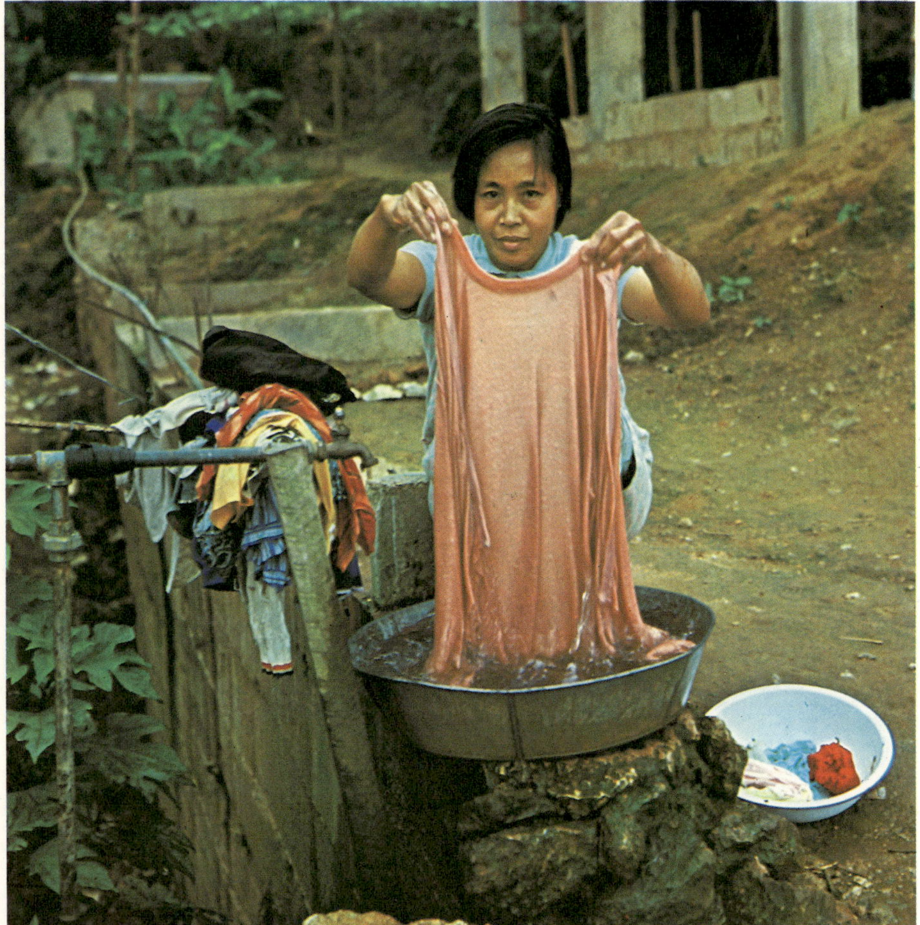

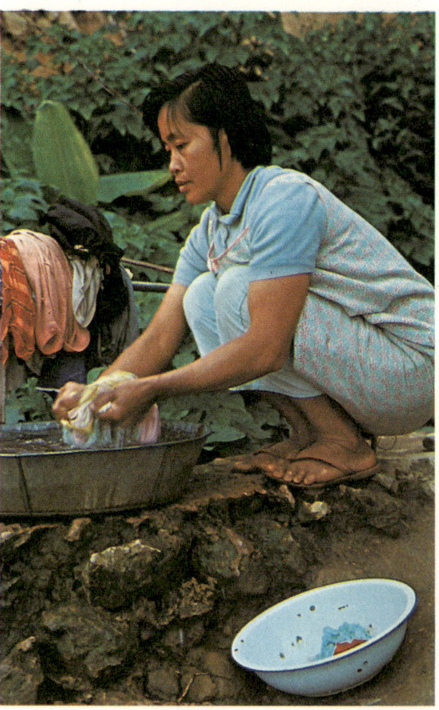

# Introduction

The Philippines has more islands than any other Asian country. For generations these Pacific atolls have lured adventurers whose reports are so varying that the armchair traveller finds it impossible to distinguish fact from fantasy. Certainly, life is not all swaying palms and exotic girls. But whatever their shortcomings as a paradise, these capricious circles in the sea undoubtedly rank among the world's most spectacular features. They have a time-defying magic and an irresistible attraction. Even their names impart a siren-like aura—Mystique, Seven Sins, Enchanted Rock, Ursula Island, Ob-Ob Beach, Pañgapuyana and Tabon Caves, to mention but a few.

Their physical attractions can be as perplexing as they are picturesque. As an island, the crater of Taal volcano rises from the lake of its original crater which in turn contains another lake and another island. Still a mystery is the origin of the Chocolate Hills, huge mounds of earth sprawled over miles of plain country. The weirdly-shaped mountains of salt dominating Bambang town are yet another geological puzzle. And at Banaue, an entire mountain range was carved with bare hands into rice terraces now 3,000 years old and considered to be the "Eighth Wonder of the World." If placed end to end, the terraces would be ten times as long as the Great Wall of China and cover the distance from London to Tokyo. It took 2,500 years of labour to raise these terraces into the clouds where torrential rains supply the rice with water.

Statistics are also impressive: of the thirteen most valuable seashells in the world, three are indigenous to the Philippines including the glory-of-the-sea which sells for more than $1000 U.S.; off Surigao Island, the Pacific Ocean plunges to 35,000 feet, the second greatest depth known to man; scores of plants, trees, animals and birds found nowhere else on earth, flourish in the tropical environment; Lingayen Gulf is acknowledged as one of the largest marine reserves; and the smallest fish known—half-an-inch when fully grown—breeds in Lake Buthi.

The Filipinos are as stimulating as their country—a race of people who are a unique mixture of many moods and traditions. From the Malays they have inherited courage. Their adventurous spirit is Indonesian. Mysterious beliefs can be traced to India. Ingenuity to Japan. The importance placed on family life shows a Chinese influence. Mohammedanism came from Arabia and Christianity from Spain. America contributed democracy and the English language.

All these influences provided the impetus for Filipinos to evolve a distinct culture which was already partly established long before the first Europeans arrived. And today's Filipino, the offspring of so many cultures, is multi-racial and multi-talented. While speaking a potpourri of Hindi-Malay with a sprinkling of Chinese, Arabic and Spanish, he also has a fluent command of English. The Philippines are, in fact, the third-largest English-speaking country.

Even though sentimentalists have often portrayed a false picture of the Philippines, no amount of misrepresentation can destroy these islands, and even devastating cyclones, floods, tidal waves and volcanic eruptions cannot lessen their appeal.

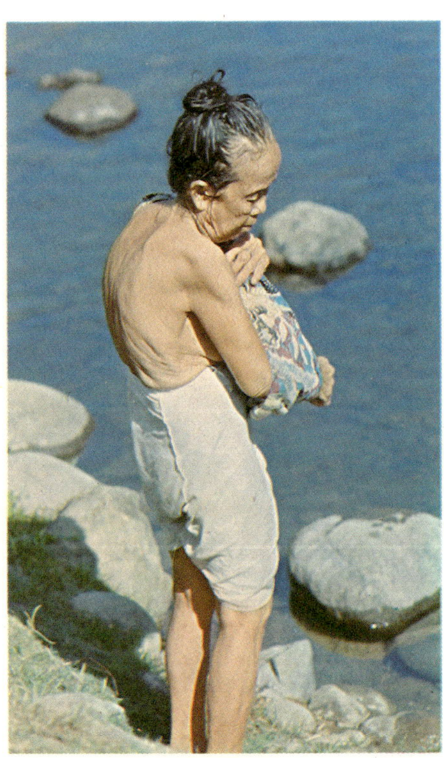

Only a few miles from the active, expanding cities, a visitor can find unspoiled rural areas where ancient women, wrinkled by sun and age, still bathe themselves twice daily in cold river water that comes from the mountains.  These people are tenacious and hardy—the salt of the earth.

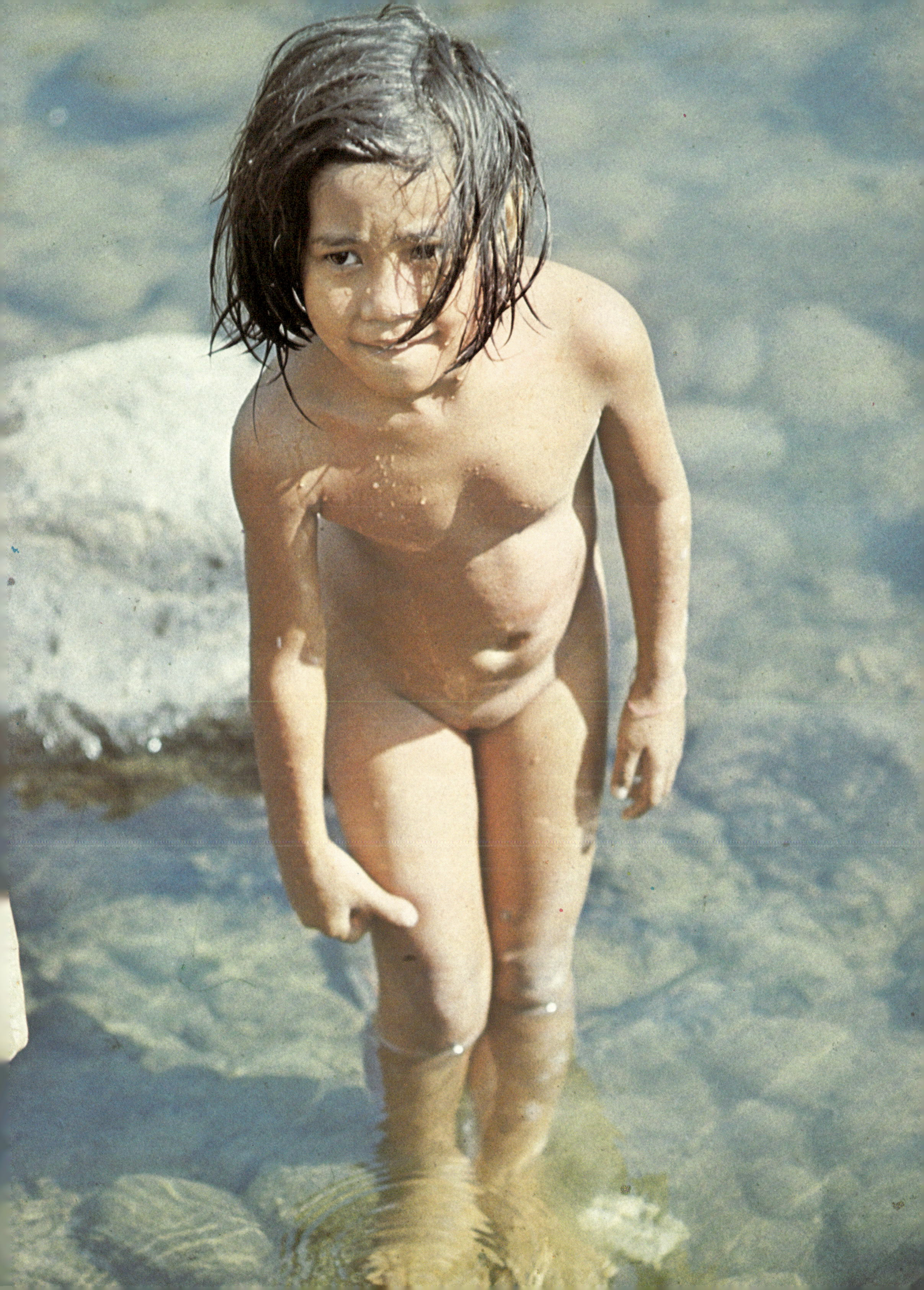

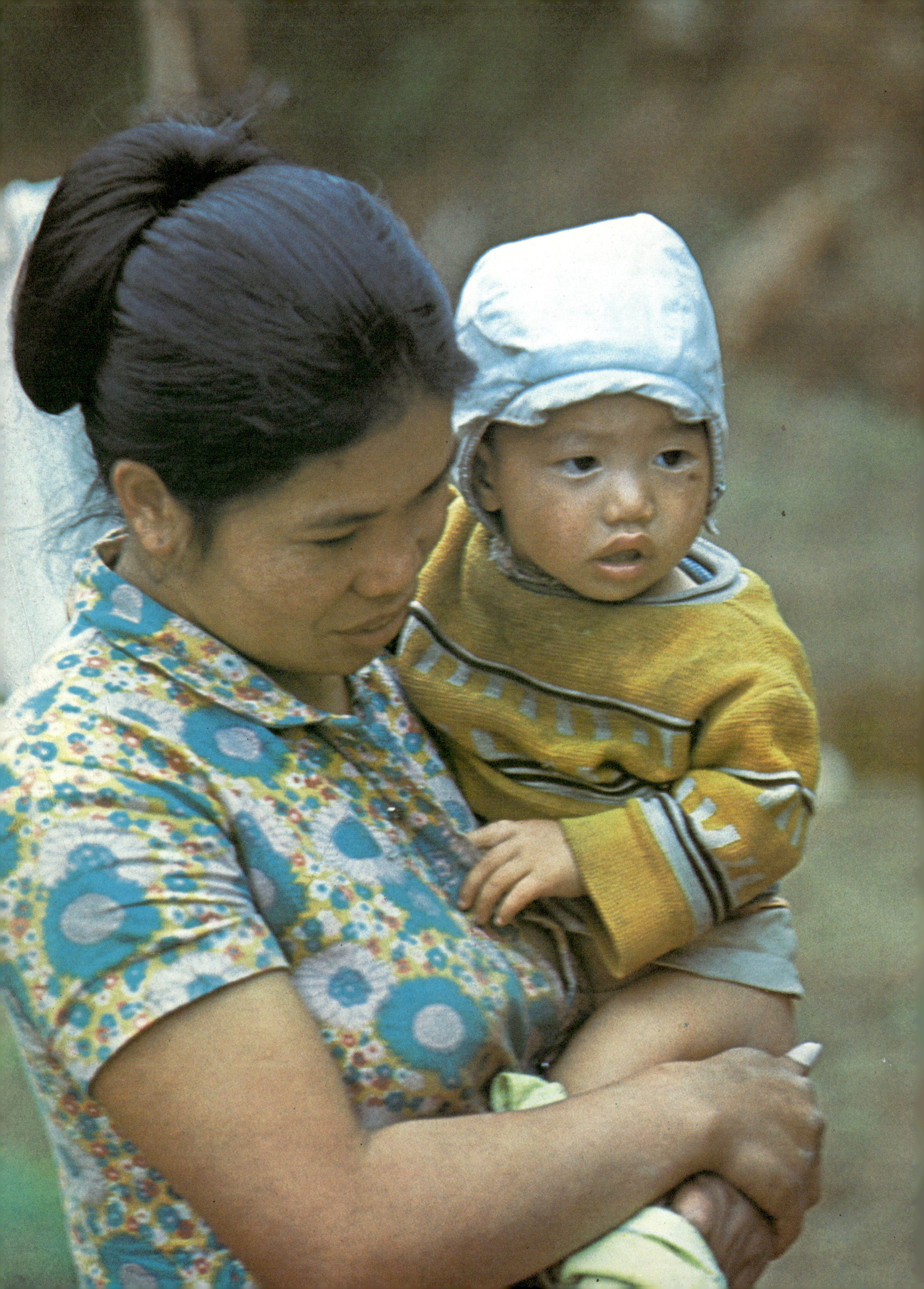

The Filipinos are a unique race of people
with many cultures, moods and traditions.
The importance they place on family life
shows a Chinese influence.

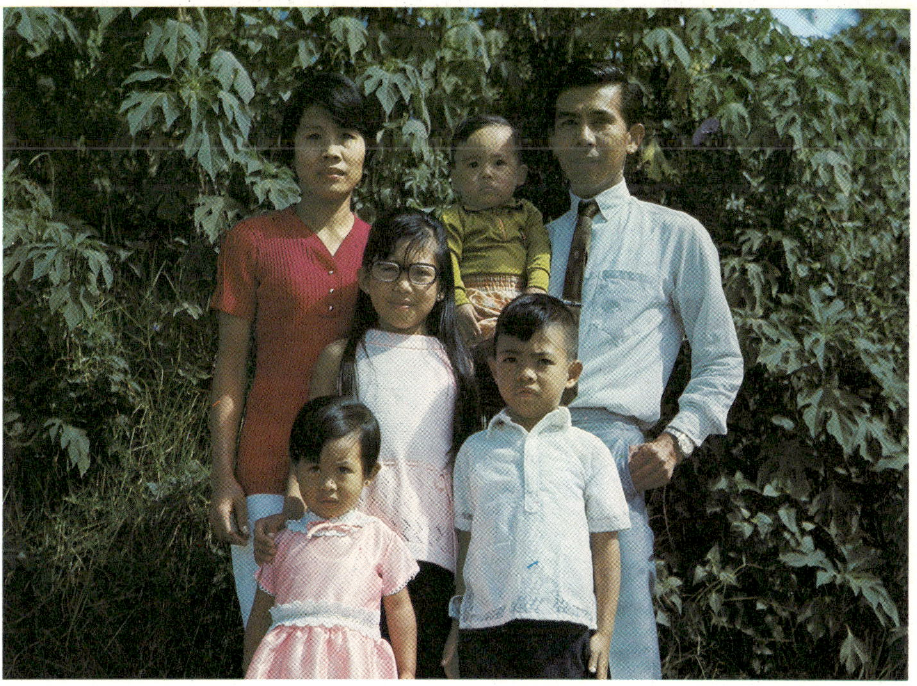

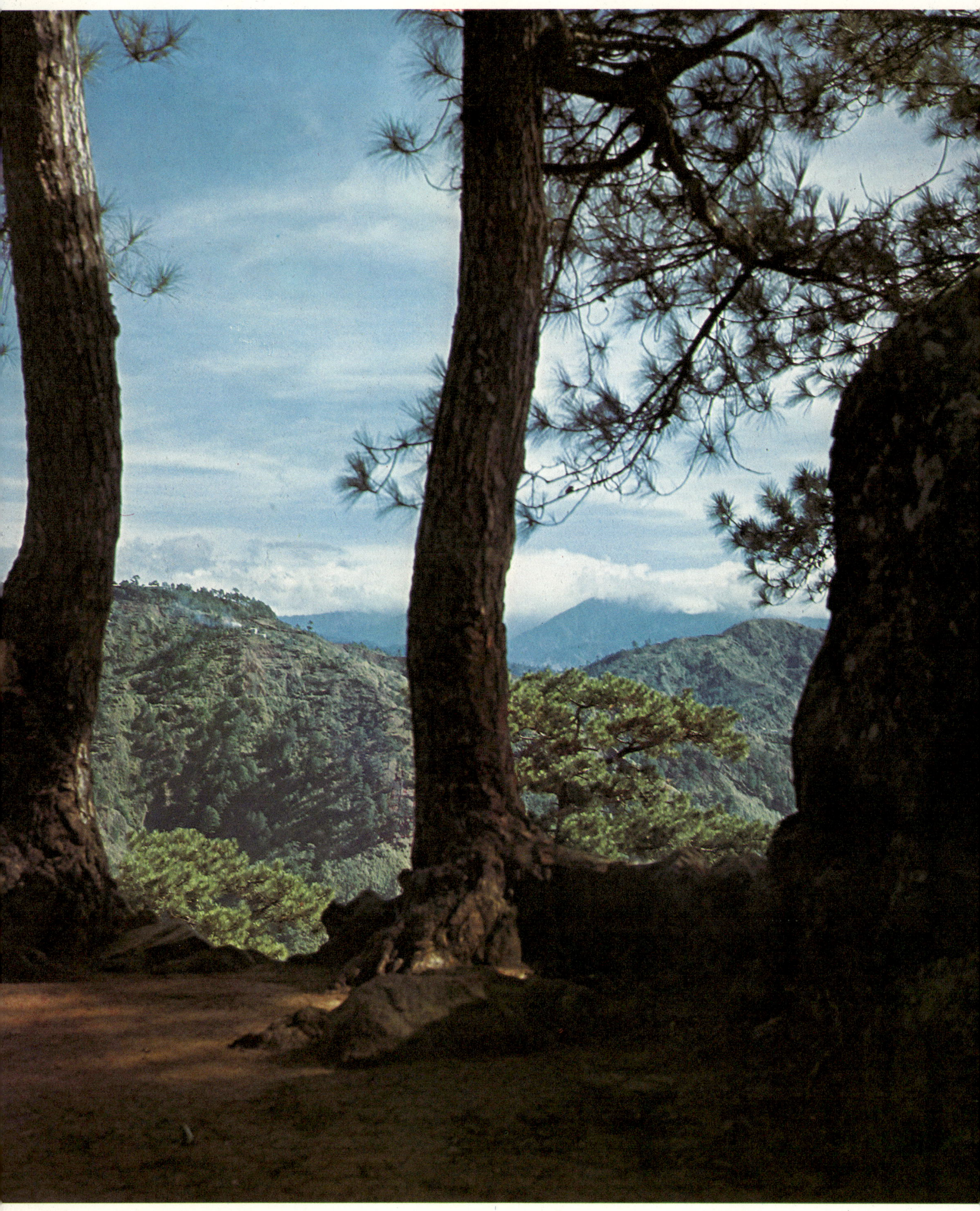

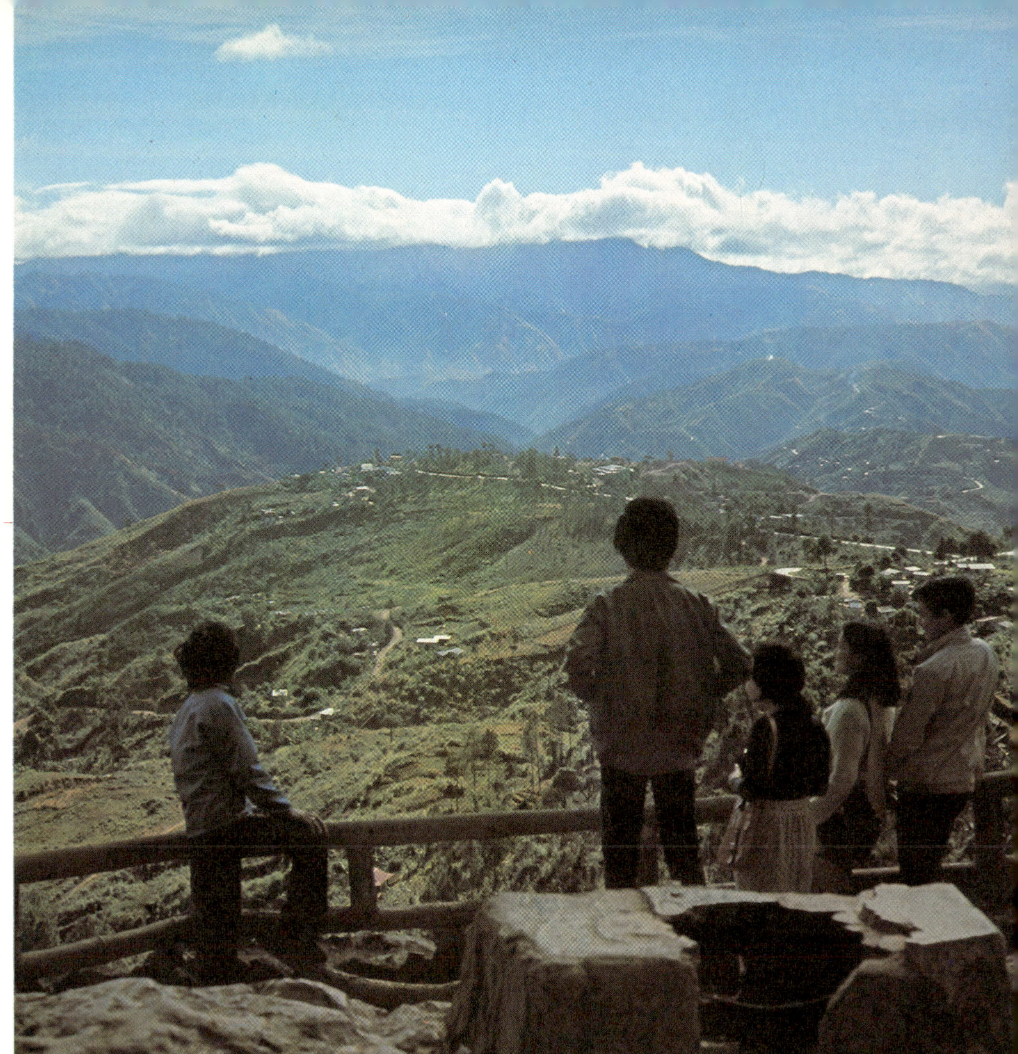

Benguet, a province in the mountains and reputed to be a vast terrain of gold. With deep ravines, waterfalls and pine-covered mountain slopes, this province offers spectacular scenic views where altitude tempers the tropical climate and brings refreshingly cool nights; on the hottest days the humidity still remains low and exceptionally pleasant by any standards. Shown in all three photographs is "Gold Valley," a panoramic tourist attraction as well as the inspiration for occasional gold prospectors.

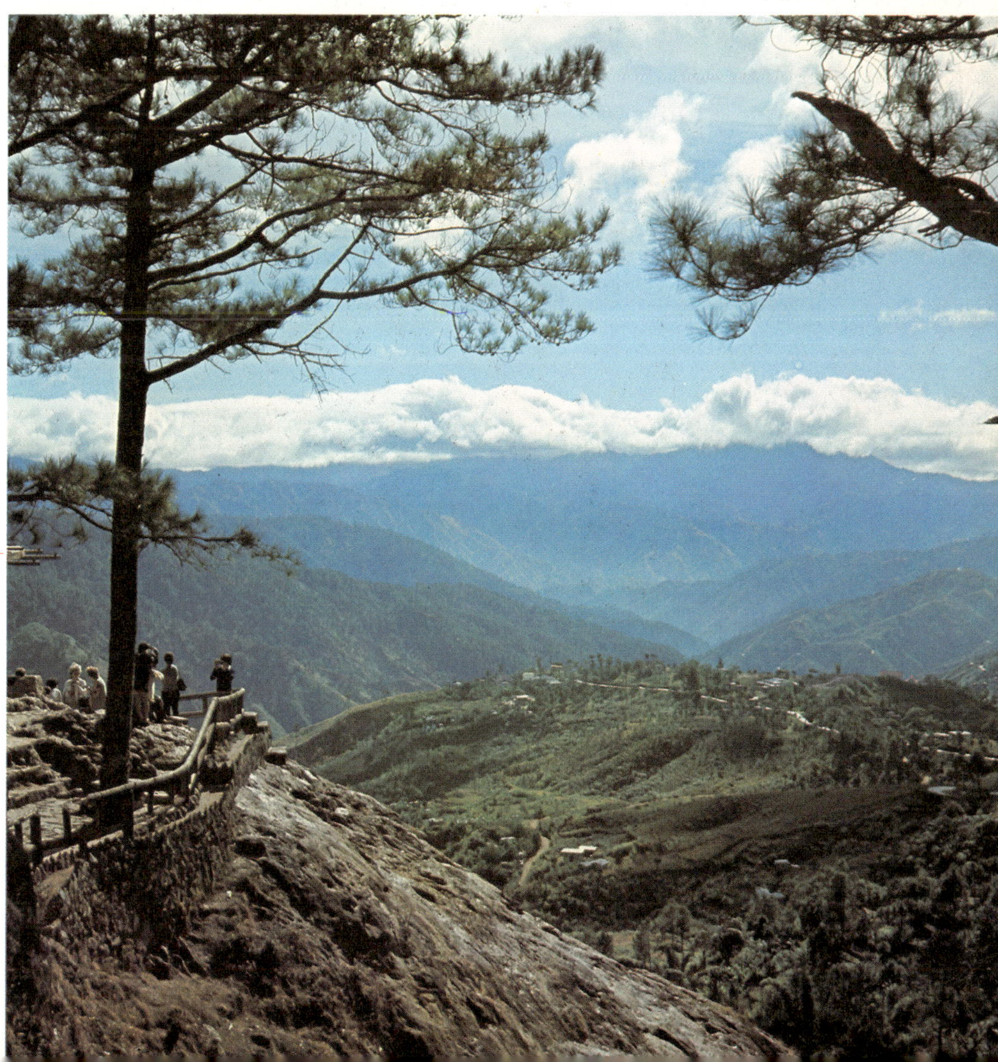

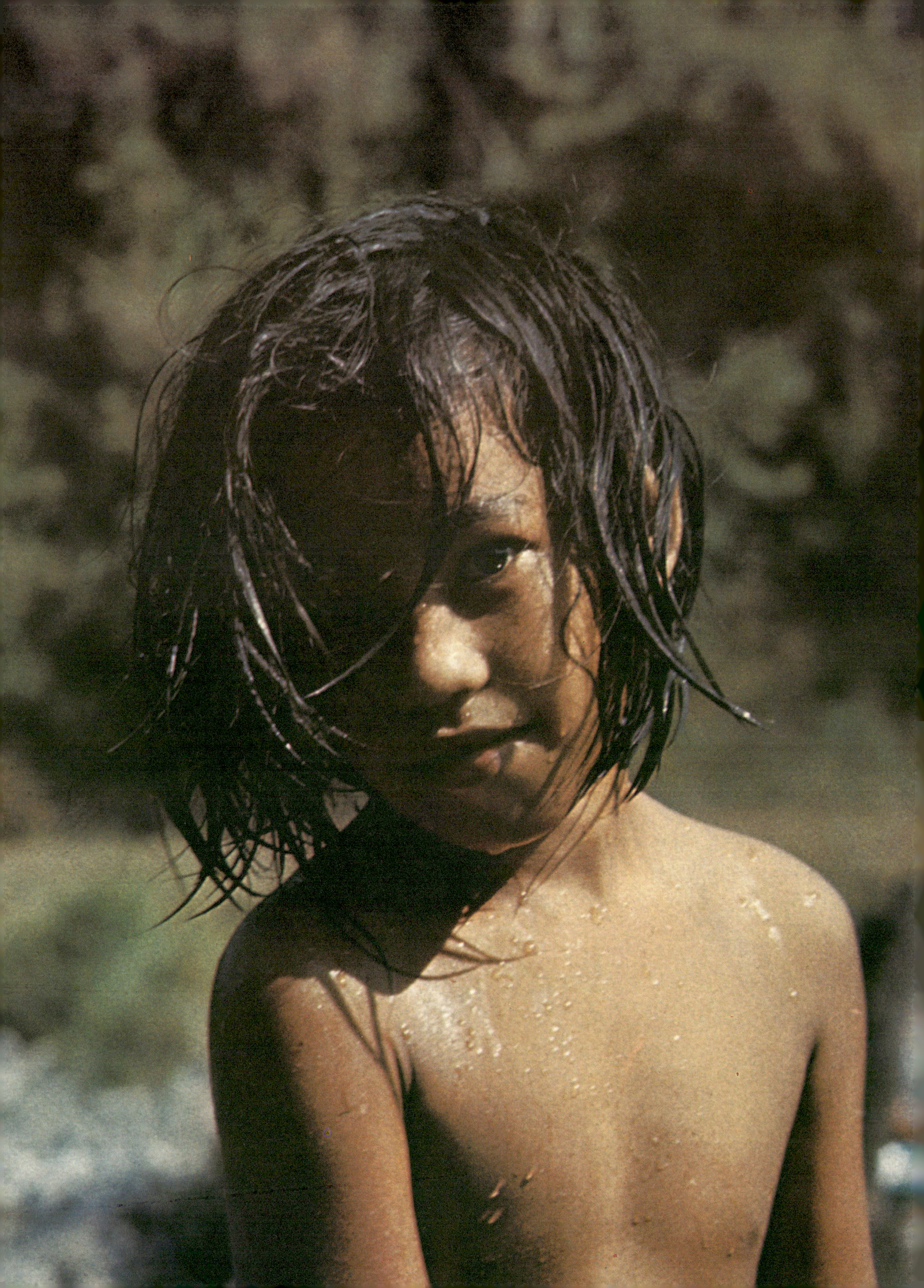

# More Than 7,100 Islands

Between the vast Pacific Ocean and the stormy China Sea is a triangular galaxy of tropical islands which, since 1946, have formed the independent Republic of the Philippines. Lying about 500 miles off South-East Asia and extending north and south for some 1,150 miles, this archipelago is named after Philip II of Spain. Luzon, at the top of the Philippines, is about 500 miles north from Taiwan; Jolo, in the south, is 150 miles from Borneo. Moving west, the neighbouring countries are Thailand, Singapore and Malaysia; to the north and northeast are China and Japan respectively; but travelling east the nearest land is Hawaii, several thousand miles away.

No one knows exactly how many islands there are; the republic states simply "more than 7,100." New islands emerge from time to time as volcanic eruptions cause great upheavals of the ocean floor. Then after a few weeks or even days, many of these, due to their own weight, sink again to become flat-topped underwater mountains.

Such eruptions are not confined to underwater. On September 28, 1965, Taal volcano, after half a century of inactivity, once again showed the gigantic natural forces which influence life in the Philippines. The volcano, forty miles south of Manila and rising as a crater-pocked island in Lake Taal, for three days blasted out innumerable tons of white-hot pumice. On the second day it ejected a mightly black cinder 1,000 feet in diameter which formed a horseshoe islet. When I photographed Taal, rain was falling gently (page 65) and, although a young boy came up and told me that a week previously "the hole was smoking real good man," it now lay serene—an impressive natural time bomb that has become a tourist attraction. At least ten other volcanoes are very active; flood, typhoon and earthquake are also quite common.

Taal's fury is only one example of nature's harshness in the Philippines. High, parallel mountain chains, deep gorges, rapids, mangrove swamps and dense rain forest isolate many parts of the islands and make it doubtful if their landscapes will be inhabited. Mindoro, the seventh biggest island in the group, remains largely unmapped. Even the southeast coast of Luzon, the principal island, is still a remote area hardly explored, while Luzon's *bundok* (mountain country) is popularly called "the boondocks," U.S. slang for the last place on earth without civilization. Less than fifty miles from Manila, it is still possible to find villages where the people, untouched by modern technology, still hunt with bows and arrows and know little of basic agriculture; yet I found these villages were marked by peaceful coexistence, strong family ties and an integrity of purpose.


*The Gateway*

The main port of entry to the Philippines is Manila and, as my Philippine Airlines DC-8 began the final approach, I looked down upon a curving shoreline, green seawater, green rivers and an even greener landscape. Everything appeared so tranquil it was hard to believe that this was a vibrant Asian metropolis of 3 million people.

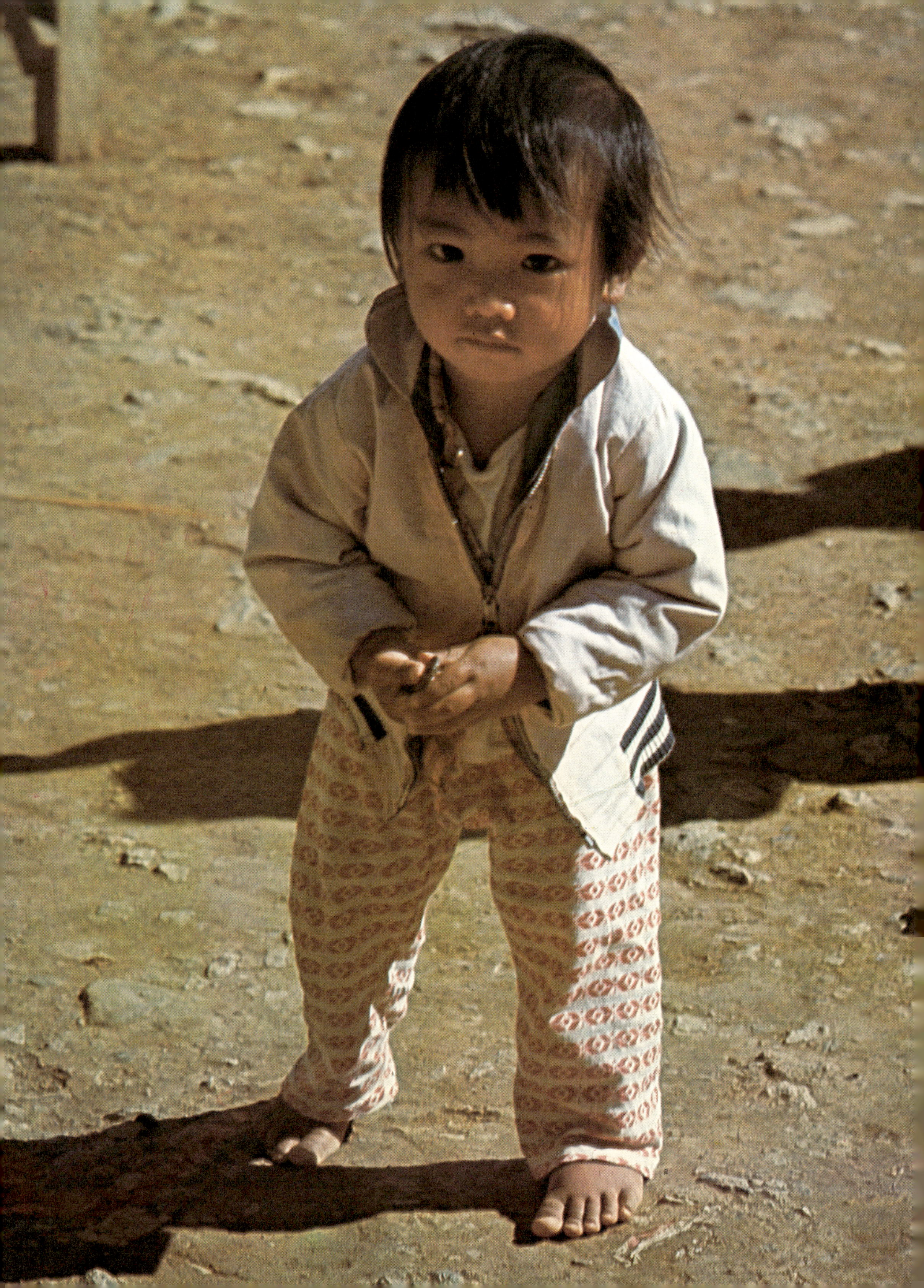

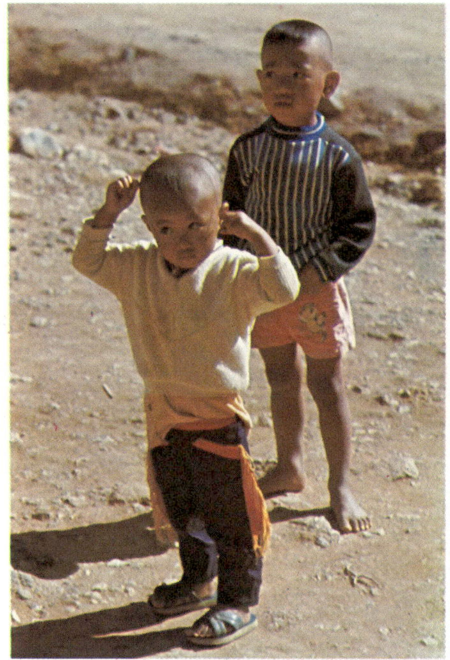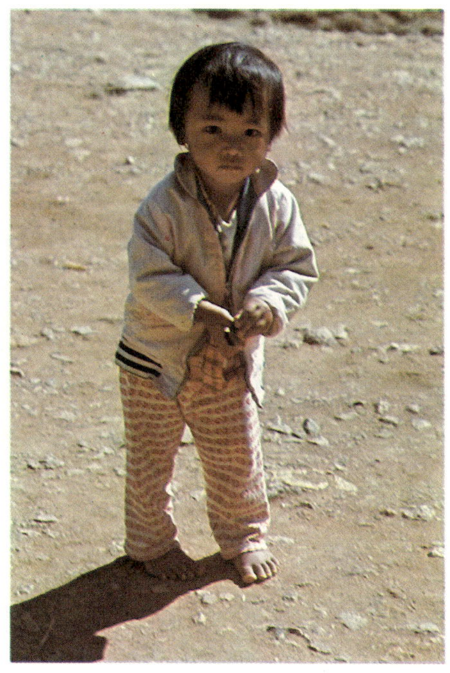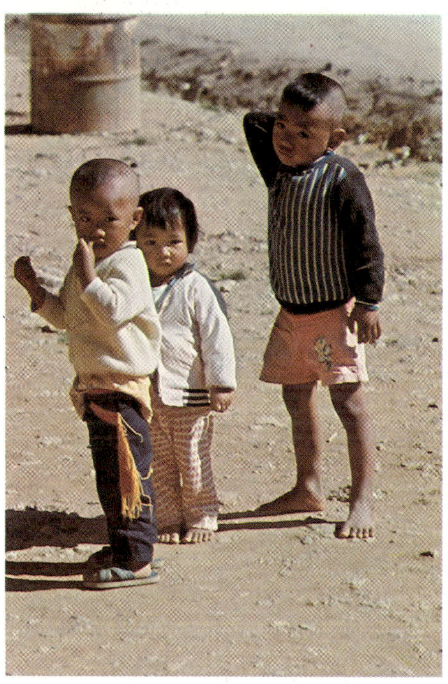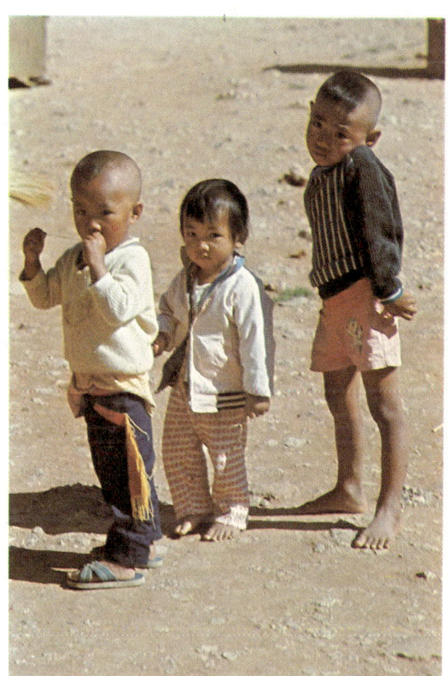

These children from northern Luzon are nomadic mountain dwellers. Their island nation, born amidst the conflict of World War II, now fights another war as it battles against long odds to make life worthwhile by developing a progressive land of opportunity.

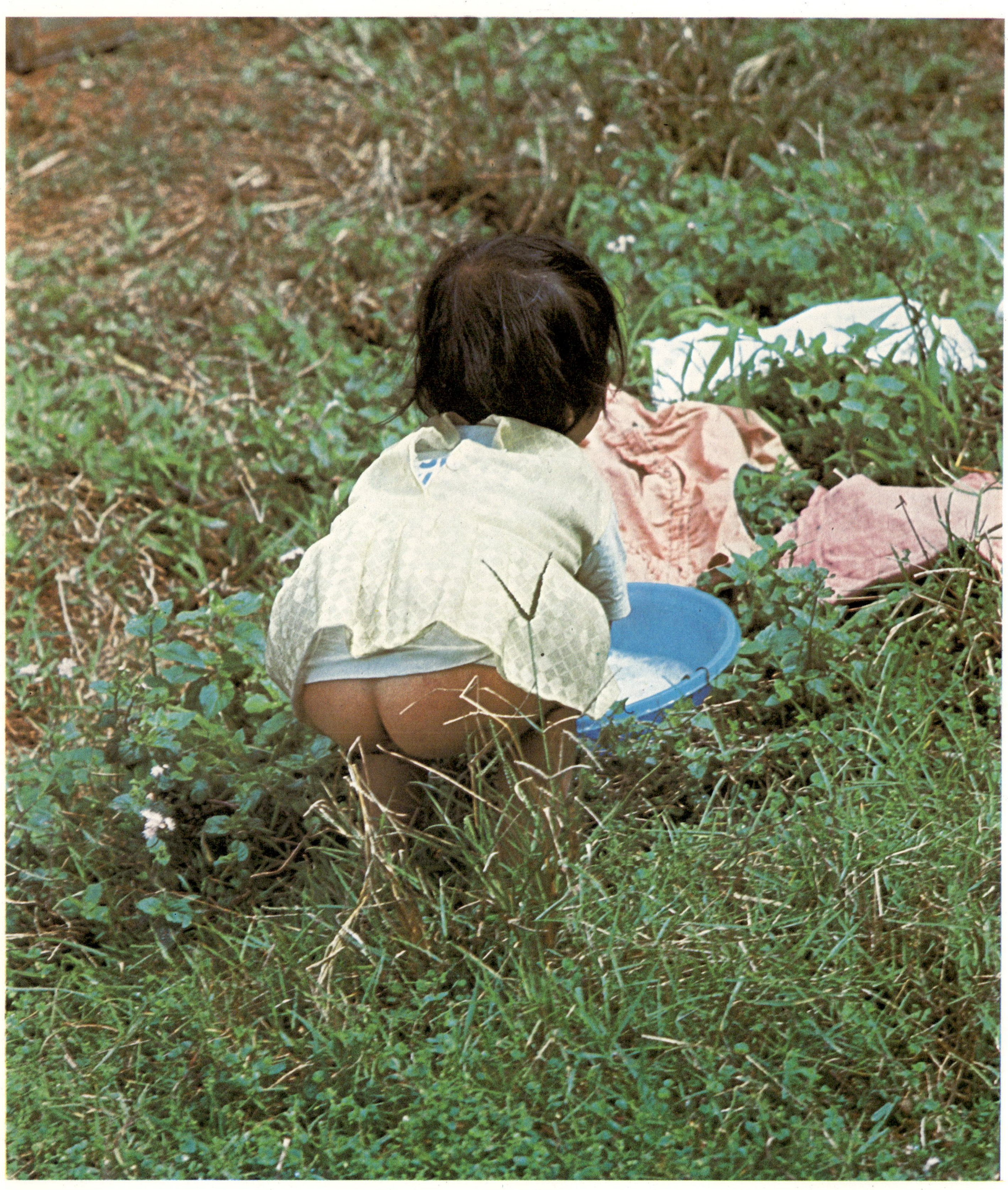

*Below Centre:* Note the small boy wearing
a helmet; it is a relic from World War II
and not a toy.


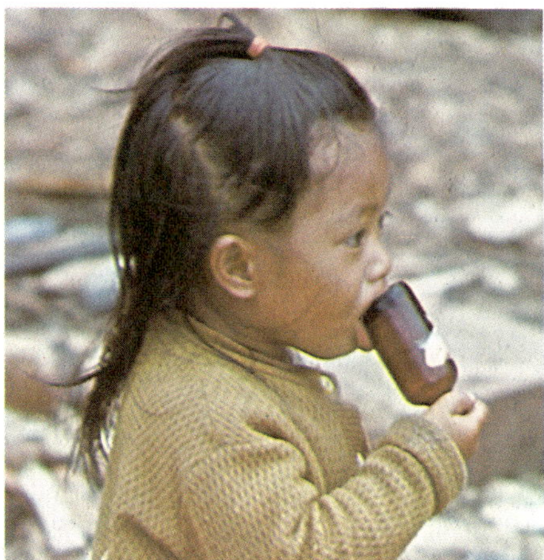

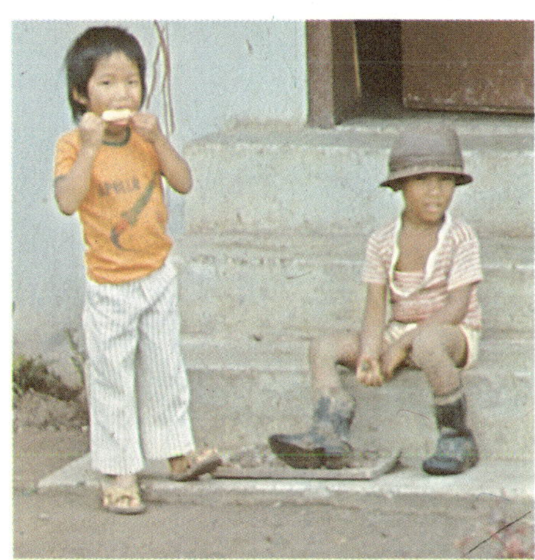

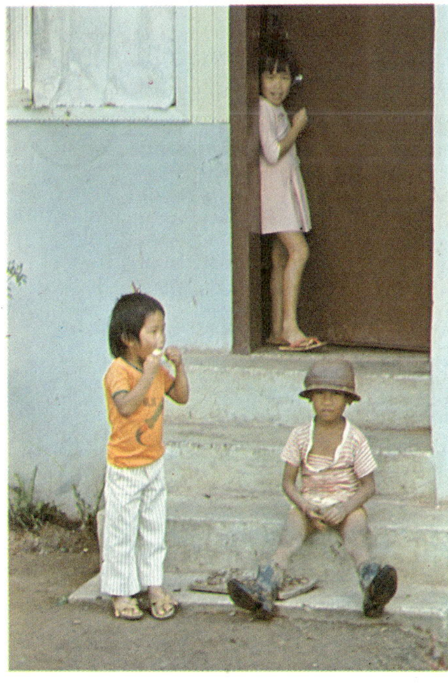

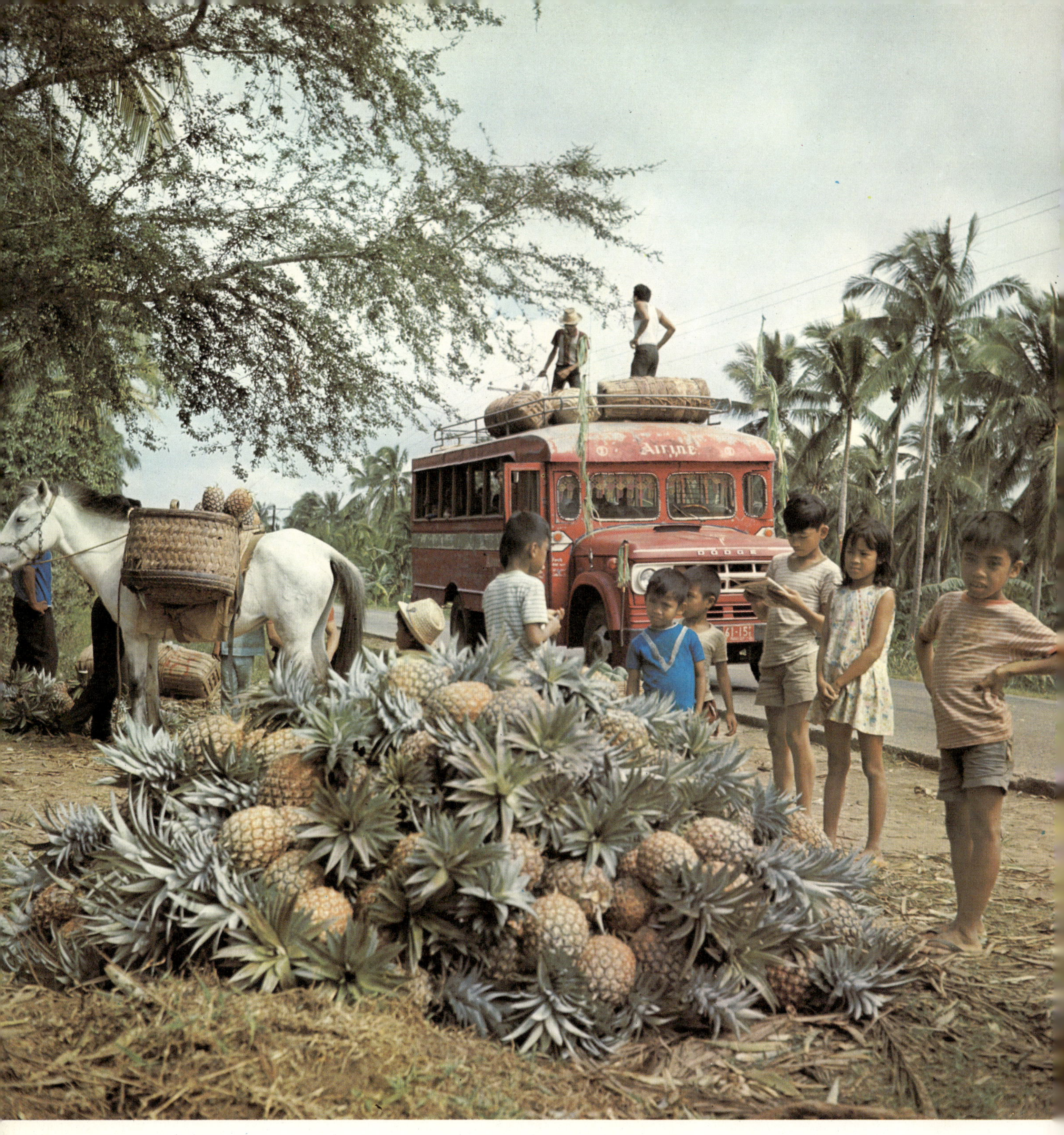

Local buses are often used to send loads of vegetables and fruit to market. The passenger service may suffer but it is an accepted way of life where timetables and speed have no place.

28

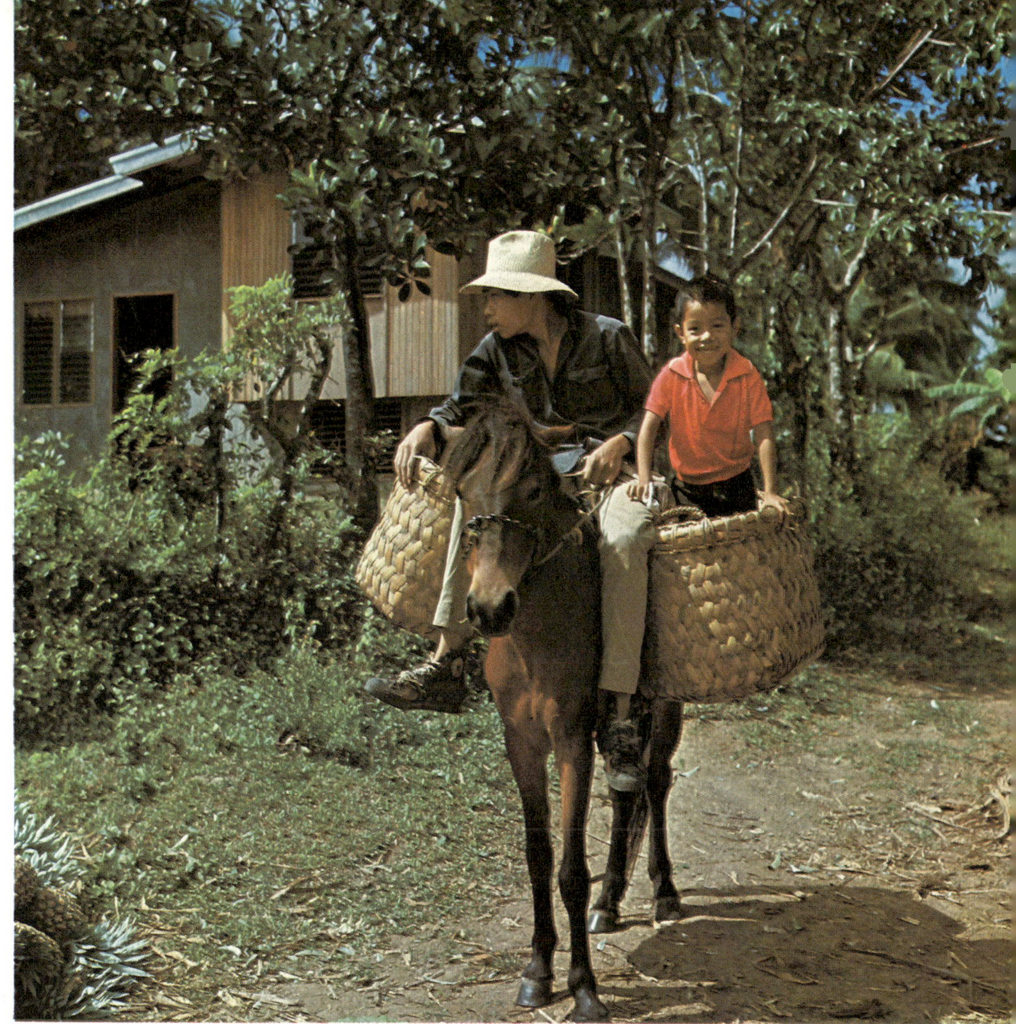

Considerable quantities of pineapples are grown for local consumption and for canning; the Philippines is the world's fifth largest producer.  The commercially productive life of a pineapple plantation is about 3½ years.  First quality breeding plants are raised from seed and it takes 10-12 years for a fruit to mature and become full-grown.  To establish plantations, crowns, slips and suckers are used. Gathering the fruit and arranging its transportation is a job for the entire family. *Right:* Toddlers watch the operation from a special place of honour.

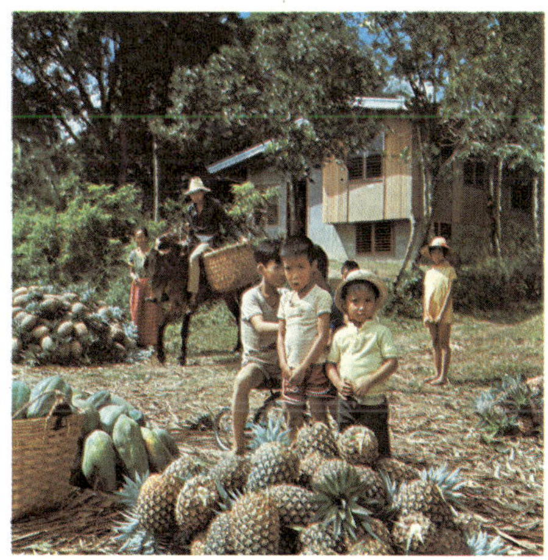

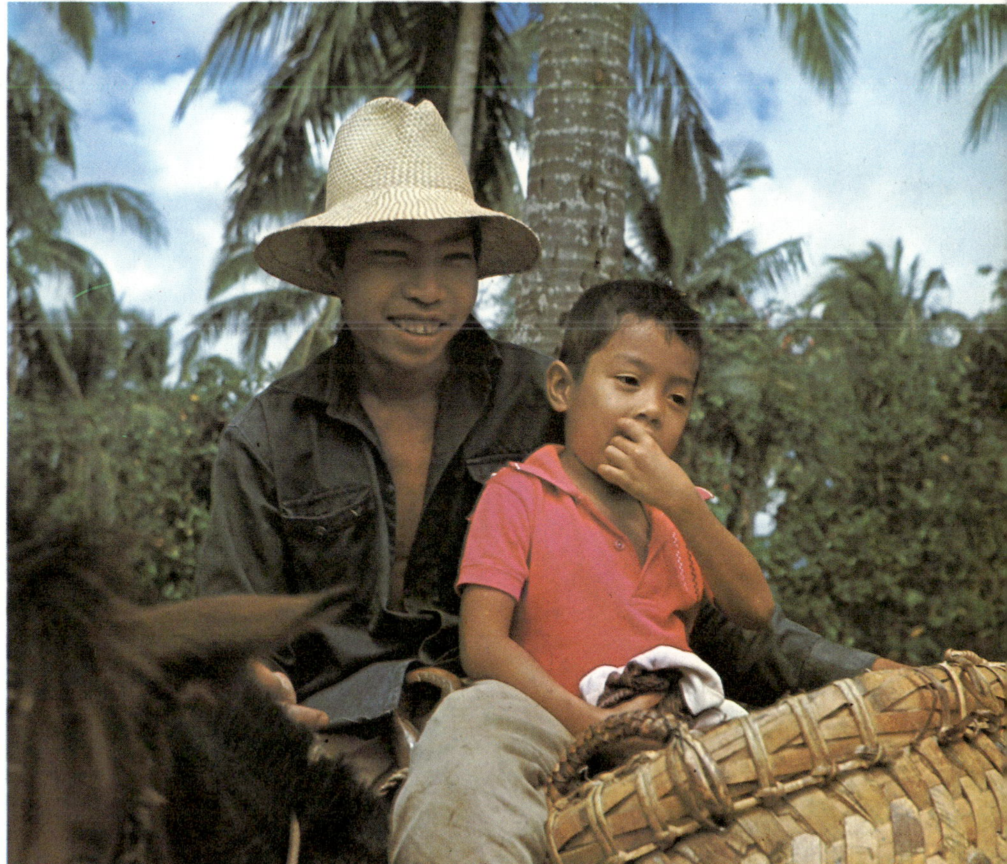

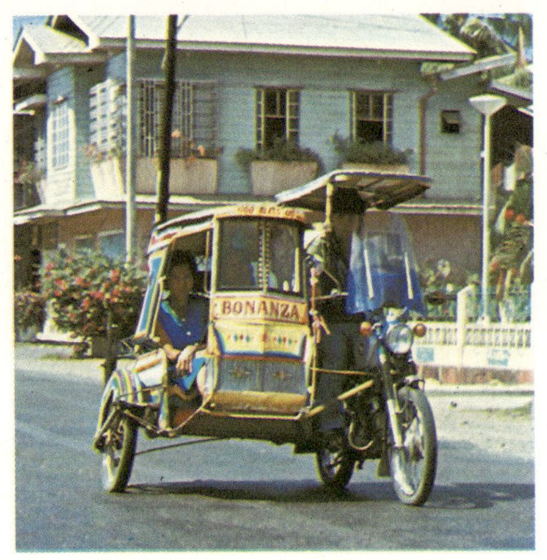

*Above:* War-surplus jeeps are converted into jeepneys, highly decorated pieces of oriental folk art.  Firms like Francisco Motors employ modern equipment and produce many of the required parts as well as oversize bodies.  (Text page 37.) *Left:* Motor scooters with sidecars add to the traffic nightmare.

Apart from jeepneys and scooters, all kinds of transport are available in the Philippines.
*Right:* The leisurely clip-clop of horse-drawn caratelas are reminiscent of a bygone age.
*Below:* Most of the buses show their age and battle scars of frequent encounters with bridges, walls, cliffsides, trees, and other hazards found along the narrow, twisting country roads.

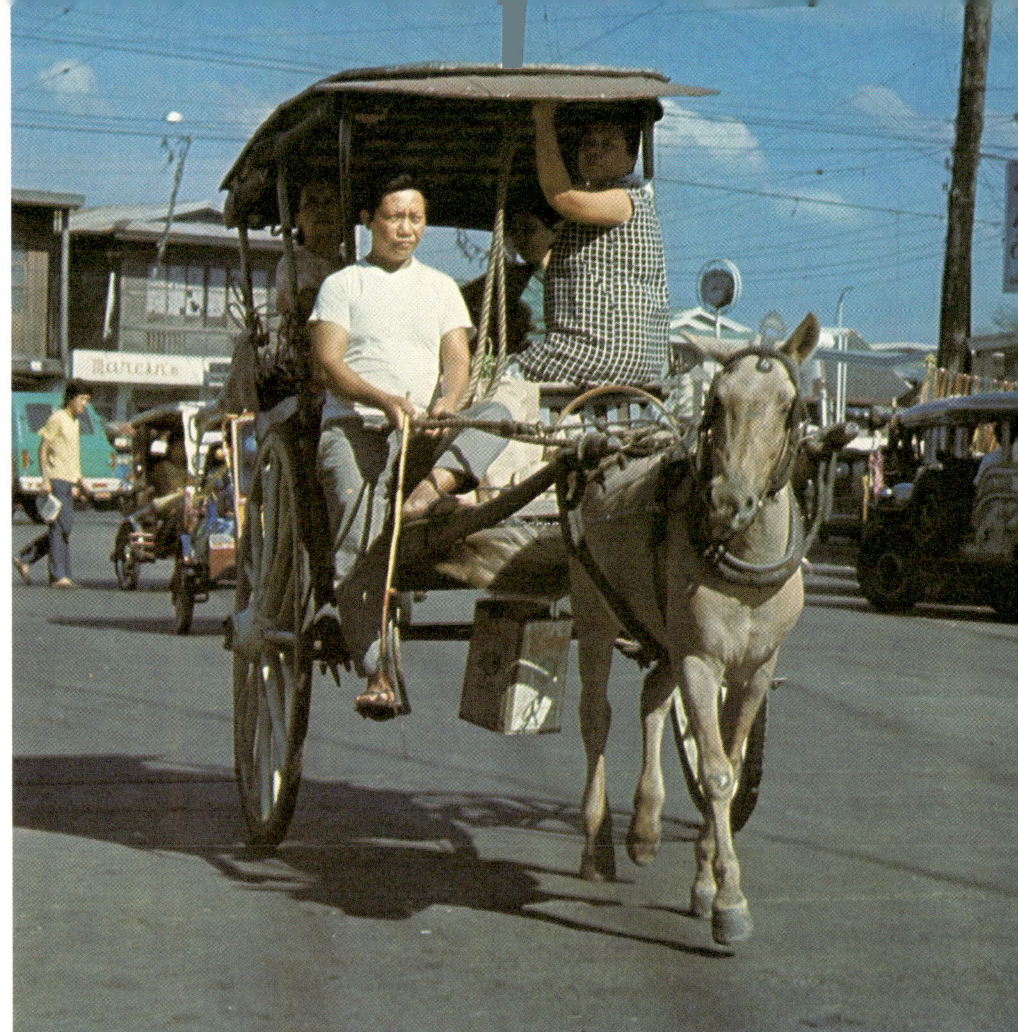

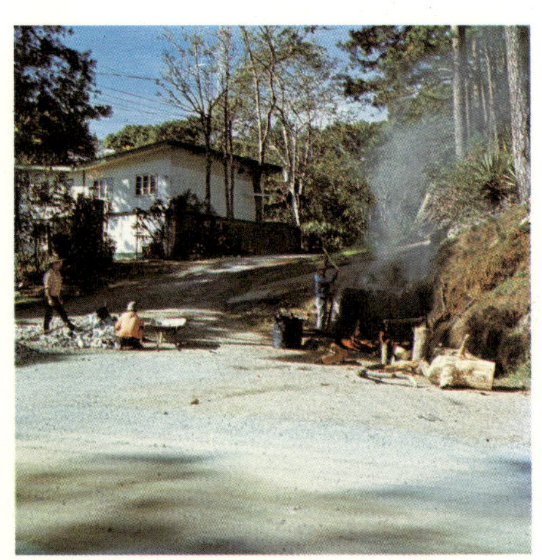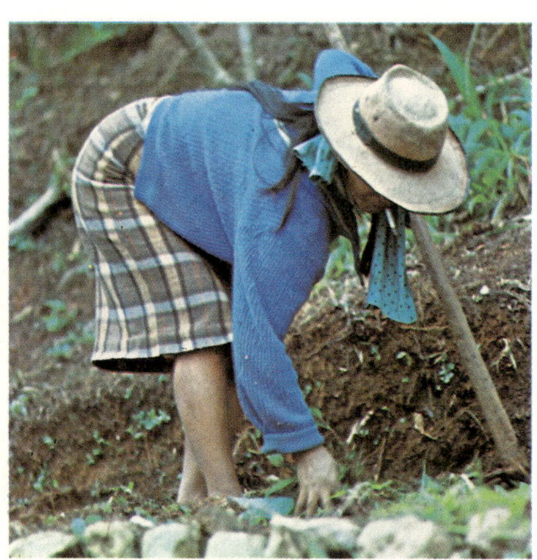

Away from the large towns, road construction and repairs are often undertaken with primitive tools and equipment. Employment is far more important than efficiency and the longer a "job" takes, the longer people are kept contented by earning a wage, small though it may be. Children always stand around and remain fascinated by the same activity they have watched every day for years. But it is a healthy outdoor existence. (Also pages 33 to 35.)

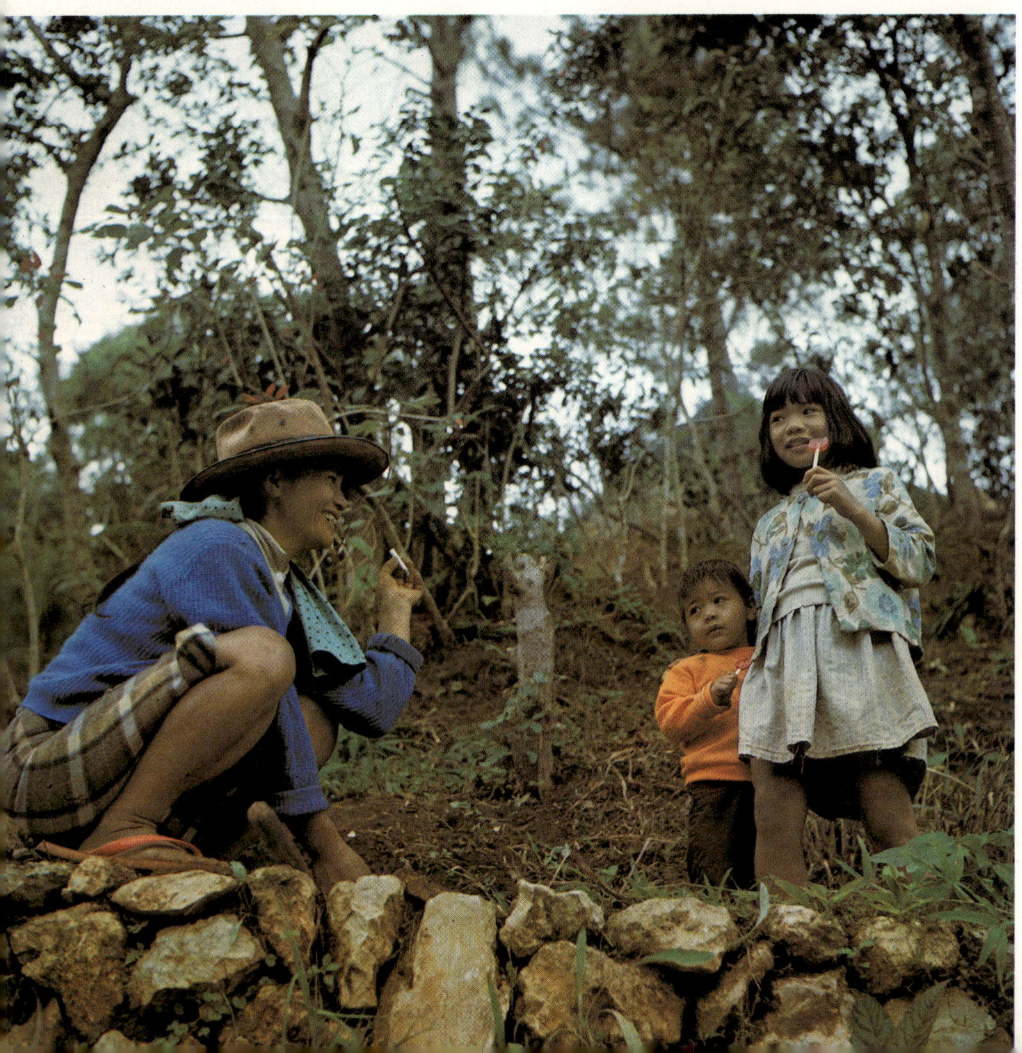

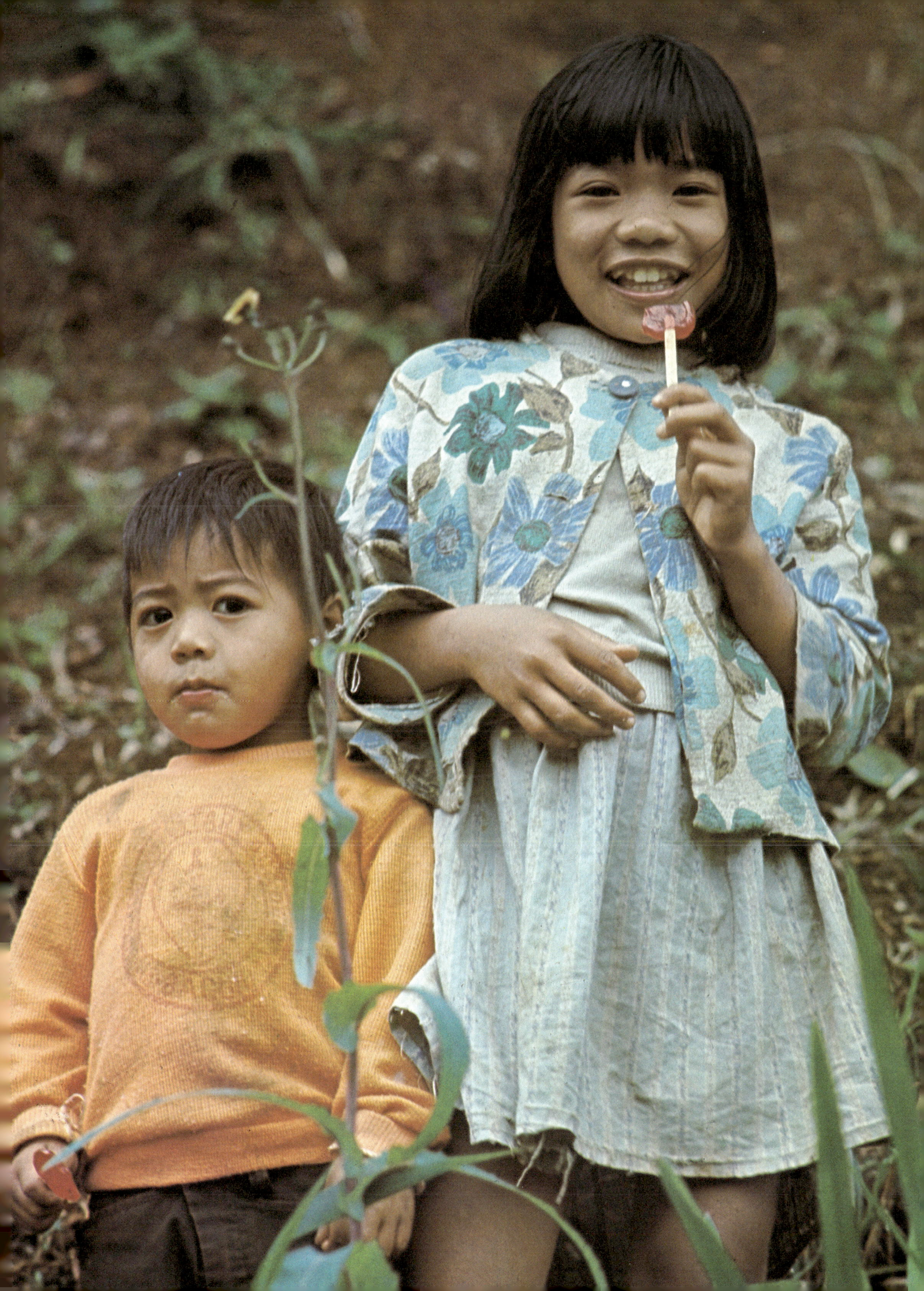

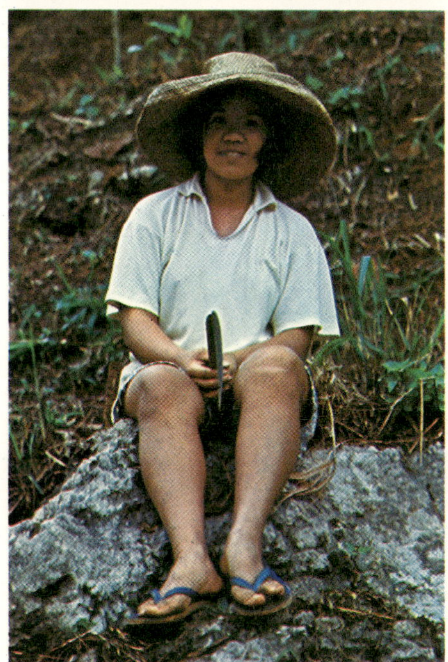
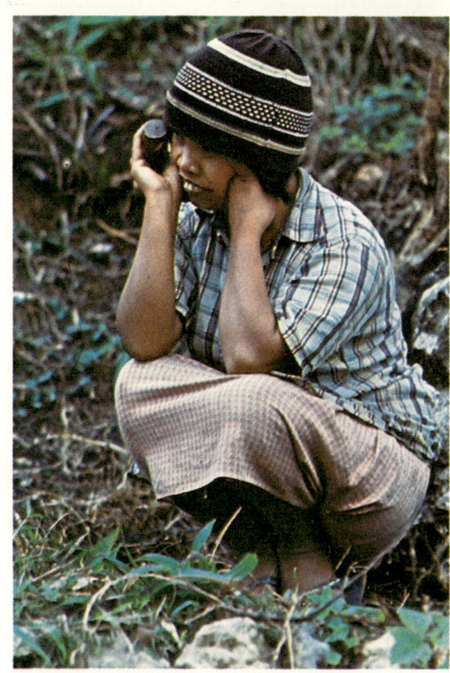



*Above:* Brushes, made locally, are always for sale in villages and displayed along the roadside.

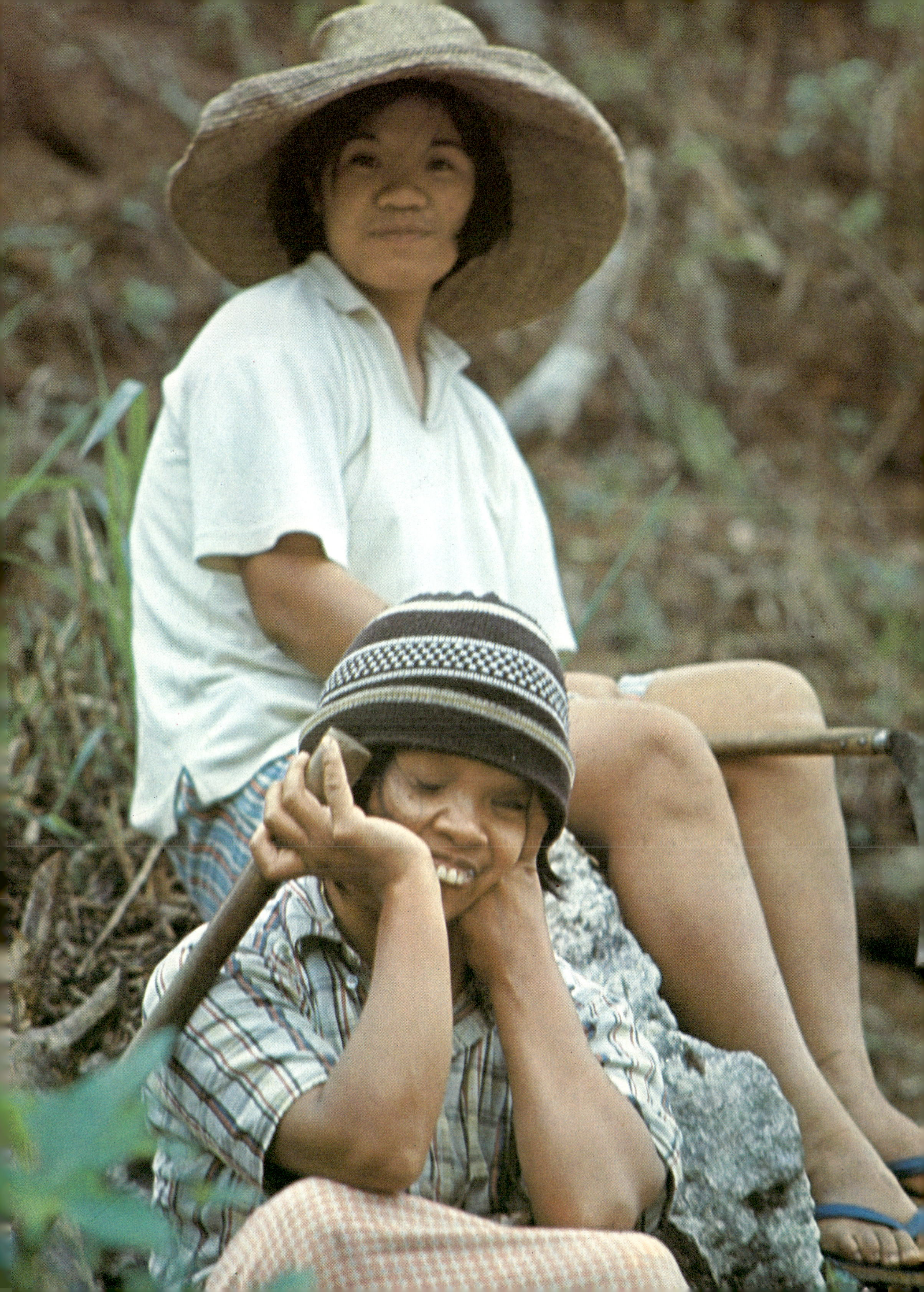

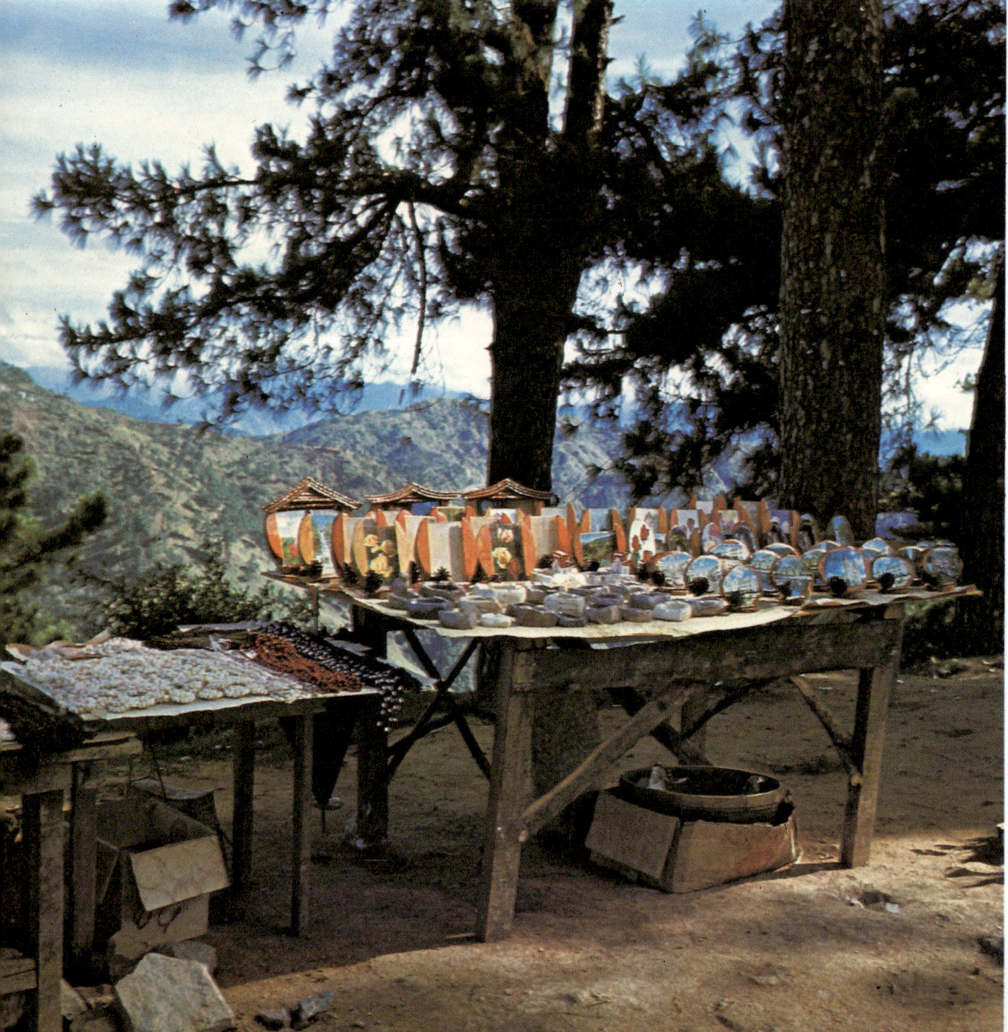

*Above:* Baskets, often made from buri palm, are sold to local people for transporting vegetables and other garden produce to the markets.  Tourists buy them to use as linen baskets.
*Left:* Gift and souvenir stalls are found even in remote mountain areas.  They sell all kinds of handicrafts from embroidered table items and pearl shells to walking sticks and dolls.

Thirty minutes later I was in a ramshackle taxi and this restless city, which throws itself at a visitor and takes his breath away, had caught me in a whirl of action as it displayed a gamut of noisy life just as the armchair traveller must imagine: there were roadside markets with tottering piles of wicker baskets, pictures, sandals, underclothes, fly sprays and matches spread among colourful heaps of pawpaws, mangoes, curry powder and cakes; small girls selling newspapers and older girls offering other favours; shops displaying Filipino made shoes, cigars, raw silks, rich cloths, grass fibre shirts—called *barong Tagalog*—with elaborately embroidered frills; traditional brasswork and wooden carvings, all offered for a fraction of the price at home. There was an incongruous mass of shoeshine boys, businessmen, housewives, lottery ticket sellers and begging urchins who flashed white teeth that brightened their dark faces like lightning in a stormy sky; the smell of incense, adobo soup and fried rice; a network of cobbled byways; and Chinatown with its atmosphere of old-time Shanghai.

My taxi continued to browbeat its way through the additional hubbub of Manila's traffic which was about as tranquil as a bullring. It has been said that driving in Manila is not a convenience, not a means of transport, but an exciting sport. And sport it is—a friendly battle of skill, cunning and bluff where the drivers take evasive manoeuvres only at the very last moment, avoiding collision by a calculated hair's-breadth: cars opposing buses, buses opposing lorries, lorries opposing horse-drawn caratelas, motor scooters with a sidecar, and the immaculate "psychedelic" jeepneys which speed everywhere in a flash of colour like rainbow fish.

The jeepneys are converted jeeps from World War II, although after renovation they bear little resemblance to their original utilitarian version. Usually they are sprayed in about six vivid colours, embellished with chromium plated trim, fitted with extravagant wrap-round fenders, gleaming roof racks, mirrors, windtone horns and extensive lighting arrays. Finally, each jeepney is "dressed" with flags and streamers before the driver christens it by painting on a name such as *Love Me Tonight, Baby Be Mine, Once Again,* or perhaps something more down to earth like *Anywhere Anytime.*

So, being driven with reckless professionalism, my ride to the Inter-continental Hotel was accomplished by keeping the horn at full blast, by outwitting all motorized opponents and by sweeping away the harassed but necessarily agile pedestrians. An unwritten feature of the Filipino highway code is that pedestrians never walk on the footpath; instead they use the road. Men, women and children will wander casually in front of a vehicle expecting the driver to stop miraculously. (Cars in the Philippines often manage a journey with only two cylinders firing and a flat battery, with one usable gear and a faulty clutch—but without a horn, quite impossible!) Chauffeur-driven, air-conditioned models are readily available and quite inexpensive—taxis are perhaps cheaper than in most other countries—and a jeepney will go anywhere for just a few cents.

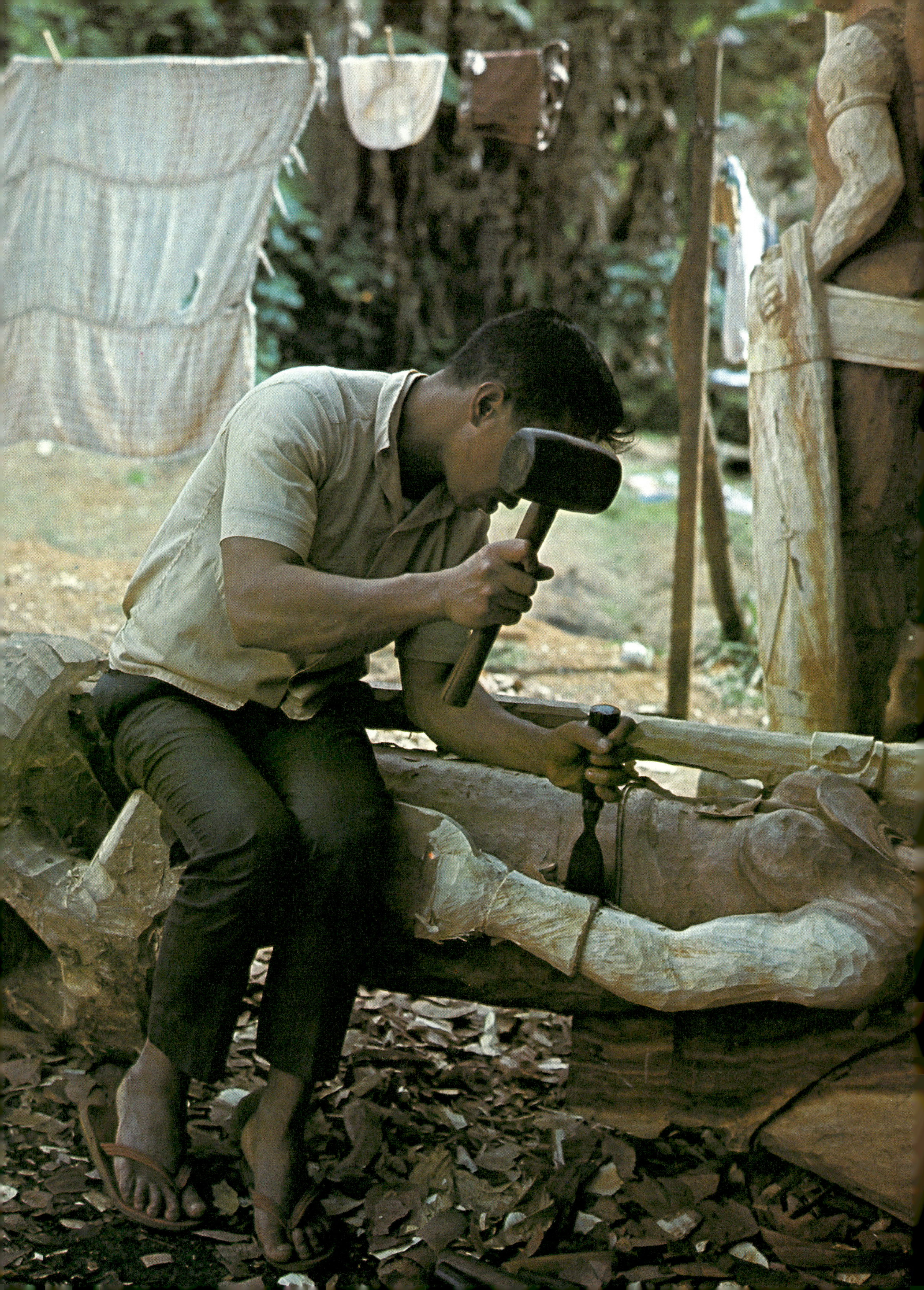

## The Ravages of War

Like Berlin and Cologne, Manila has risen from the ashes of World War II,
during which period it took more bombs and shells than any other capital in the
world with the possible exception of Warsaw. A million people died,
thousands of them in prison camps. Almost half a million had their homes
destroyed. Historic churches and the venerable walled city of Intramuros (built
fifty years after the Spanish discovery of the Philippines) were erased for ever.

Miraculously, just as the famous Cathedral survived in Cologne, so did many
great edifices remain undamaged around Manila; others have been renovated
perfectly. For instance, San Agustin Church, the oldest building in the
Philippines was relatively unscarred; with a long history of survival from
earthquakes and fires it is now affectionately known as "the durable one."
Yet, Manila Cathedral (built in 1581 and an important example of Spanish
architecture), only yards from San Agustin, crumbled in 1945 after intensive
shelling. Previously, the Cathedral had been destroyed five times by fire or
earthquake—it was rebuilt in 1958.

After the overall devastation, a new city finally emerged where, except for the
American Memorial at Fort William McKinley, there is little to remind the
casual visitor of war. But at this Fort, the Americans who died are
commemorated by 17,180 sad white markers. Often the marker bears no
identification apart from the inscription, "Here rests in honored glory a comrade
in arms known only to God." The names of other men who lie in unknown
Philippine graves are recorded on two curved stone arcades—there are 36,279
names.

## Risen from the Ashes

Proudly straddling the Pasig River, today's bulging, ever-expanding Manila is a
unique city. At first, it may seem incongruous to come across a stone church
with a baroque facade, or a beautiful Filipino girl with Chinese-Malay features
who speaks English and has a Spanish name, or narrow cobbled streets which
are little changed from the fifteenth century yet merge into wide boulevards
where flashing neon signs advertise nightclubs, theatres and restaurants.
But where geography has made the Philippines an Asian country, history
has made it a fascinating blend of Oriental and Occidental culture that is to be
found nowhere else. In one word, Manila is a paradox. Pockets of culture still
remain from the ancient empires of Shri-Vishayan and Madjapatit, elegant
mosques and Indonesian dress in the South reflect the Moslem expansion of a
bygone age, and the architectural remnants of former Spanish glory are now
combined with a skyline dominated by new buildings which are a tribute to the
genius of young Filipino designers.

To mention but a few of these varied attractions—there is the Cultural
Centre, an imposing Athenian temple-like structure with Manila Bay as a
backcloth; and the massive Rizal Stadium can accommodate thousands of

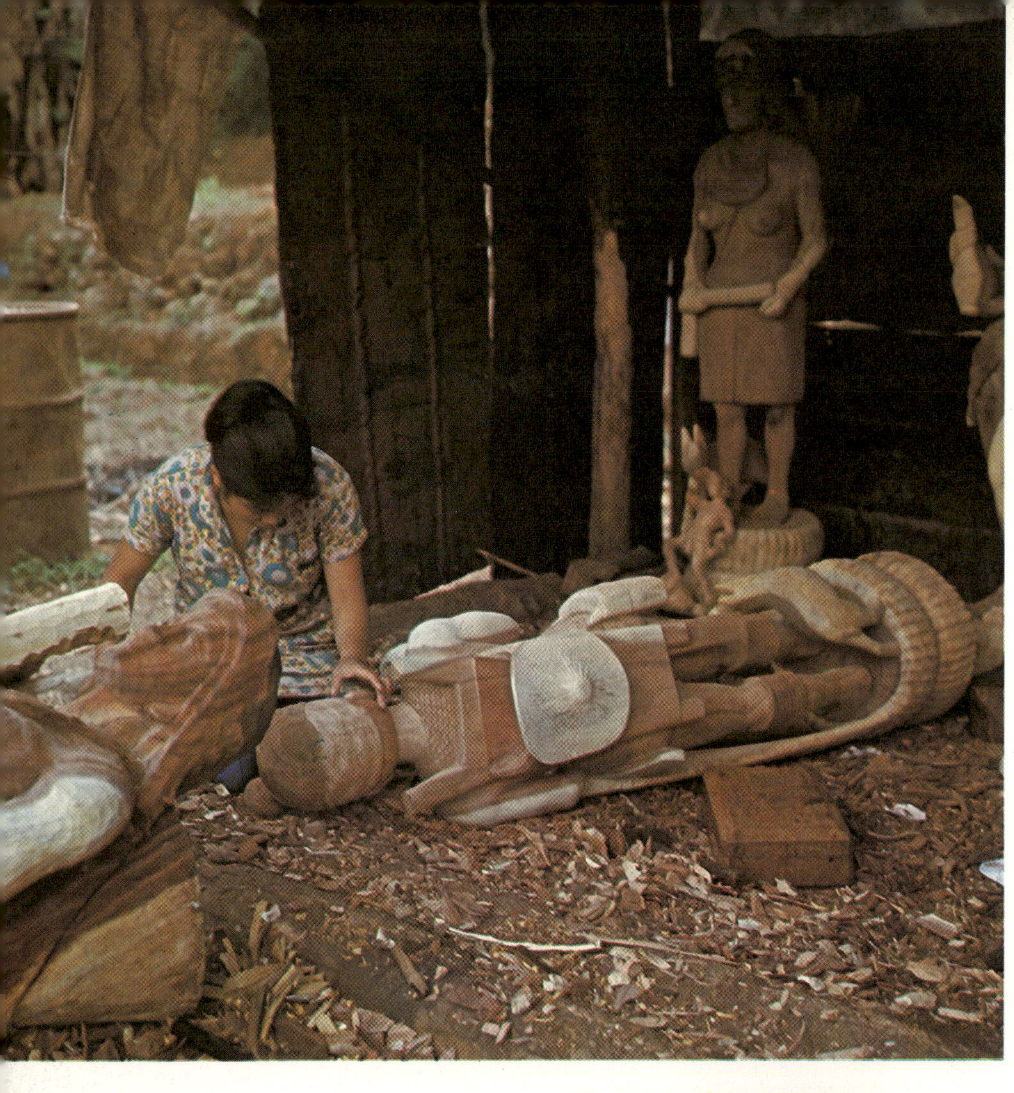

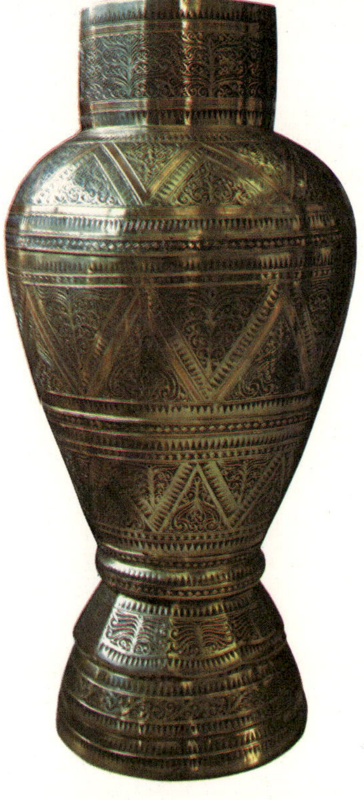

*Above:* Women carvers of the Igorot tribe handle their chisels and hammer with as much dexterity as the men. During recent years, these sculptures have made a great impression in the Western art world. There are numerous tribes who specialize in this art; they all have individual traits, and experts can usually name the tribe or region from where a particular carving originated.

*Left:* Muslim brass handicrafts are extremely popular and their display occupies large sections of souvenir shops. At Zamboanga City, the capital city of Mindanao (text page 131), Muslim brass-ware is especially cheap and there is a wide range from which to choose.

*Right:* A carving has just been finished. Wooden shavings are left to burn and the smoke will help to darken the statue.

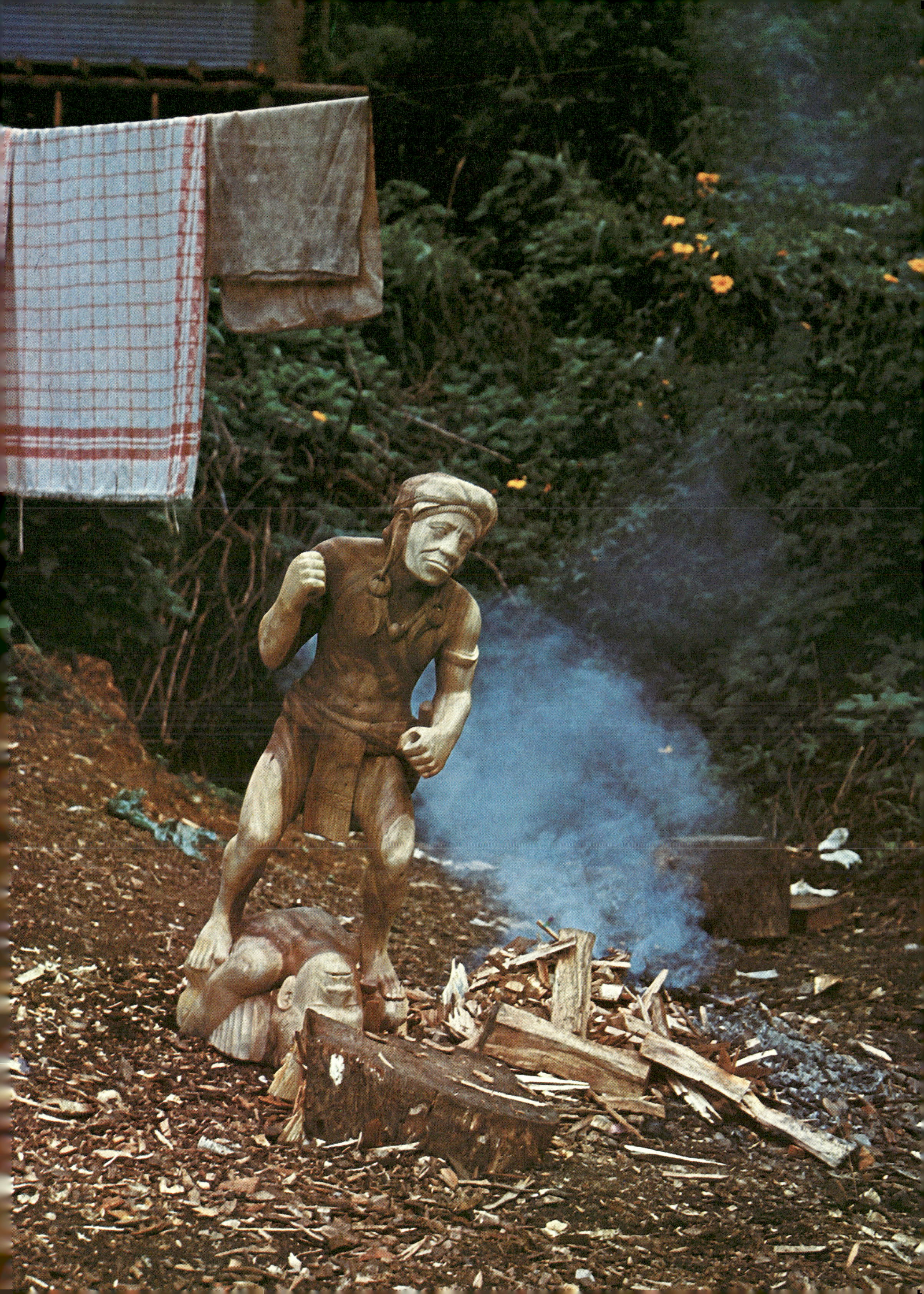

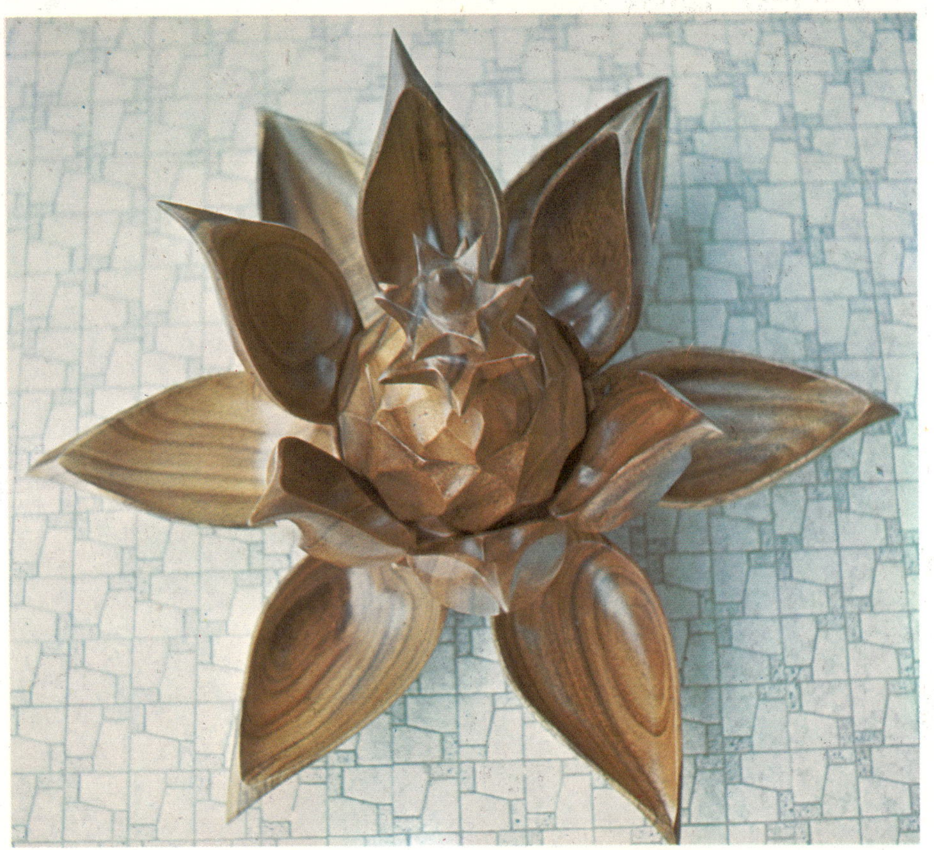

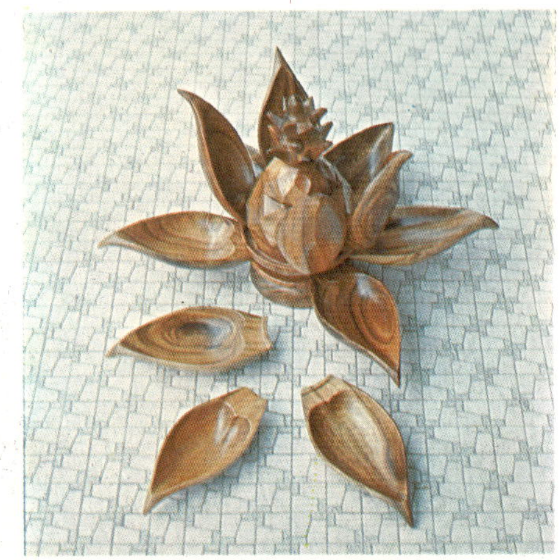

Above left/right: Many carvings have a practical use. Here, in the shape of a pineapple, and exquisitely made, is a set of hors-d'oeuvre dishes which can be revolved as well as removed individually.
Right: A punch-bowl set with an intricately carved design. Smooth and shiny. Perfect in every detail.

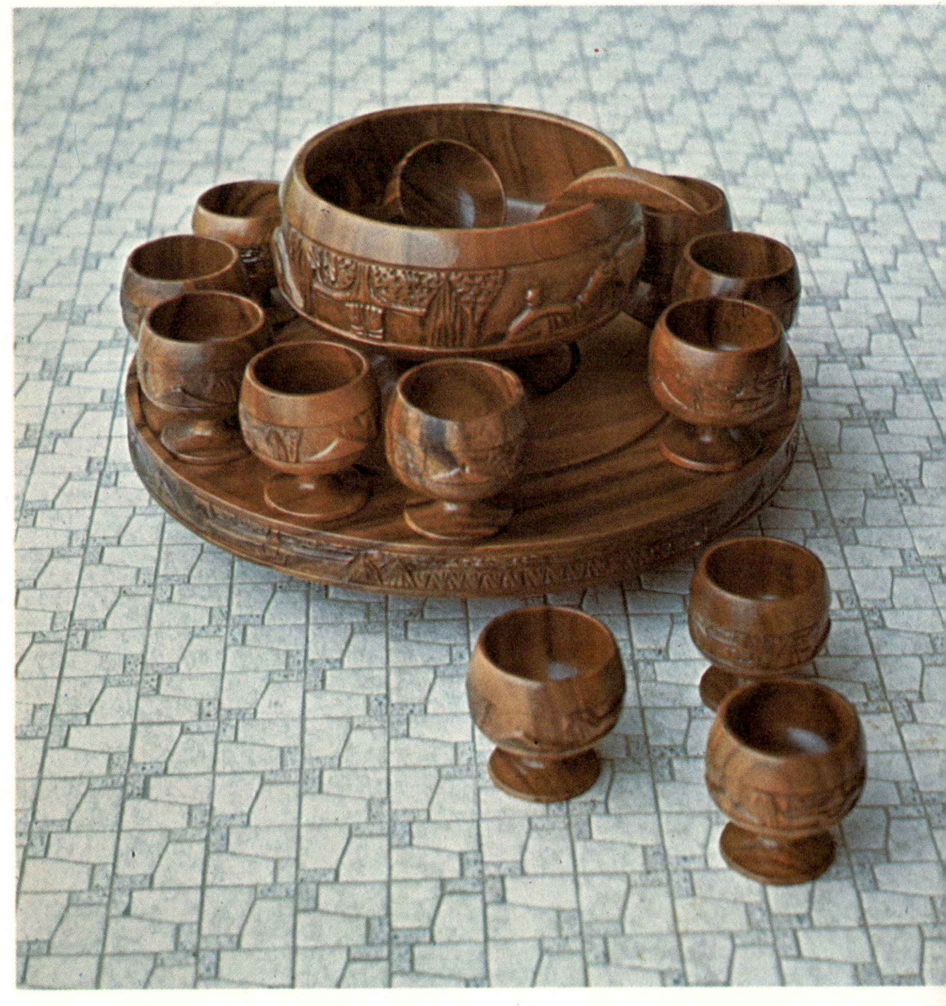

spectators for every kind of sport. Ayala Avenue, an ultramodern satellite city
of Manila, is the country's showpiece of commerce and trade, with banks,
trading firms, insurance companies and office blocks towering in elegant display
in an area that seventeen years ago was snake-infested swamp. Art galleries,
exhibiting the work of Filipinos, attract entrepreneurs from Europe and America,
while several museums are renowned for their displays of native art relics that
date back to the earliest centuries of Philippine civilization.

Along almost every road in Manila there are tropical flowers and trees while
numberless public gardens have acres of lawn as green and unblemished as the
felt on a billiard table. On several afternoons I sat by a willow-and-palm
bordered lake in the Chinese Gardens. Here, I watched mating dragon flies of
metallic lustre dance a *pas de deux* just above the surface where water lilies and
ferns grew in profusion near a cooling man-made waterfall. Whenever I moved,
butterflies, which had been absorbing moisture, rose in a blue snowstorm.
It was hard to believe that the endless horn-blowing, tyre-screeching traffic
was so near at hand.

Close to the Chinese Gardens is Fort Santiago, the Spanish dungeon where,
before his execution, the national hero Dr José P. Rizal, wrote his immortal
*Mi Ultimo Adios* ("My Last Farewell.") Translated, it begins:

> Land that I love: Farewell: Oh land the sun loves:
> Pearl in the sea of the Orient: Eden lost to your brood:
> Gaily I go to present you this hapless, hopeless life:
> Were it more brilliant: had it more freshness, more bloom:
> Still for you would I give it: would give it for your good!

A great Filipino patriot and the inspiration of Philippine nationalism,
José Rizal devoted his career to proving that Filipinos were, in art and
culture, equal to their Spanish masters. His death by firing squad on
30 December 1896 stimulated national sentiment and enhanced his already
great prestige among Filipinos.


*Houses for the Rich and the Poor*

A few years ago, Santiago was an eyesore of unsanitary squatters' shacks, but
Mayor Antonio J. Villegas, with determination and foresight, ordered in the
bulldozers. The Fort, rebuilt and beautifully landscaped, is now a national
shrine.

The squatters from Fort Santiago were resettled in communal housing estates,
but since those days the overcrowding of Manila has become a chronic problem.
Before the war, its population was about 575,000; the current figure is closer to
3 million.

Although the republic is not yet rich enough to do more than scratch the
surface of its housing shortage, a start has nevertheless been made and the
planned community "village" of Makati is a fine example. Twenty years ago,

Makati was a vast wilderness of swamp land, rice paddies and impenetrable snake-infested vegetation. Today, it is an impressive complex of houses, parks and commercial centres. While the Forbes Park section is equal to any prestigious residential area in the world, Makati is not exclusively for the rich. Some parts have been subdivided and sold to former squatters at low cost on long-term payments that return an annual total of more than 15 million pesos and have thereby changed large numbers of people from non-productive government liabilities into tax-paying citizens.

*Heritage from the War—a lingua franca*

Although there are some eighty-seven dialects of the national language, the most common tongue is English, a legacy from the war years when English was the medium of instruction. The most important dialect is Tagalog (pronounced Tuh-GAH-log) which, declared as the national language in 1946, was subsequently renamed Filipino in 1962; English and Spanish became the other official languages. However, Spanish was never popular and its use declines yearly. Those visitors who wish to practise their Spanish will be disappointed because the average Filipino will fail to understand one word; but English, the lingua franca of 38 million Filipinos, is spoken fluently even in remote areas.

The other dialects, including Filipino, have assimilated words from Arabic, Chinese, English, Indian and Spanish, but they all originate from the Malayo-Polynesian people who inhabit Oceania.

*A Culture before Christ*

For Europeans, the Philippine archipelago became known on 16 March 1521, when it was discovered by Ferdinand Magellan. But there are authentic Chinese records of trading voyages as early as the tenth century; in exchange for sandalwood and spices, the Filipinos were given porcelain, silks and cheap jewellery. Some of the porcelain, now extremely valuable, is occasionally found in "junk" shops and inadvertently sold very cheaply.

An acquaintance of mine who lives in Makati showed me a dozen genuine pieces from the Ming dynasty that had cost him only a few dollars. And in the National Museum I found an incredible display of Sung, Tang and Ming dynasty pottery and porcelain ware. Also, there were similar exhibits from Siam. In fact, the Philippines has far more rare Chinese pottery and porcelain than China, and more Siamese ware than Thailand. The explanation is simple. In China and Siam, such things as drinking vessels, urns and plates were made for everyday use and consequently became damaged, broken, or simply thrown away. But in the Philippines, these wares played an important part in rituals and were kept for burial "gifts;" the extensive display in Manila's museum had been excavated from more than one thousand graves.

By the middle of the fourteenth century, Indochina was likewise trading in porcelain, although as early as 200 B.C. the Philippines is known to have had contact with empires centred in Indonesia or Indochina.

*Above right:* Some sculptures are characterized by a striking and grotesque distortion of limbs and features. Others are entirely the opposite and, apart from being magnificently balanced, they also have great beauty and fine detail. Many of the more beautiful carvings were made to be used in religious or tribal rituals.
*Right:* Book ends; an ideal pair of matched ornamental props worth a place in every home where fine workmanship is appreciated.

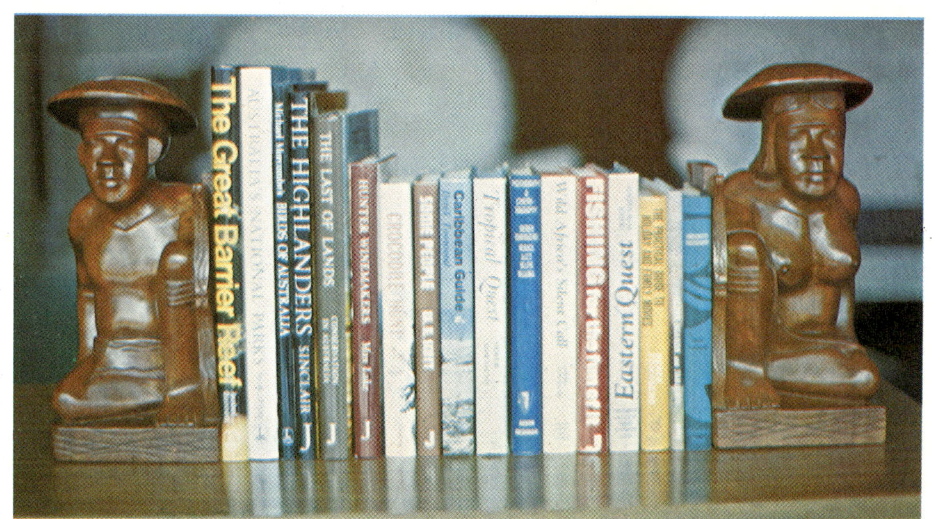

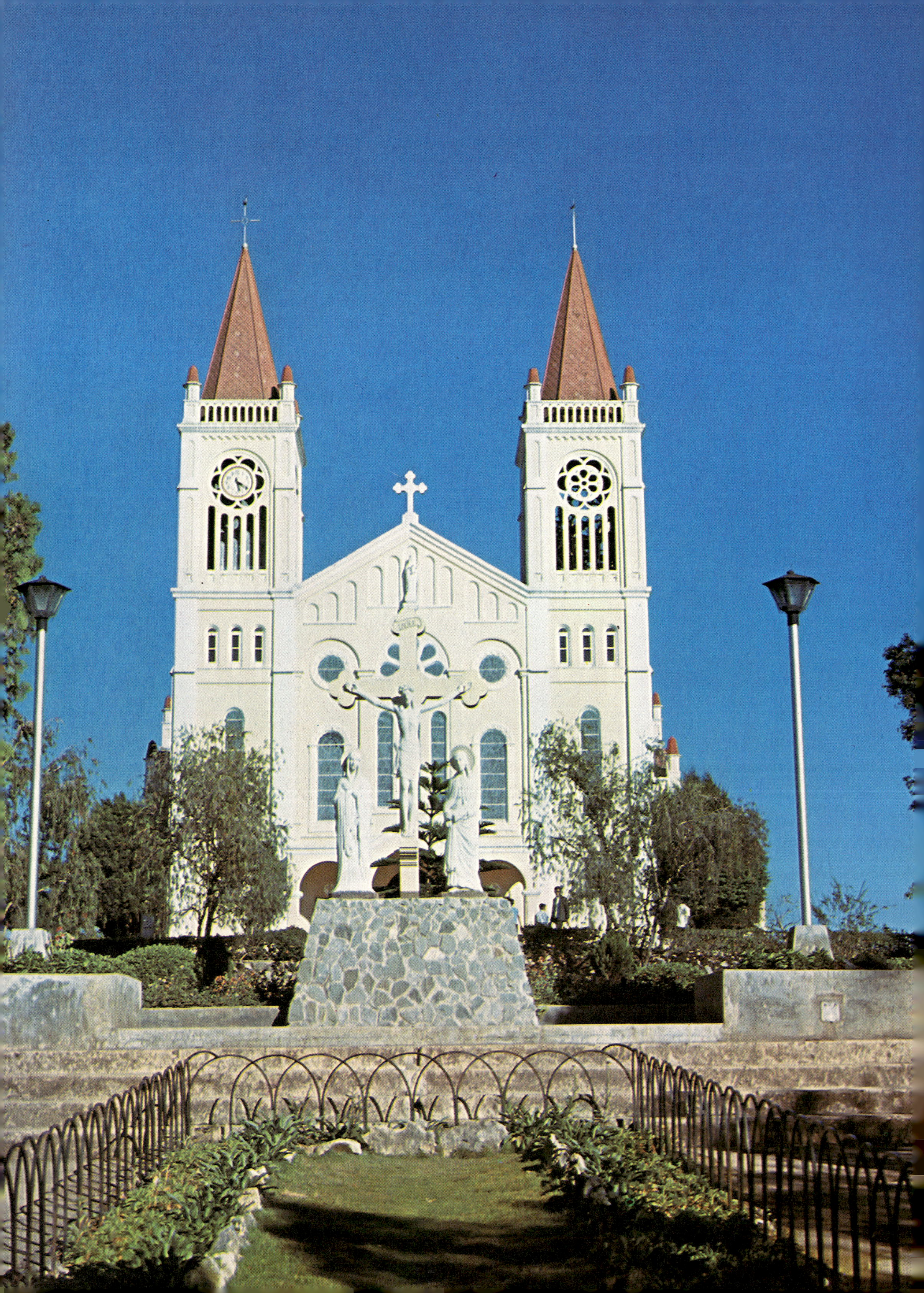

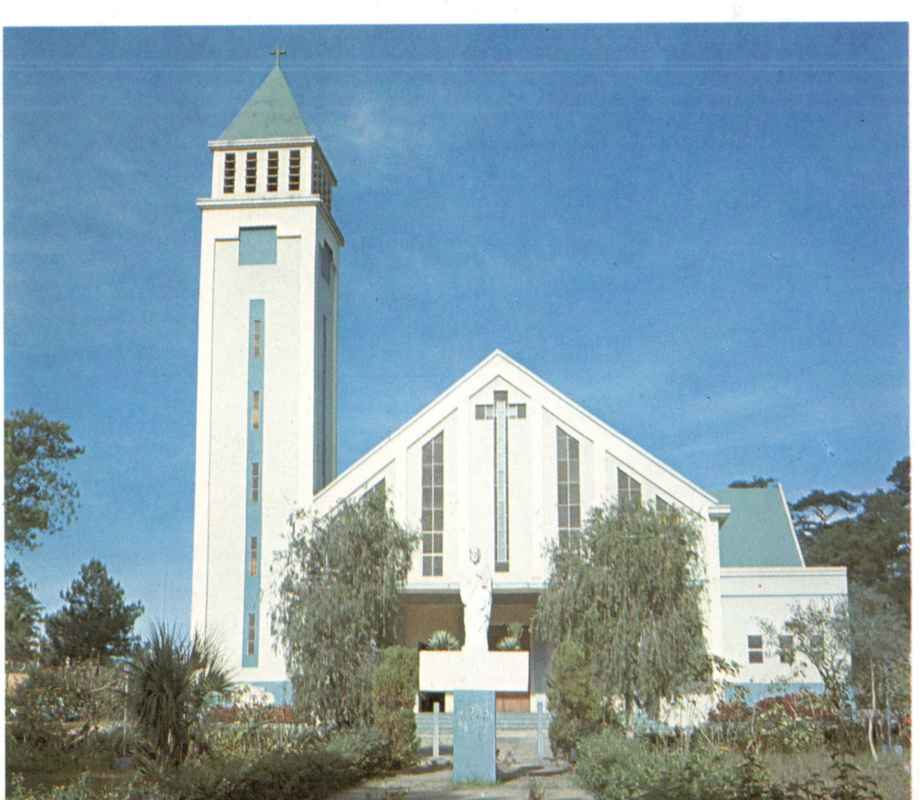



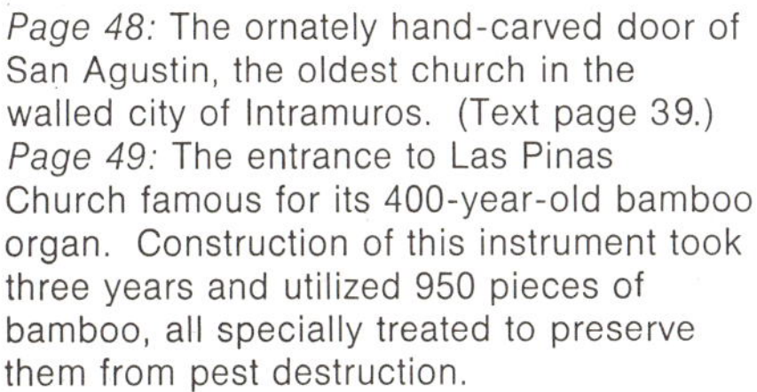

*Left/Above right:* Baguio City Cathedral.
*Below right:* Saint Joseph Roman Catholic Church built in 1957, Baguio City.

*Page 48:* The ornately hand-carved door of San Agustin, the oldest church in the walled city of Intramuros. (Text page 39.)
*Page 49:* The entrance to Las Pinas Church famous for its 400-year-old bamboo organ. Construction of this instrument took three years and utilized 950 pieces of bamboo, all specially treated to preserve them from pest destruction.

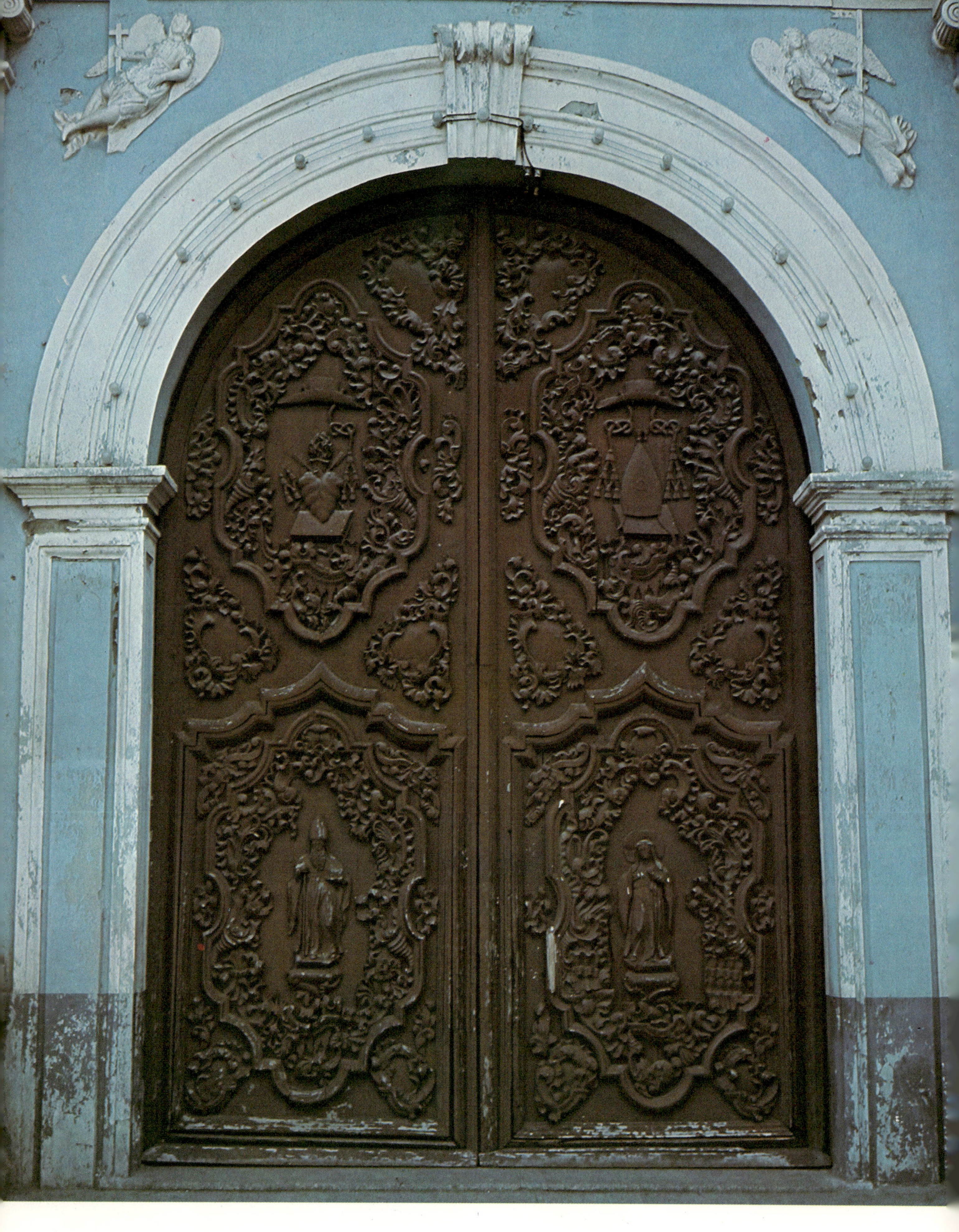

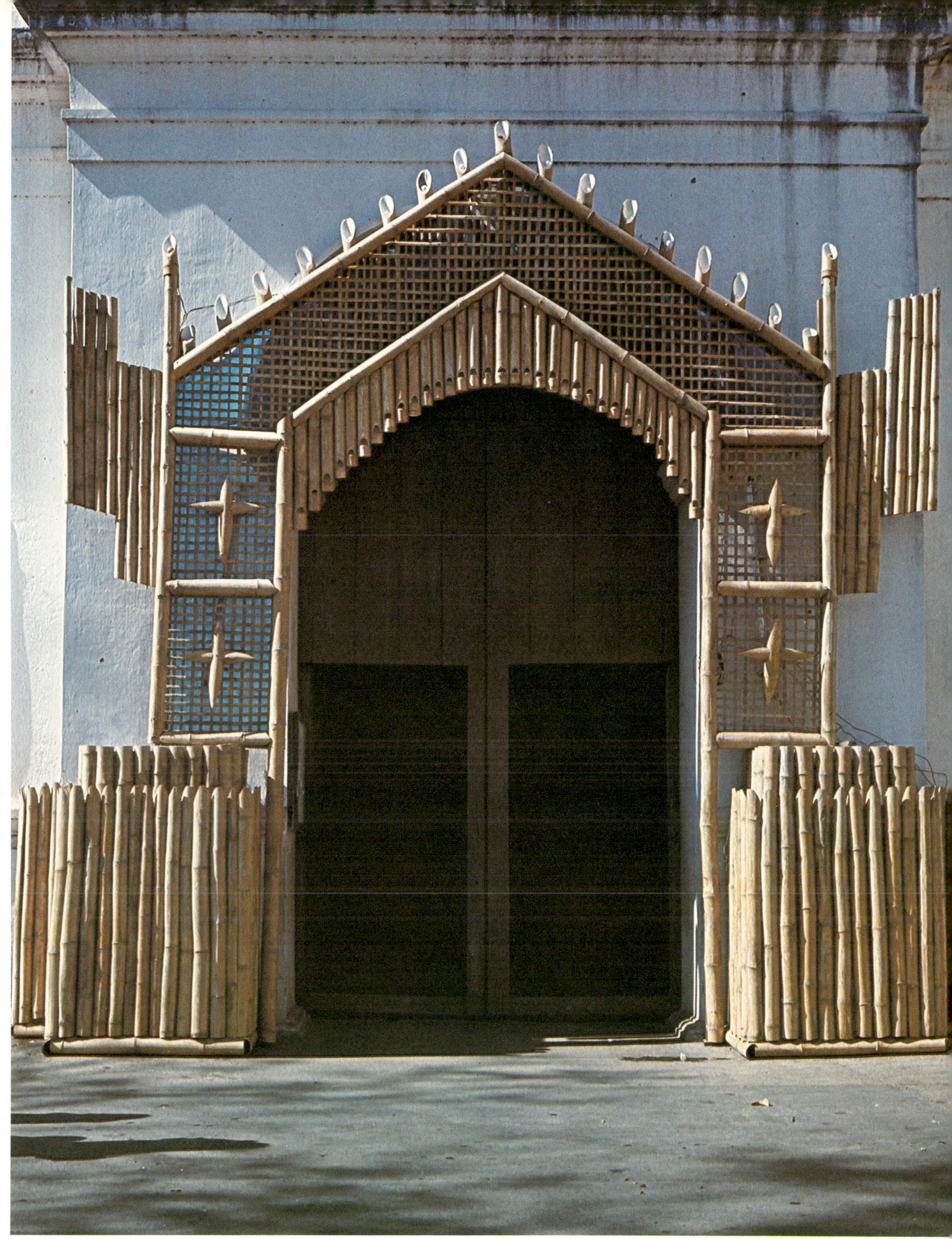

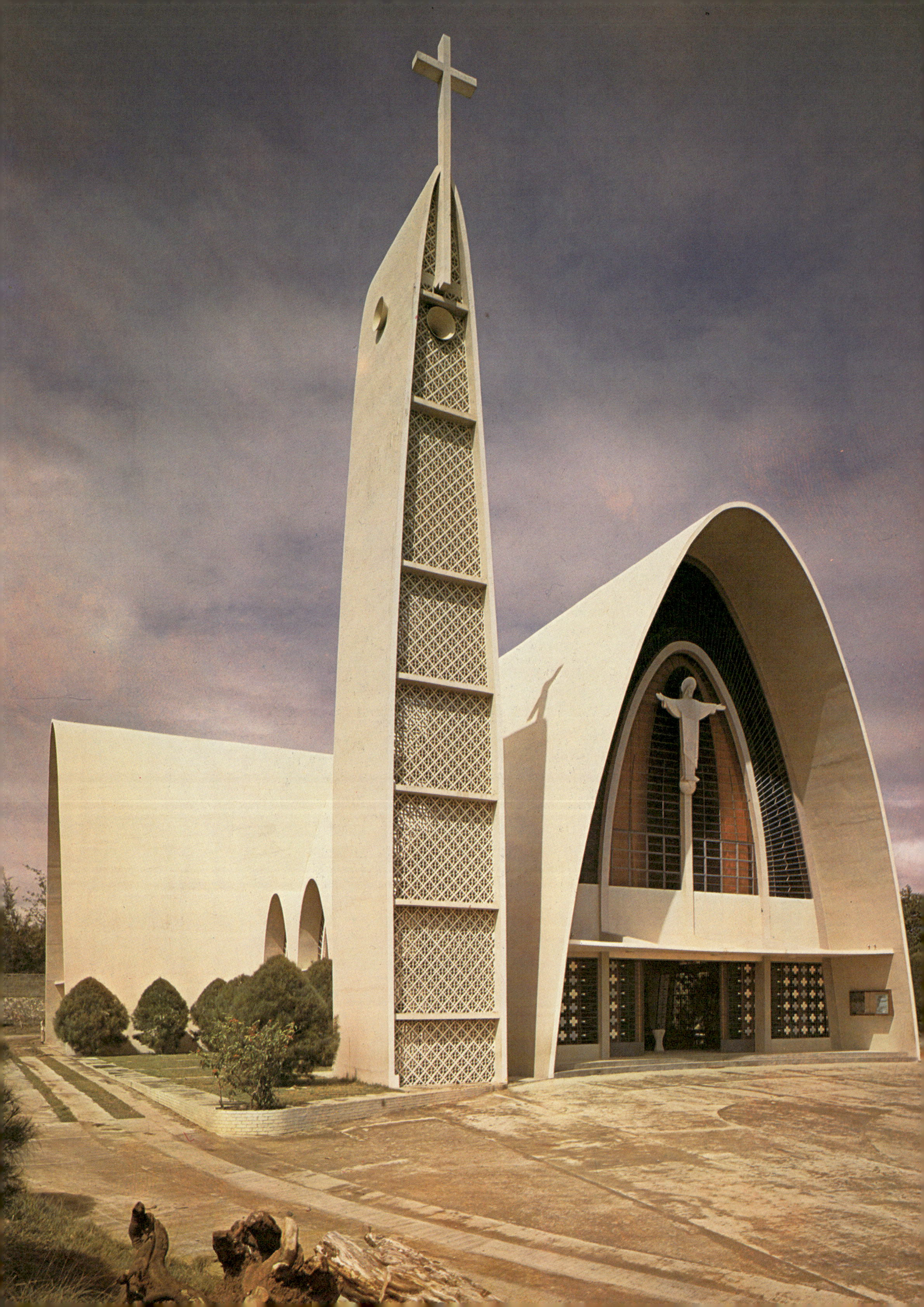

The very first inhabitants of the Philippines were almost certainly of
Polynesian origin, a theory enforced by the similarity of language and customs
between people from the Pacific islands of Indonesia, Melanesia, Micronesia and
Polynesia. While Europeans still believed the world to be flat and were afraid
to venture even into the Atlantic, the Polynesians, with skill, courage and
seamanship that have never been equalled, completed all the major Pacific
explorations. With primitive boats, and navigating only by a self-taught
knowledge of the stars, they spread in all directions, using Tonga, Samoa and
Tahiti.as bases for travelling south almost to the Antarctic, and north as far as
Hawaii. Yet, these amazing brown-skinned people had none of the resources
available to the later more famed explorers like Magellan, Bougainville, Cook,
Drake and Fernandez de Quieros.

Facts suggest that, in about the fourth century before Christ, after the Hindus
were known to have arrived by way of the Malay Peninsula and Java, the
Polynesians made a general exodus from the Philippines and began their
journeys into Oceania.

Other early migrations brought Asian people from the Chinese Gobi Desert
area or from the Himalaya Mountains—small, tough people who were the
ancestors of present-day mountain tribes in northern Luzon. These tribes, then
living along the coast, were found by the first Chinese traders, but inevitably
business encouraged more and more foreign settlers with whom the tribes were
reluctant to mix. Consequently, they moved gradually further inland where they
now reside in rugged mountain areas at more than 5,000 feet above sea-level.

One of these tribes, the Ifugaos, was responsible for the spectacular rice
terraces at Banaue which were carved from steep hillsides more than three
thousands years ago. Classed as an eighth wonder of the world these terraces,
if placed end to end, would stretch more than halfway round the world
(photograph pages 54-55).

*Spanish Rule*

After Magellan's discovery of the Philippines, the potential spice trade attracted
several further unsuccessful Spanish expeditions, but it was not until Miguel de
Legaspi arrived at Cebu on 13 February 1565 that Spanish occupation became
a reality. At first, the Spanish conquest was precarious and hazardous, being
challenged by Chinese pirates, the Japanese, the Dutch, the Portuguese and the
British. But when Legaspi died in 1572 he had already established Manila as
the capital (it was previously a Mohammedan outpost), the northern and
central islands were held securely and conversion to Christianity was
proceeding fast. In October 1762 the British captured Manila and soon
occupied most of the islands, but they were returned to Spain in 1764.

Later, during the nineteenth century, Filipino discontent with Spanish rule
reached a climax with the execution of Dr José Rizal. Several rebellions
occurred including the Spanish-American War which formally ended with the
rebels in absolute control. On 10 December 1898 the Treaty of Paris gave the

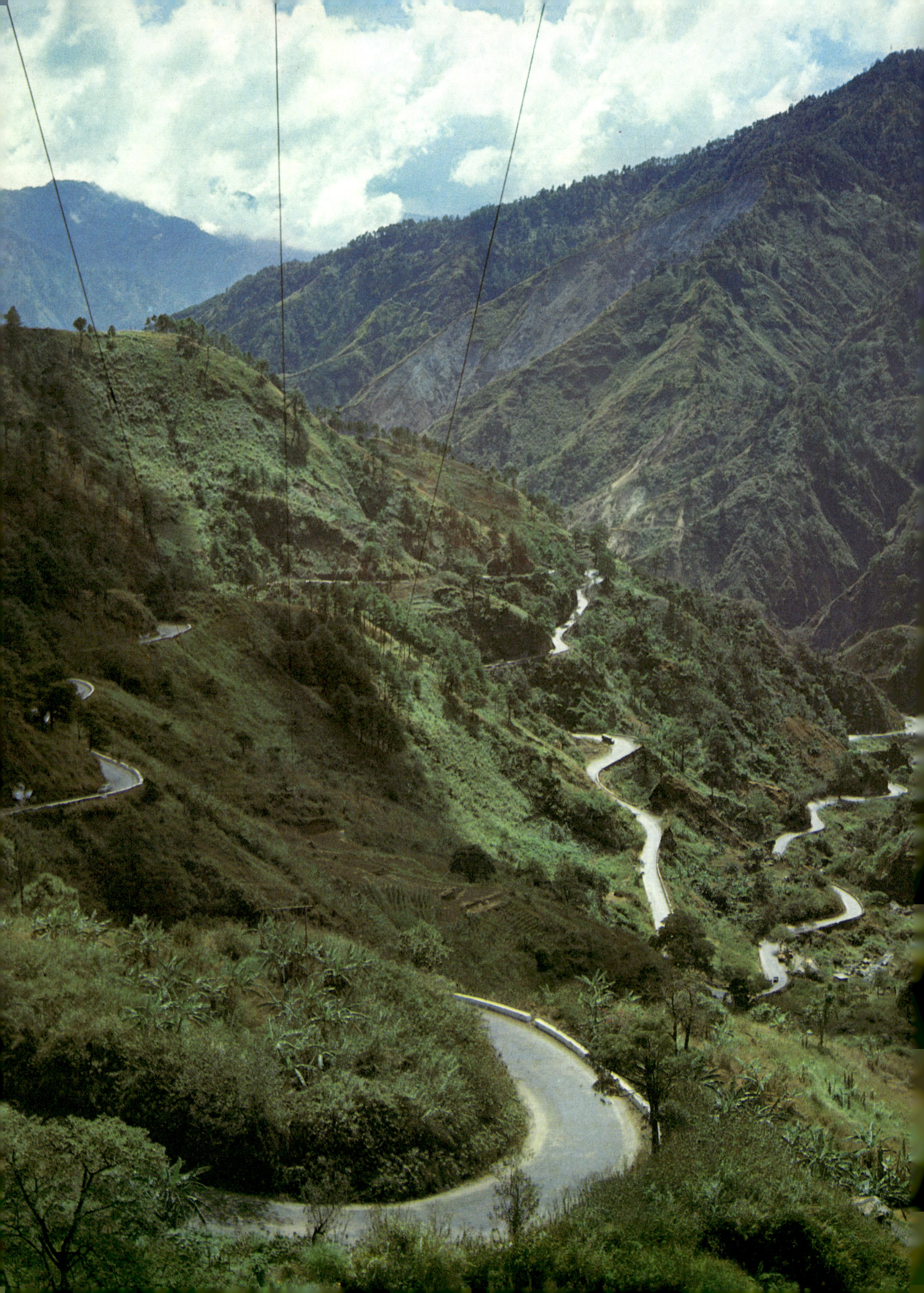

U.S.A. sovereignty over the islands, but fighting, which broke out between American and Filipino forces, was not settled until 1901 and complete independence came only on 4 July 1946 after World War II.  But the Filipinos, artistic and creative by nature, managed to extract the best things from their turbulent history.

Spain influenced the Philippines with its language, its civilization and its Christian religion.  America contributed widespread education and a higher standard of living.  (Damian Domingo, known as the "Father of Filipino Painting" and famous for his miniature water-colours depicting the Filipino way of life, was appointed by the Spaniards, in 1826, as director of a school of fine arts; later, Europe gave Filipino artists the recognition they deserved.)

On the outer islands I was able to see Spanish influence in the industry of making guitars and ukuleles.  Generally, young boys did the work, producing each instrument by hand, polishing it to perfection and inlaying designs with mother-of-pearl.  However, the Filipinos had traditional music long before the Spanish conquest.  The Europeans, with their great composers like Beethoven, Schumann and Brahms, merely widened the range of the Filipinos' appreciation, thereby enabling them to find their own musical identity by merging the technique of Western composers with the existing Filipino rhythms and melodies of Indo-Malayan origin.

During the American occupation the arts were further encouraged with the initiation of numerous colleges, training centres and workshops.  In particular, Filipino literature began to flourish, and it now ranks highly everywhere in the world.

These contacts with the Hindus, Chinese and Arabs not only influenced the Filipinos but also provided the impetus for them to evolve a distinct culture which was established long before Magellan arrived.

Hindu influence is indicated by the many Sanskrit words in the languages and dialects of the Filipinos as well as in the original formation of their alphabetic letters. Folklore, metal-work, dress and art also show a link with Hindu life.

By the sixteenth century, the Filipinos had their own alphabet and they wrote on pieces of earthenware by scratching them with pointed sticks of bamboo; but their literature, which included songs and plays, had begun centuries before the Europeans arrived.  They also had a 356-day calendar; a system of weights and measures which utilized different units for length and capacity, as well as taking into account the difference between dry and fluid measures; an adequate system of law that encompassed everything from divorce to murder; and economic policies to handle loans, money-lending and financial contracts.

*The Filipinos*

As a result of the Philippines' varied historical relationships, the population comprises three main groups separated by religion.  The majority group is Christian, followed by Muslim (these belong to the southern islands) and, from isolated areas, a minority group of different ancient religions that originated centuries before the Muslims and Christians arrived.

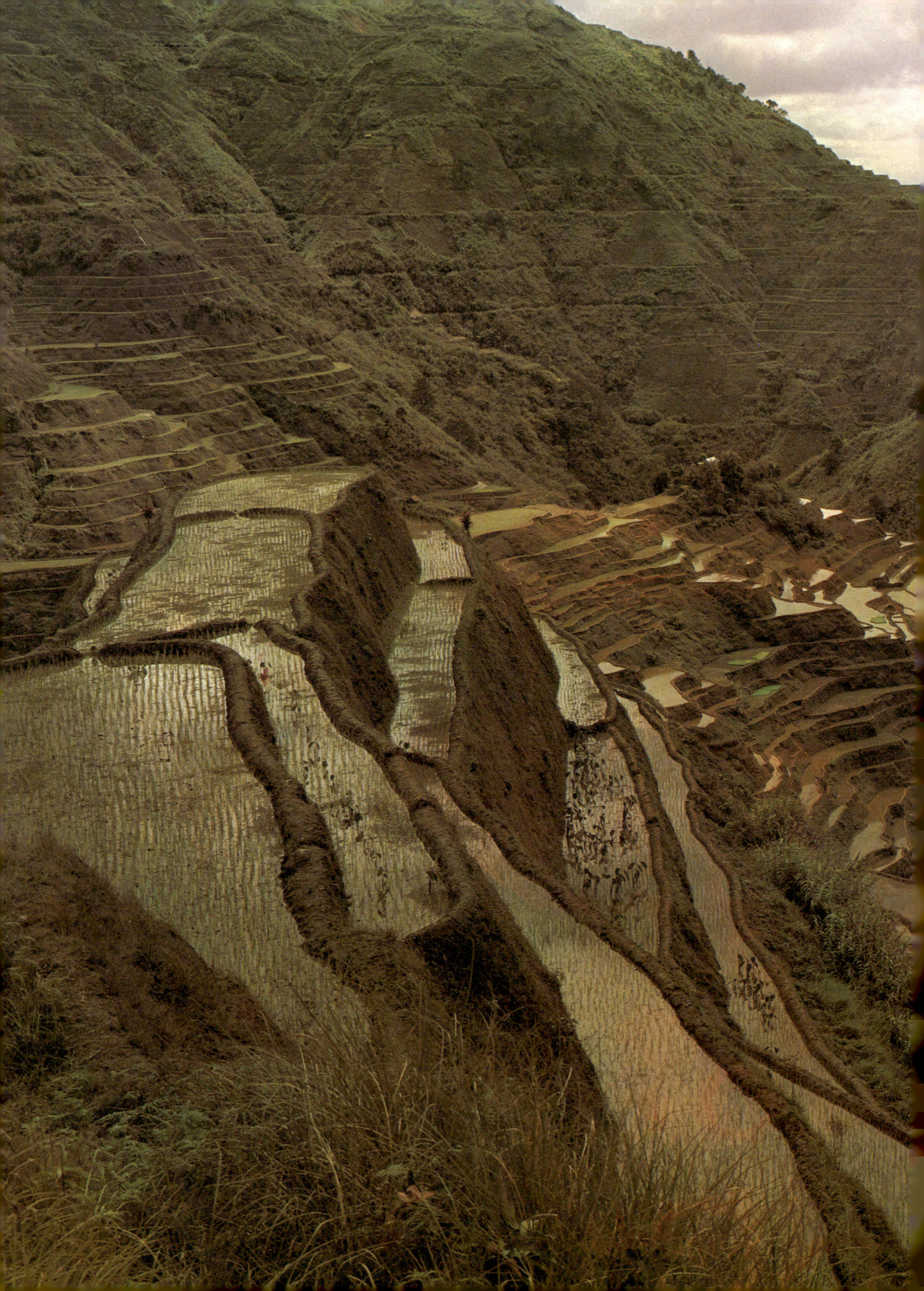

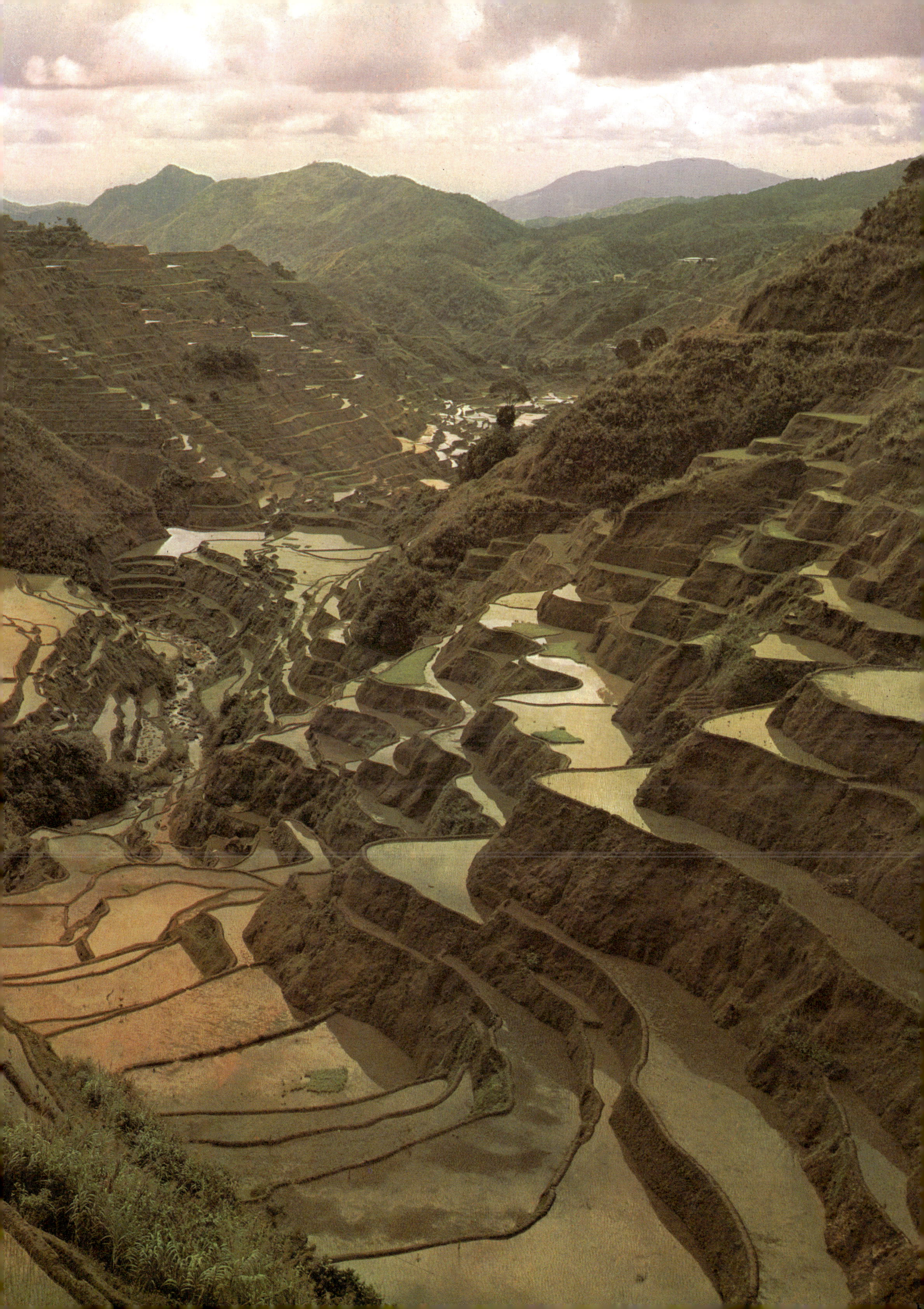

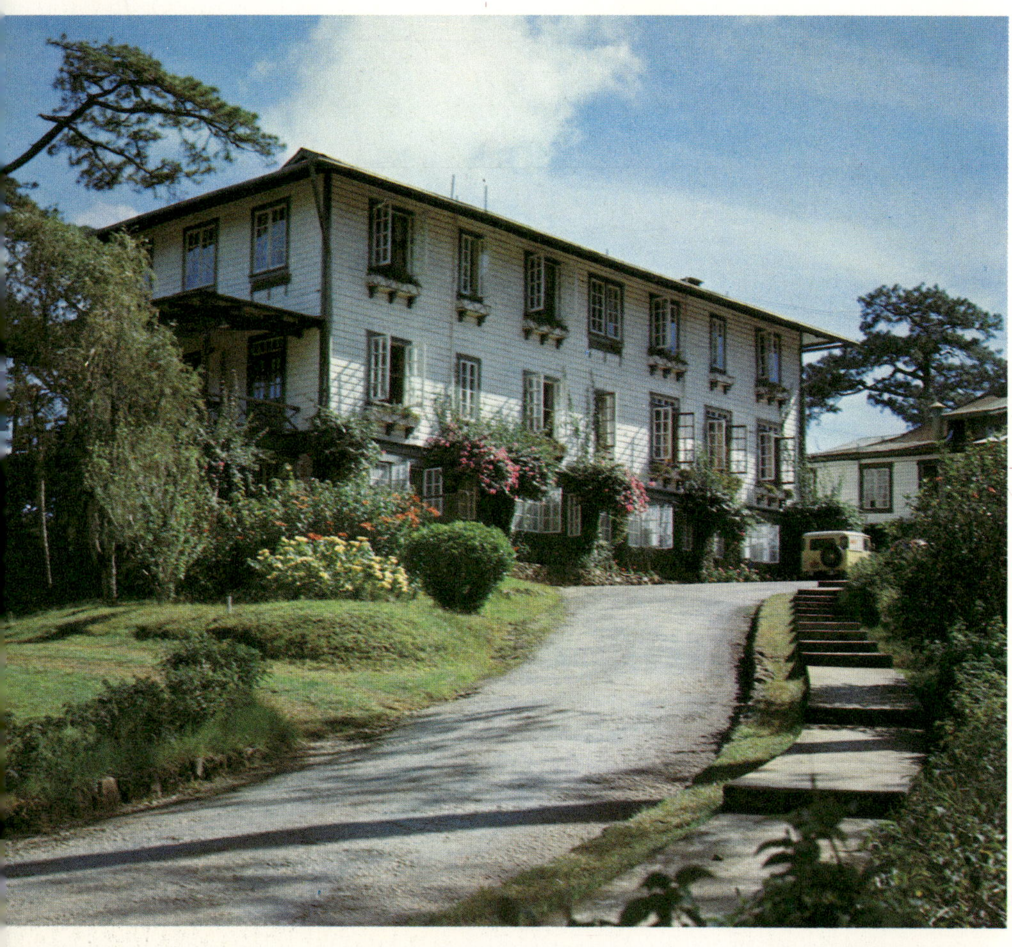

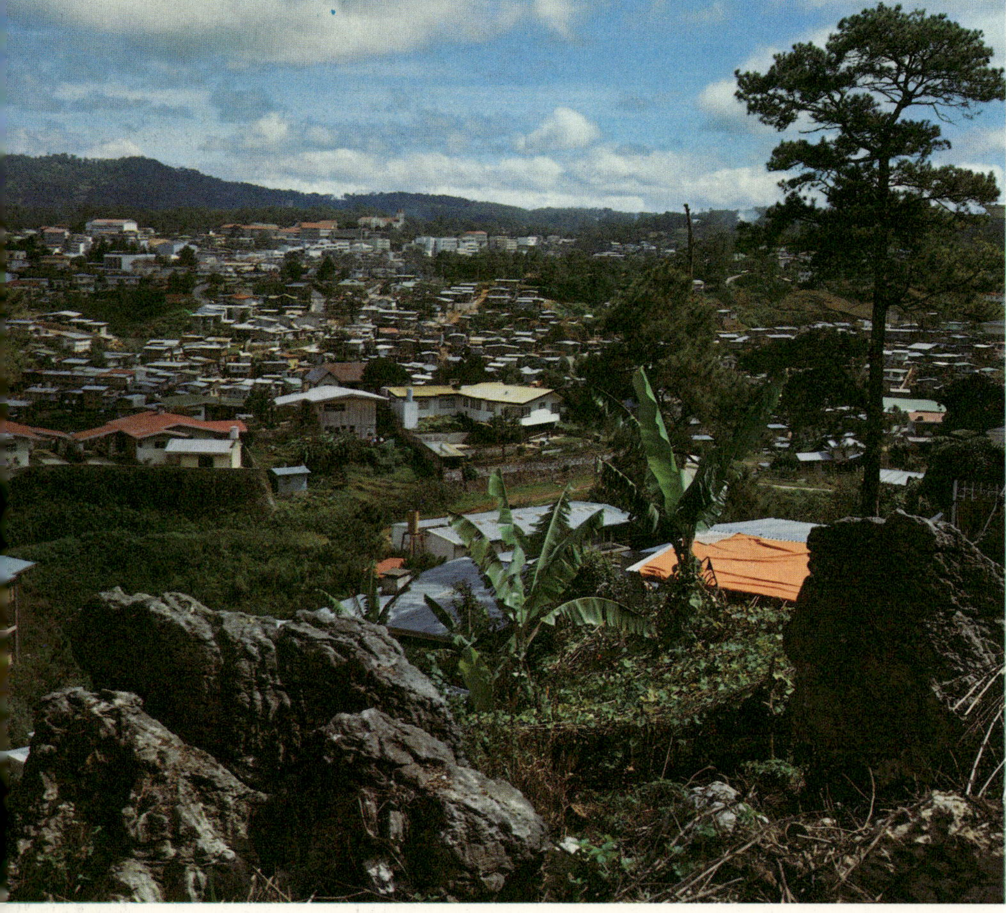

*Above left:* Baguio City Country Club where visitors can enjoy fine food and a round of golf.
*Below left:* Baguio City viewed from high ground.

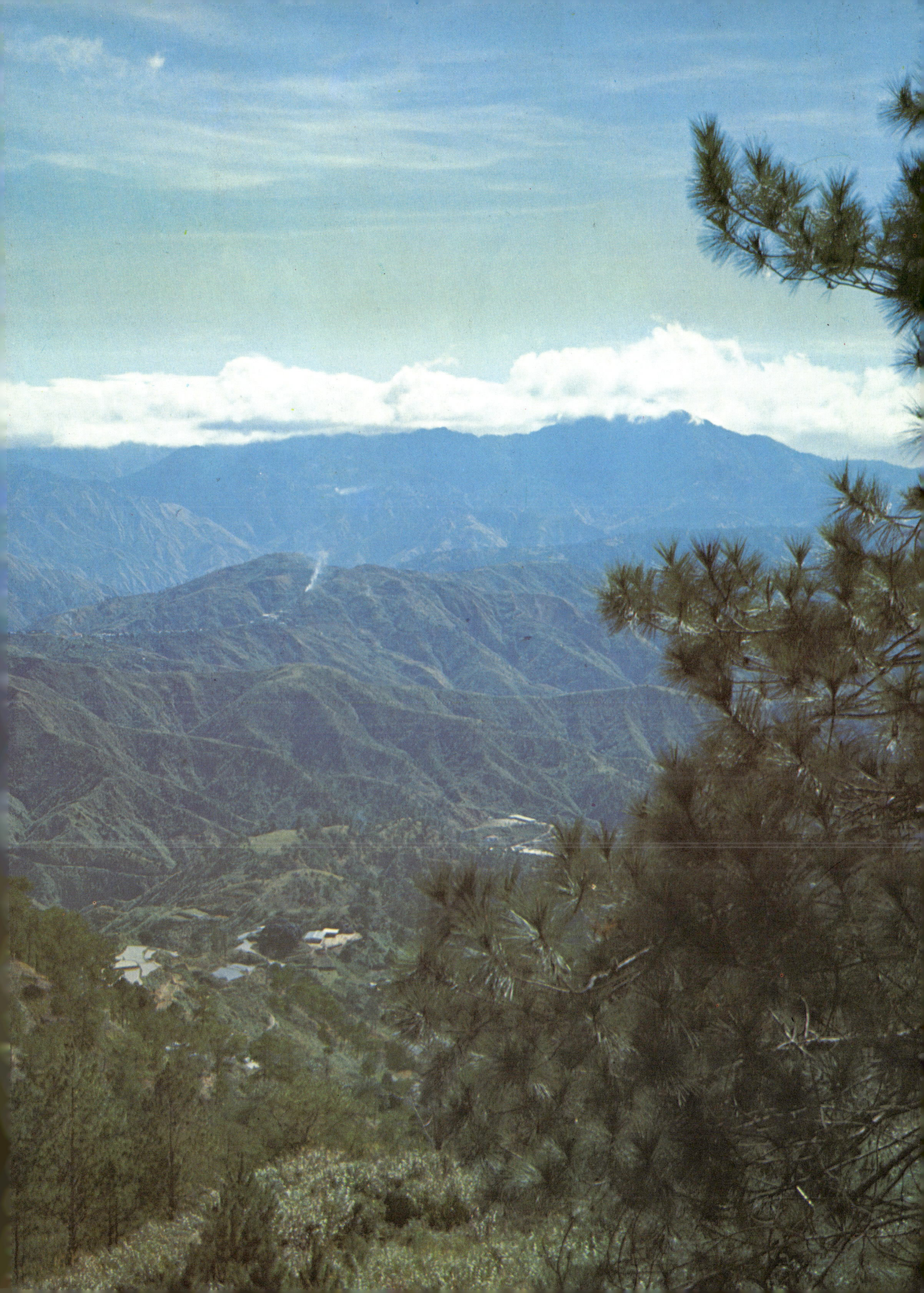

''I'm from Baguio City. Yes Sir!'' These children spoke fluent English as well as Filipino. (Text page 44.)

In the southern islands life grinds on
slowly.  And children are always children
wherever they are.  These little girls have
been washing themselves, including their
hair and teeth, with soap.

Curiosity eventually overcame her shyness as this Igo girl examines the photographer who, carrying three cameras and two lenses, must have looked formidable to any child!

*Top right:* Manila harbour and waterside gardens.
*Top left:* One of Manila's numerous illuminated fountains with changing light patterns and colours.
*Bottom left:* One of the many attractive statues in Rizal Park, Manila.
*Bottom right:* The Rizal Memorial Sports Centre.
*Page 65:* Taal Volcano on a rainy day. An impressive natural time bomb that has become a tourist attraction.  (Text page 23.)

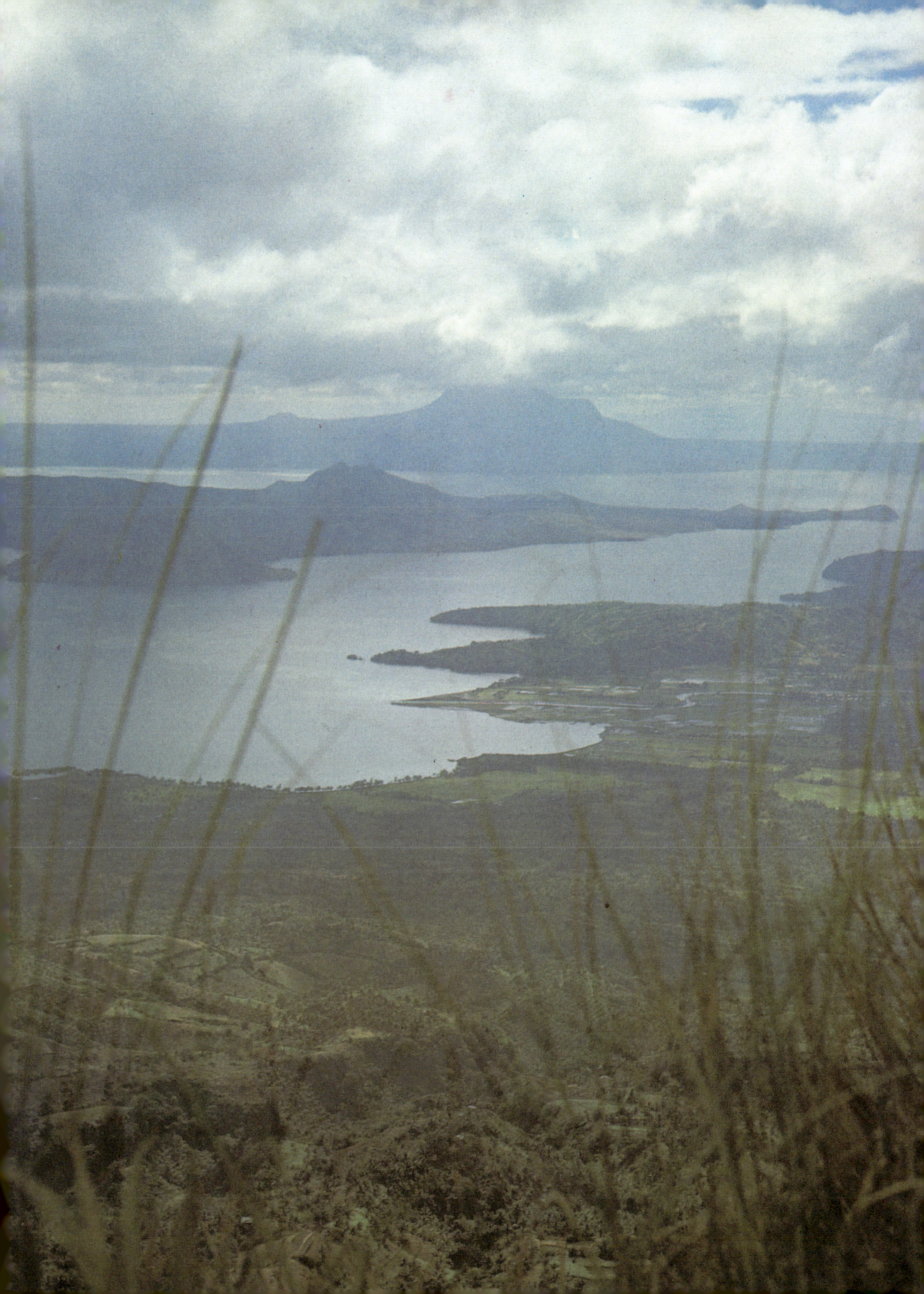

_Above:_ Ruins of the Cagsawa, an ancient Spanish church destroyed when Mayon Volcano (background) erupted. Dominating Legaspi City, Mayon is the world's most perfect cone-shaped volcano.
_Right:_ Shooting the rapids at Pagsanjan in Laguna. (Text pages 83, 85-86.)

During recent years Filipino paintings, sculpture, metal and brass work have made a great impression in the Western art world. Wooden carvings produced in the mountain provinces are sold in practically every Manila store and handicraft shop and are much sought by tourists and collectors; the magnificent statues in the churches are all carved by these craftsmen.

The Muslims, particularly those from Mindanao, are especially famous for their brassware and intricately fashioned silver filigree jewellery and inlay work. Deep in the mountain ranges, the people continue to follow a way of life older than Western civilization. Here, ornate brass sword hilts, magnificent works of art prized by collectors, are produced from crude forges with a craftsmanship nurtured for centuries. To mould these hilts, the natives employ an ancient process: a facsimile, carved in beeswax, is covered with clay. After drying, the clay is then heated and the liquid wax poured away to leave a cavity for the molten brass which is generally obtained from empty World War II shell casings!

Those tribes unaffected by Muslim, Christian, Spanish or American influence remain pagan, their villages outposts of civilization where they pursue traditional forms of dancing, singing, music and sports. Inhabiting the high altitude regions, these people continue many old ways of life, even to wearing no more than a brief loin cloth (hand-woven and colourfully decorated with complex patterns) despite the cold climate. All these people were once headhunters, but now only a small group continues this custom. These people, a racial mixture of the Igorot and Negrito, inhabit the desolate ranges of Northern Luzon and are thought to originate from the New Guinea Highlanders*, although unlike the Highlanders, they were never cannibals and took heads only as trophies which, in their society, were important items in rituals of puberty.

Filipinos have always believed in spirits and many of their superstitions— which are comparable with throwing spilled salt over the left shoulder—can be traced to ancient folklore. The Igorots still worship a variety of gods, one of the most important being the granary god; idols of this god stand in the rice paddies to protect the workers and to ensure a healthy crop. When the rice has been harvested the god is then placed with the precious grain to frighten away thieves and evil spirits. The home god is also of great importance in every dwelling place. (Here is a remarkable similarity to the Siamese Spirit Chao Ti or "Lord of the Place" which in modern Thailand is acknowledged by having a Spirit House—built like a miniature palace—in *every* house. Each day, offerings of fruit or flowers are made to the spirit and lighted candles and incense sticks are placed before the shrine. Even factories are guarded by these Spirit Houses.)

But all Filipinos, irrespective of tribe or religion, have an impressive sense of design and colour. They excel in weaving—as they have done for over 400 years—and three of the more unusual hand-woven fabrics are *piña,* woven from pineapple fibres; *jusi,* loomed from raw silk; and *patadiong,* a soft, fine cotton.

* *The Highlanders,* also published by The Jacaranda Press

Needleworkers are famed for their exquisite embroidery of table linens, infants' clothing, skirts, blouses, dresses and handkerchiefs. Even when I wandered around country markets, I found the fruit and vegetables arranged in kaleidoscopic patterns that made full use of their different sizes, colours and shapes. Certainly, no race of people can be more talented, more courteous or more friendly, while the beauty of Filipino women is renowned.

*Nights Alive*

The philosopher Nathaniel Branden once stated: "Pleasure for man is not a luxury, but a profound psychological need," and he qualified this by explaining how man can understand the value of life through pleasurable living. Such philosophy is typified in Manila where, since time immemorial, Filipinos have closely followed the pursuit of pleasure through romance, eating and drinking, singing and dancing, and through all the creative arts.

This unique cultural trend has resulted in "the business of pleasure" being a major industry employing an incredible number of people in hotels, restaurants, bars and nightclubs. A brochure produced by one of the official Philippine Tourist Associations says of the night-life—"Manila and its suburbs offers more entertainment than any city in Asia. Name it, and we'll lead you to it. Legit or illegit, nice or naughty, chic or cheek, breezy or bawdy, wild or weird."

Long before the sun has set over Manila Bay, the night people are already hard at work: the musicians, the hostesses, the chefs, the singers and the gambling operators, all advertising their attractions in an extravaganza of flashing lights and music. In the plushy hotels, there are excellent supper clubs of international standard; dress is formal and you can dine in continental style while enjoying floor shows that feature leading entertainers from Australia, Europe and America. For the younger generation these same hotels offer more groovy pleasures in their disco pads.

At the Jai-Alai Building, from the safety of the Sky Room cocktail lounge, you can watch Jai-Alai (pronounced "high-lie") being played, one of the fastest, most vigorous ball games in the world. This game originated in the Basque country of Spain and was derived from handball and squash, but it is much faster than either. The ball *(pelotari)* is hit with a scoop-shaped basket *(cesta)* which can hurl the ball to a great height at speeds of up to 150 miles an hour. For those who like to be "where the action is," go into the stadium below and join the shouting, excited onlookers as they place large bets with the bookmakers.

But variety is the password of the night. Hear progressive jazz at the Indonesia, get an Iberian flavour at Mecca, watch the "in-crowd" at the Manhattan Club, see local talent at El Patio, go to the Mutya Room's spectacular "acquacade," enjoy the companionship and dancing skills of a hostess at the Bayside, or look for the naughtier spots like Adam & Eve, Quezon City, and Champagne.

Most of the better clubs are discreetly hostessed with only elegantly dressed

No ghosts of the past ennoble these heights.
No recorded Hannibal has struggled
across them.  No conquering armies have
marched here.  Nevertheless, all mountains,
like the sea, must command respect; they
are a power unto themselves.

*Above:* Manila Bay from the Cultural Centre—one of the many new buildings which are a tribute to the genius of young Filipino designers.

*Right:* In the mountain provinces especially, there are many secluded places where a city girl can relax and enjoy the sunshine.

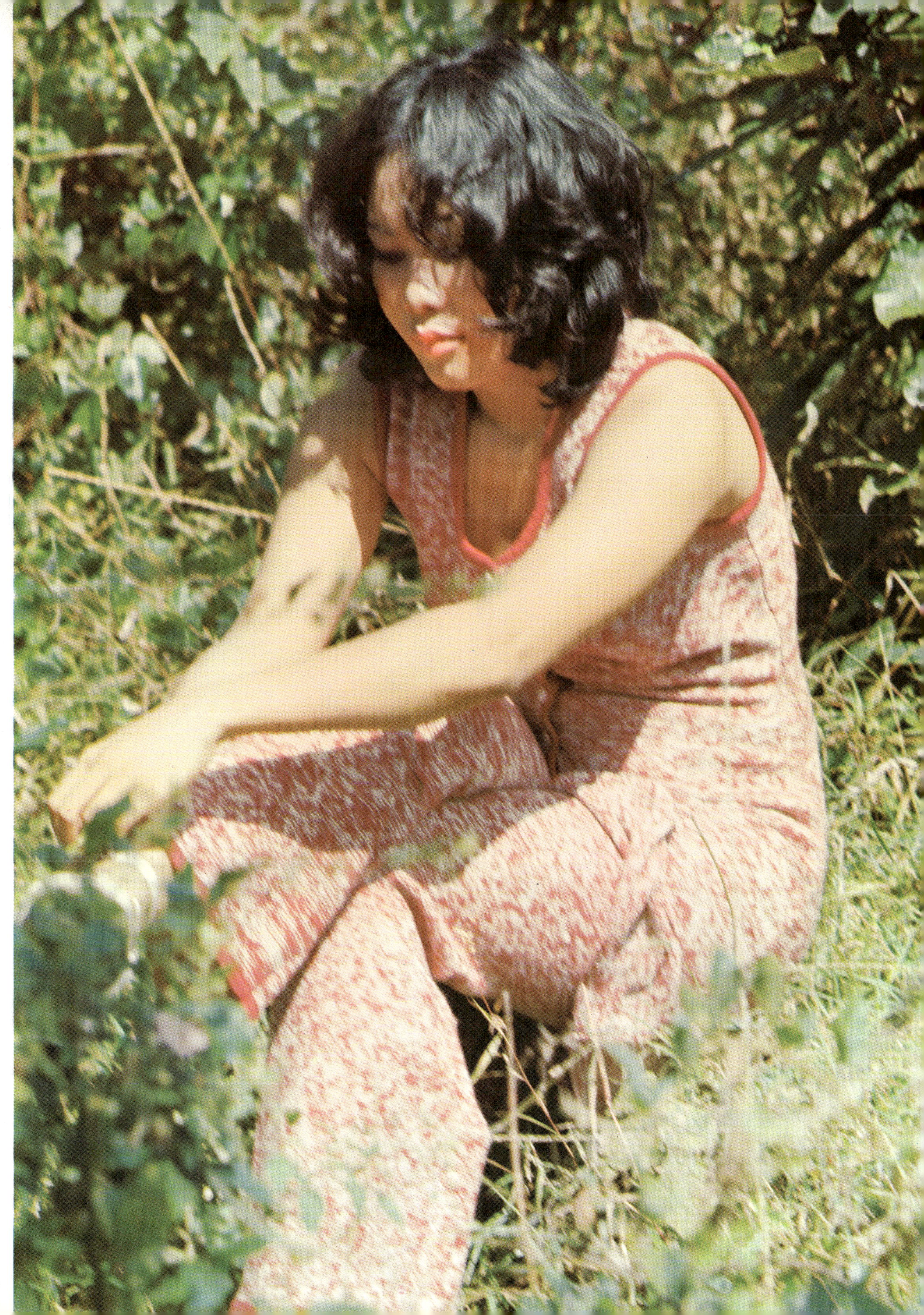

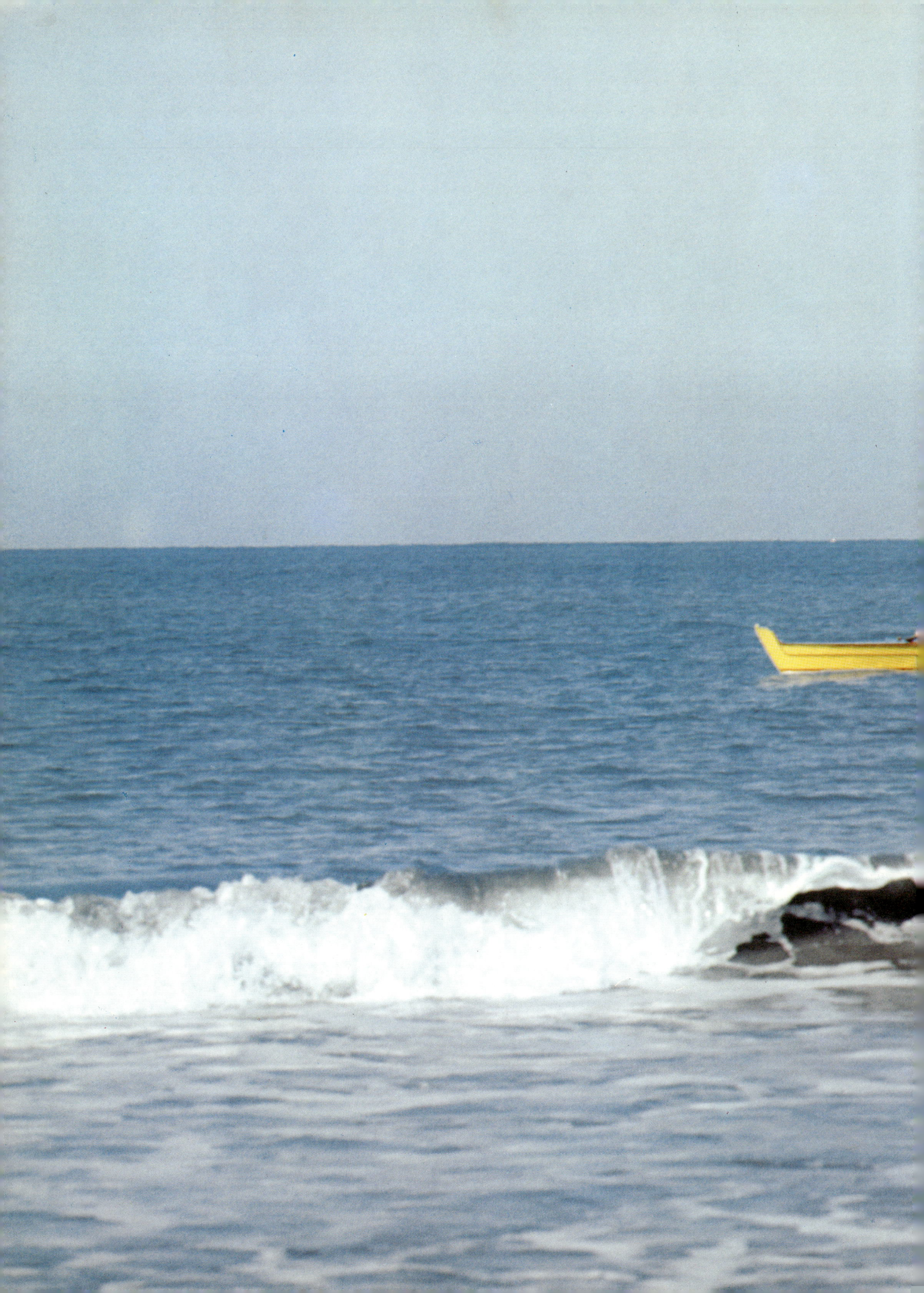

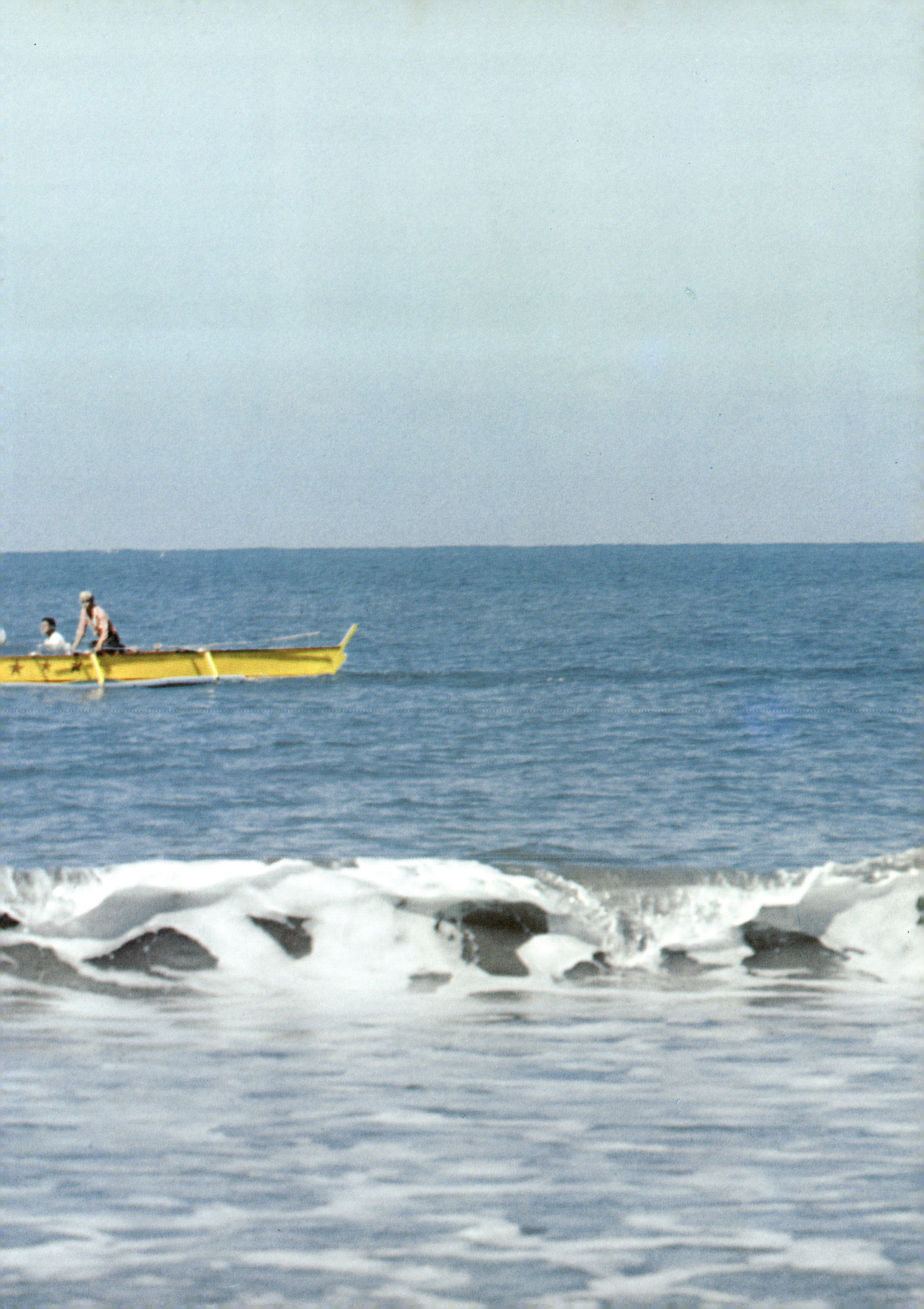

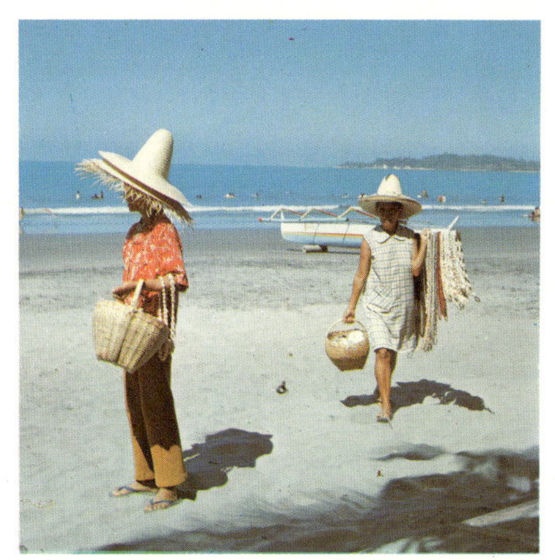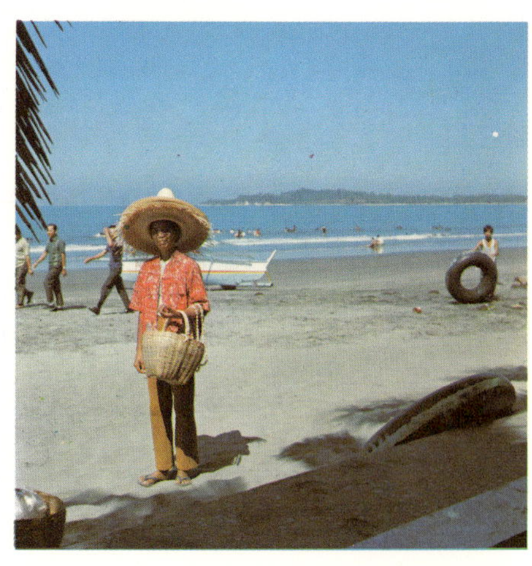

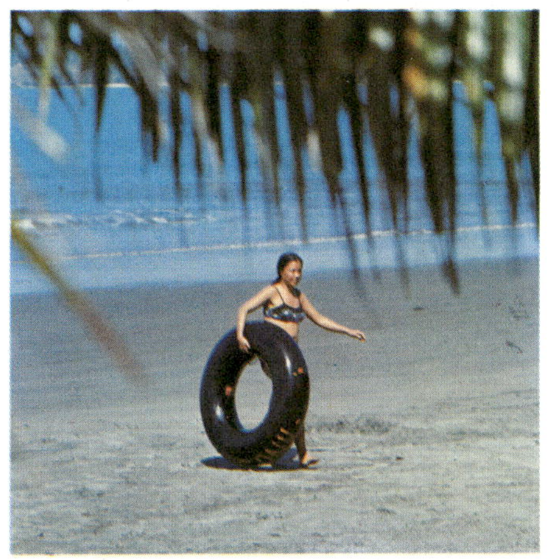 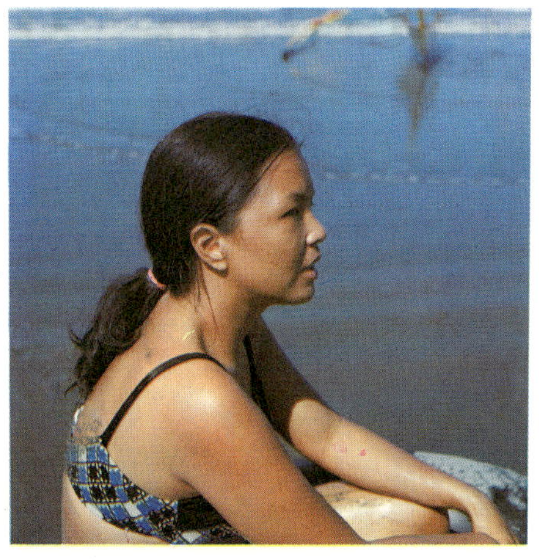

Beaches in La Union are among the best in the Philippines. Along this coast, fine sand stretches north and south for many miles. The provincial capital is San Fernando.

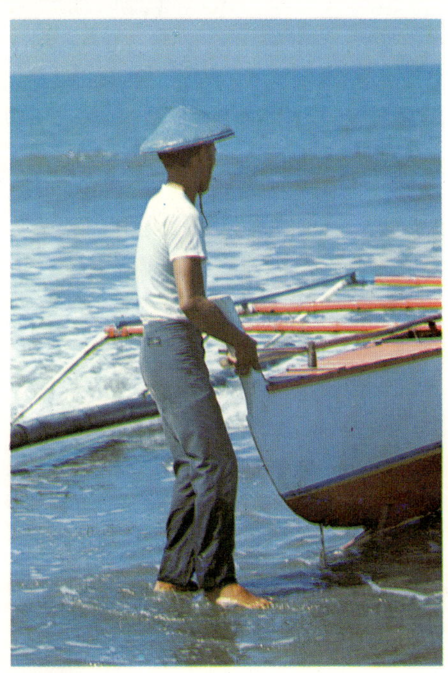 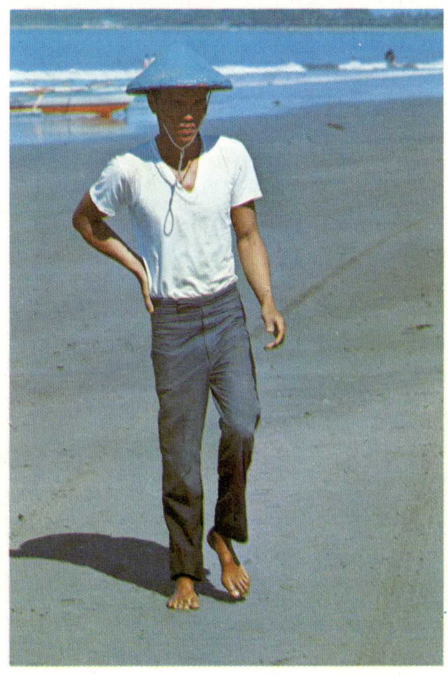

The most popular beaches in La Union are Bali-Hai, Malaysia, Mar-Pil, Cresta Ola, Long Beach and Nalinac. Resort facilities are excellent and boats—of all shapes, types and sizes—can be hired.

men and women in sight. But call the manager, whisper your requirements and he will whisk you away to where "a companion," well-clothed and intelligent, can be chosen through a one-way mirror. Less pretentious establishments display a board on which the name of available hostesses are illuminated. The cheap clubs merely have girls sitting in one corner of the room, displayed like fruit and chosen in the same manner.

Hostesses are expected to encourage customers to drink as much as possible; they receive a percentage of the cost of any drinks which are bought for them. Even so, I never found the Philippine bar girls to be outrageous "hustlers" like their counterparts in Hong Kong and many other Asian countries. Certainly they drank a lot, but never enough to frighten off their investment and never without first asking if they could order another drink. Furthermore, these girls were usually quite satisfied with beer. (In Hong Kong particularly, the bar girls order what they call "ladies champagne"—lemonade at champagne prices. They clap their hands and in a flash another glass appears on the table which almost certainly is a double or a triple. So, the girls clap with the speed of a flamenco dancer and drink with the thirst of someone just emerged from the desert; visitors quickly find their wallets empty!) Fortunately, Manila is different. It is quite possible to visit a score of different nightclubs, to enjoy the company of pretty, English-speaking hostesses, to watch several floor shows and to drink and to eat, all for little more than ten dollars.


*Gourmet's Potpourri*

The food served in Manila's nightclubs and restaurants—even the smallest—is excellent. Three centuries of Spanish occupation have left their mark on the country's cuisine, but the Filipinos have naturally gone one step better; they blended into their cooking the disparate cuisines of the Chinese, the Mexicans, the Indonesians, the Japanese, the Thais, the Malaysians and the Americans. Filipino cuisine is therefore said to be a subtle reminder of the country's varied history as well as being reflective of the Filipino soul.

Perhaps the finest example of this distillation of both Oriental and Western cuisines is to be found in the Filipino national dish, *adobo,* a stew which contains chicken, pork and beef whipped with garlic, soya, onions, spices, vinegar and coconut. It is as Mexico-Spanish in origin as it is Chinese-Malay in flavour. The use of garlic and bay leaves is typical of Spanish cookery; the soya makes it Chinese, the pepper and spices give the Malay influence and the use of vinegar is typical of the Philippines. (Indonesians, Malaysians and Thais are continually amazed at the similarities between their own food and that of the Philippines. This is particularly true of cooking in the southern Philippines where turmeric, curry powder, coconut milk and steamed rice are extensively used.)

Dining in the Philippines is therefore a gastronomic adventure. Every region produces its own specialities and in the greater Manila area there are a number of excellent Filipino restaurants offering authentic regional dishes which,

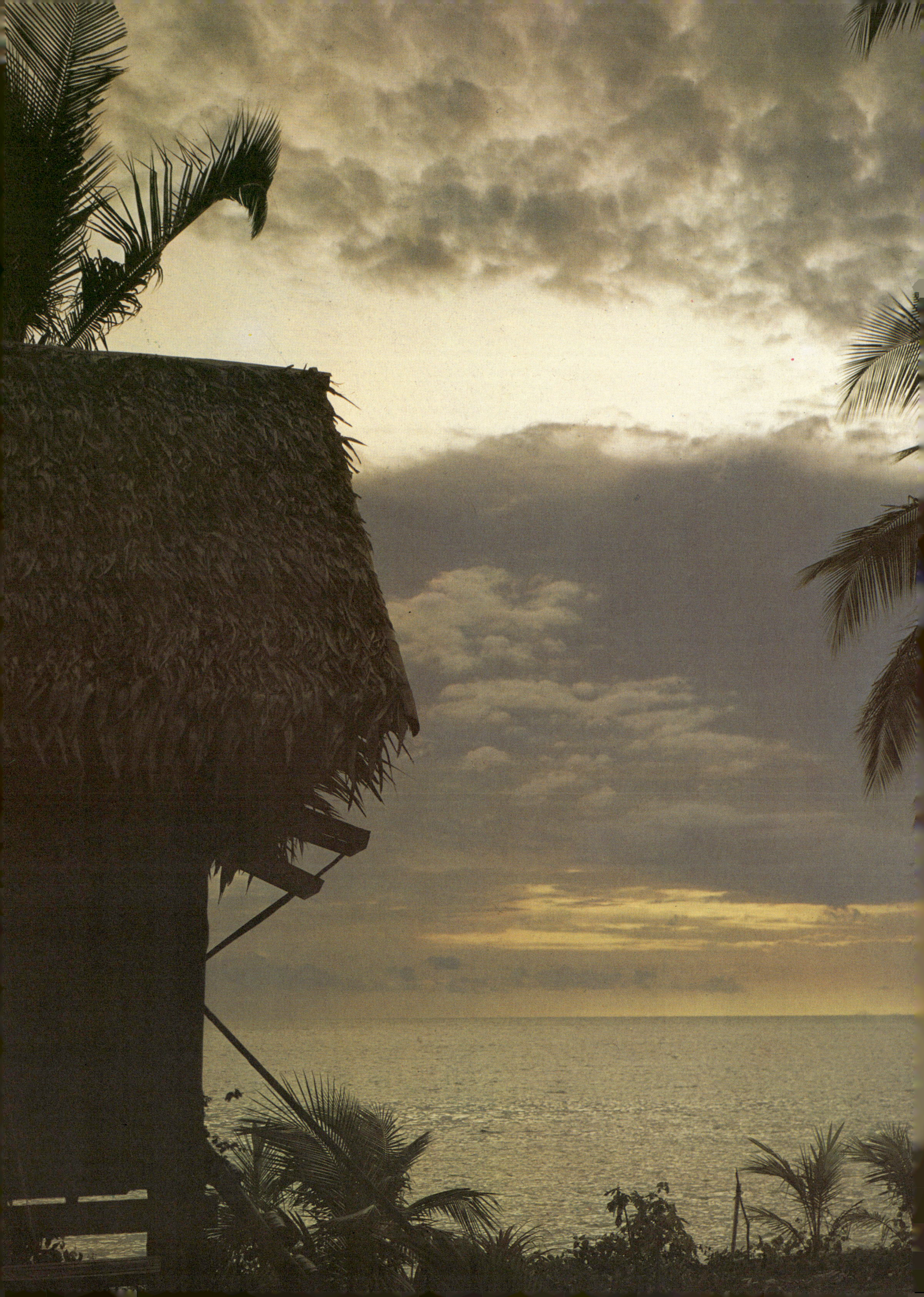

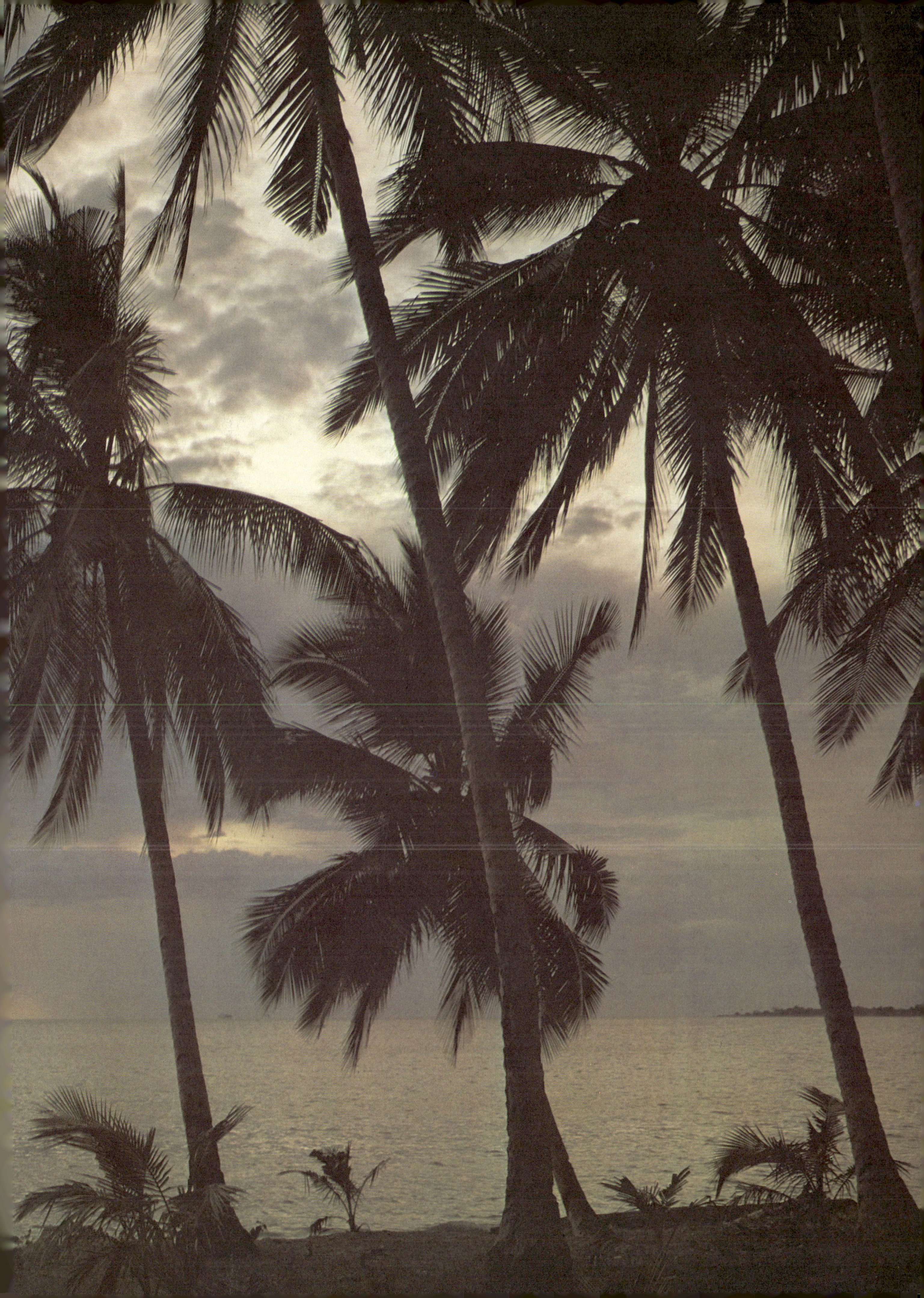

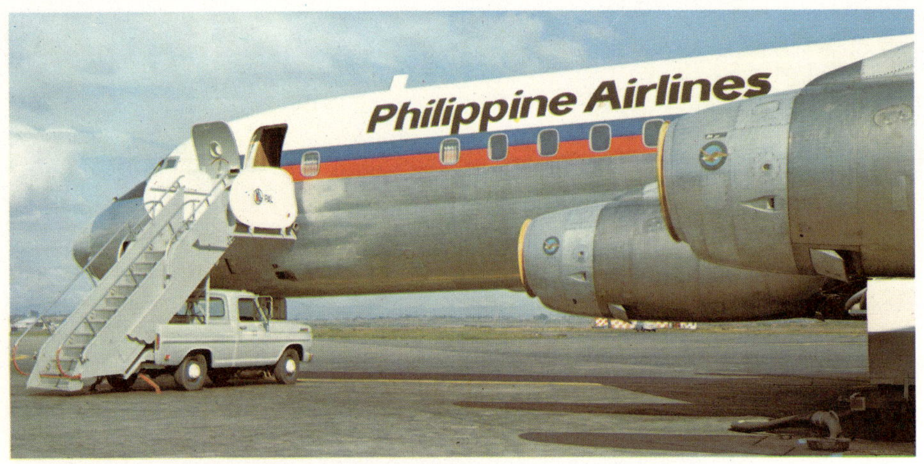

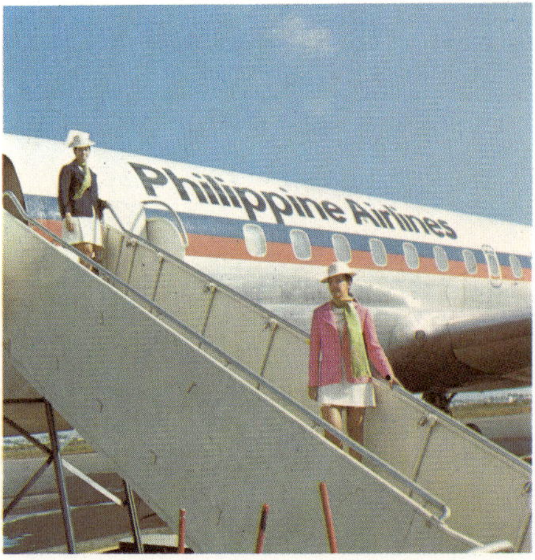

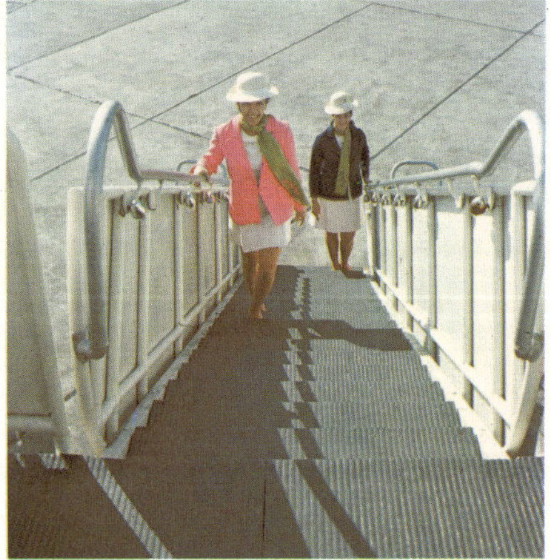

Hostesses from Philippine Airlines (PAL), attractive and colourfully dressed in national costume, not only give tourists a friendly welcome but also make the visitors' farewell—inevitably a sad moment—a little brighter.

following tradition, are displayed in clay pots. Popular dishes include *lechon* (a whole, charcoal-roasted suckling pig served with liver sauce), *lumpia* (an egg roll filled with the heart of a coconut palm that is sautéed with pork and shrimp), *kare-kare* (oxtail stew cooked in thick peanut sauce with bananas and egg plants) and *pancit luglog* (steamed rice noodles topped with red sauce, pork, shrimps and hard boiled eggs.)

Despite the richness of these foods, Filipinos generally manage to enjoy a heavy lunch and dinner—both meals consisting of several courses. In between, there is the Filipino *merienda,* or afternoon snack, which consists of something like *champurrado,* a chocolate-flavoured rice porridge.

Why is it that Filipino women keep their slim, fragile beauty?


*To Pagsanjan Falls*

Every visitor who has time available should go to the Pagsanjan Falls in the southeast province of Laguna which is about an hour-and-a-half's drive from Manila.

On the way you can pass Nichols golf course; Pansol village, a spot favoured by Spanish colonists; Los Baños, a holiday town at the foot of Mount Makiling, and numerous beach resorts situated on Laguna Bay, the largest inland lake and a popular area for hunting snipe during the open season in September. A short detour can be made to Calamba and the house where Dr José Rizal was born; it is now a national shrine. Most of the furniture and household things that belonged to the Rizal family have been restored.

The Agricultural College of the Philippines' University is not far from Los Baños and is set in mountainous terrain where countless varieties of tropical flowers and trees grow, many of which yield gums (including rubber), fruit, nuts, spices, drugs, oils and other useful substances. In the Philippines, about ten thousand species of flowering plants and ferns have been classified, more than one thousand different woods of commercial value (some of the timber trees attain huge sizes and are especially useful in making large pieces of furniture), nine hundred species of orchid, some extremely rare, and several hundred fibres, among them the *abacá,* from which Manila rope is made. There are also scores of palms, bamboos and rattans. This wide variety of flora is essentially Malaysian, but Himalayan elements do occur in the mountains of Northern Luzon, while a few Australian plants are found at all altitudes.

Nearby is the International Rice Research Institute which, by producing high-yield species, has helped the Philippines to become self-sufficient in rice production. Certainly I saw mile upon mile of rice paddies where country folk were working and children waved as I passed.

At Pagsanjan town I left my car and rented a slim, light *banca* which, manned by an expert boatman, was to take me upriver and negotiate fourteen rapids before reaching the Falls.

The main river was wide. On either side there were banks of lush, tropical vegetation in tangled growth, coconut palms, bamboo, and patches of a

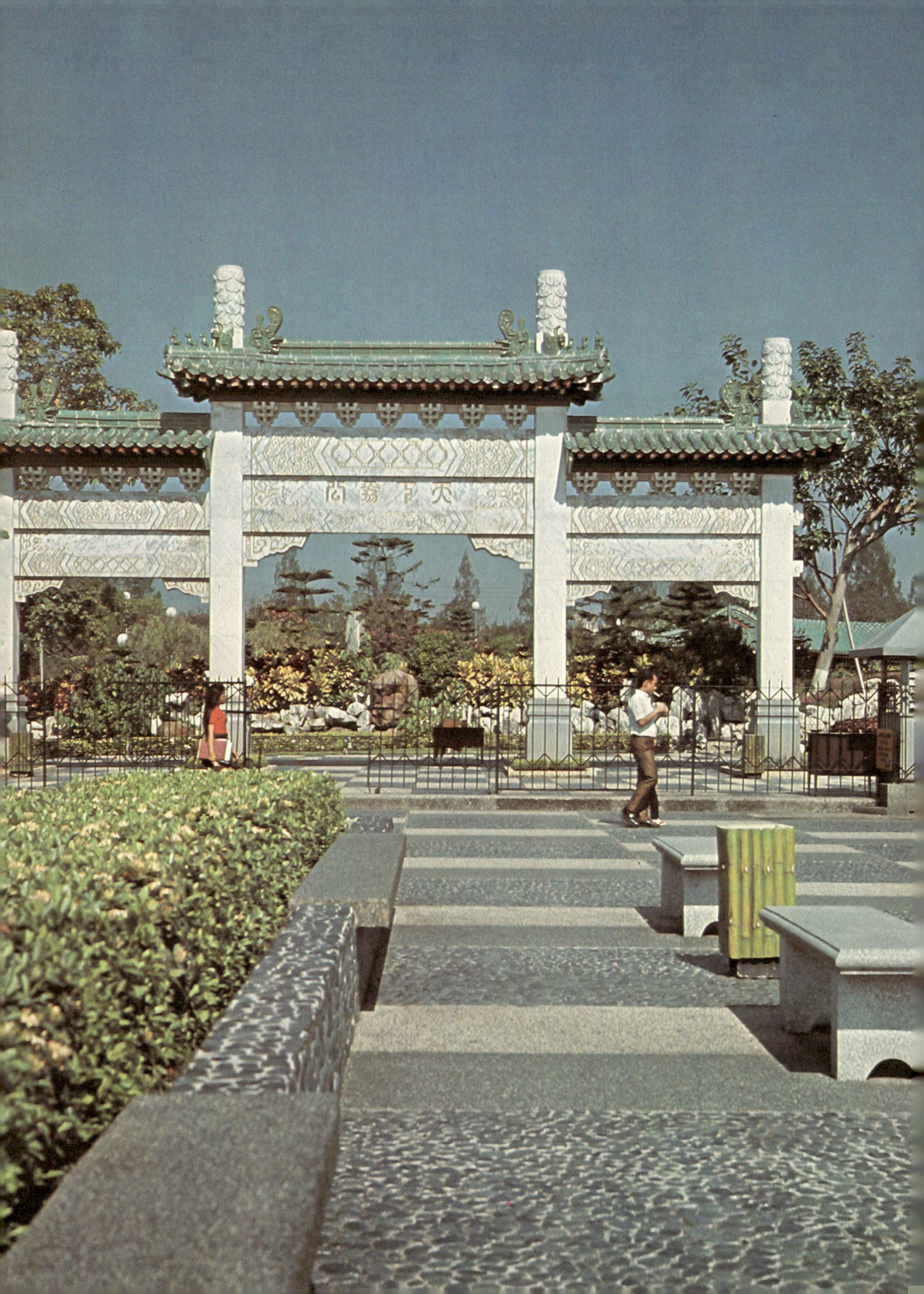
天篤閣

waist-high, broad-bladed type of imperata grass with attractive, white fluffy seed-heads.

A dazzling white-headed fish eagle zoomed, rolled and looped through the air in a thrilling display of aerobatics. These birds cannot fly if their feathers become wet and consequently they can take only small fish, but often a greedy eagle can be seen struggling towards land with quite a large catch. Even if the load is really too heavy, the bird is usually unwilling to release his fish and would rather fall and drown than forgo the anticipated meal.

Enormous rafts made entirely from coconuts were being propelled and steered by young boys using a single oar. Dried coconut meat, called copra, is essential for the manufacture of soap, margarine and cooking fats. It is one of the country's main exports and lines of this rancid smelling material were drying outside river homes. The rafts are locally termed "floating banks" and the coconut palm is known as "millionaire's tree" because every part of this palm has a use. The juice from the roots is an excellent medicine for indigestion and similar ailments; nut fibre is a natural fuel and the palm trunk is ideal for building while the leaves can be quickly plaited into hard-wearing mats, waterproof roofs and heat-protective coverings. (Once planted, a palm requires no attention and in five years it will grow to a sturdy tree, bearing fruit through every season for between fifty and one hundred years.)

Gradually, the river narrowed and as we swept closer to its muddy banks, the buzz of insects and the screech of birds swelled into a crescendo. Species of tamarind, acacia, trichilia, balanites and ambatch trees curved towards us.

A few herons and bitterns were standing on the mud flats waiting erect and motionless. Waders, with bright yellow legs and orange beaks, used white, purple and crimson water lilies as stepping stones to walk over the water as easily as on land. More than seven hundred species of birds have been recorded in the Philippines. Fifty of them are birds of prey which range in size from sparrow-like falcons to the giant monkey-eating eagle. Barbets, broadbills, flycatchers, honeyeaters, jungle fowl, kingfishers, larks, orides, parrots, parrakeets, shrikes, sunbirds, swifts, swallows, weavers and woodpeckers are all common; there are some thirty-five species of sunbird alone.

Now we were ploughing through papyrus and masses of green aquatic plants I could not identify. But soon this debris disappeared as the previously still water began to swirl and foam, surging over large boulders as we entered a gorge with sheer rock walls that rose to more than three hundred feet; arrogant peaks obscured the sun, and waterfalls tumbled from sharp ridges. Moving against the current, the boatman skilfully negotiated the powerful cascades and boulders, pointing out to me the wrecks of less fortunate *banca* trips, but hastening to add that nobody had ever been drowned. Apparently, the *bancas* take such a pounding that, inevitably, they just fall apart without warning. "It could even happen right now," I was told cheerfully. "In fact, this boat is three years old; how she holds together is a mystery," he added. I was glad that I could swim well!

Almost two hours later, my exhausted boatman navigated the final rapid.

And there were the Falls, angry and treacherous, cascading down the ravine to produce clouds of dense spray that seethed with repetitive patterns as they were propelled into the air with infinite energy.  Up and up and up; patterns which created spiralling columns of flashing marble before they collapsed to form a magnesium-bright firework cascade.  While the sun shone a rainbow encircled the cataract.

On the return trip we were travelling *with* the current, speeding "downhill" on the crest of turbulent water.  The *banca* was flooded but the journey took only half the time.  It had been an exhilarating day.

The gardens incorporate a willow-and-palm
bordered lake, miniature waterfalls, several
pavilions festooned with multi-coloured
lanterns, quaint wooden bridges, vari-
coloured flowers, lawns, Chinese trees and
evergreens.  (Text page 43.)

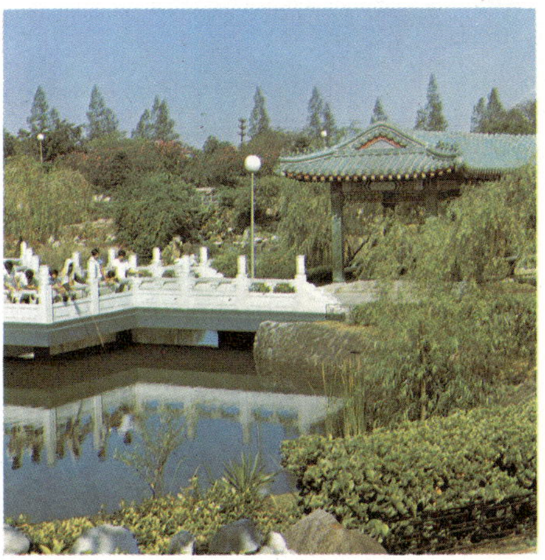

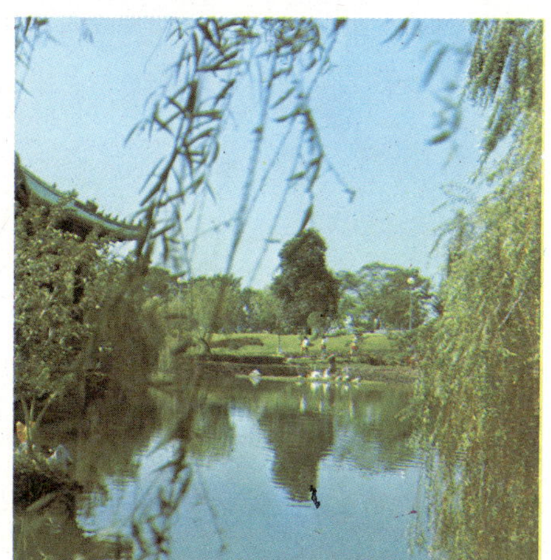

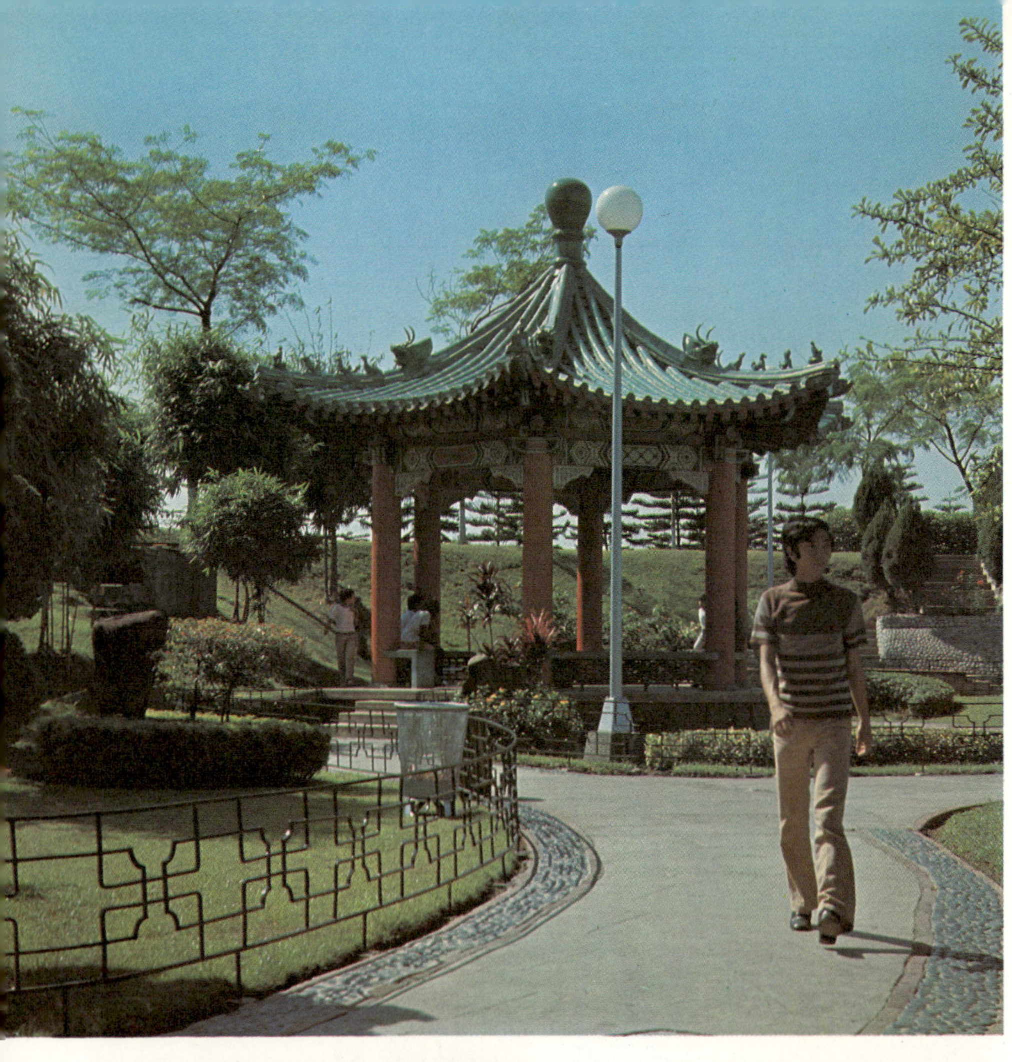

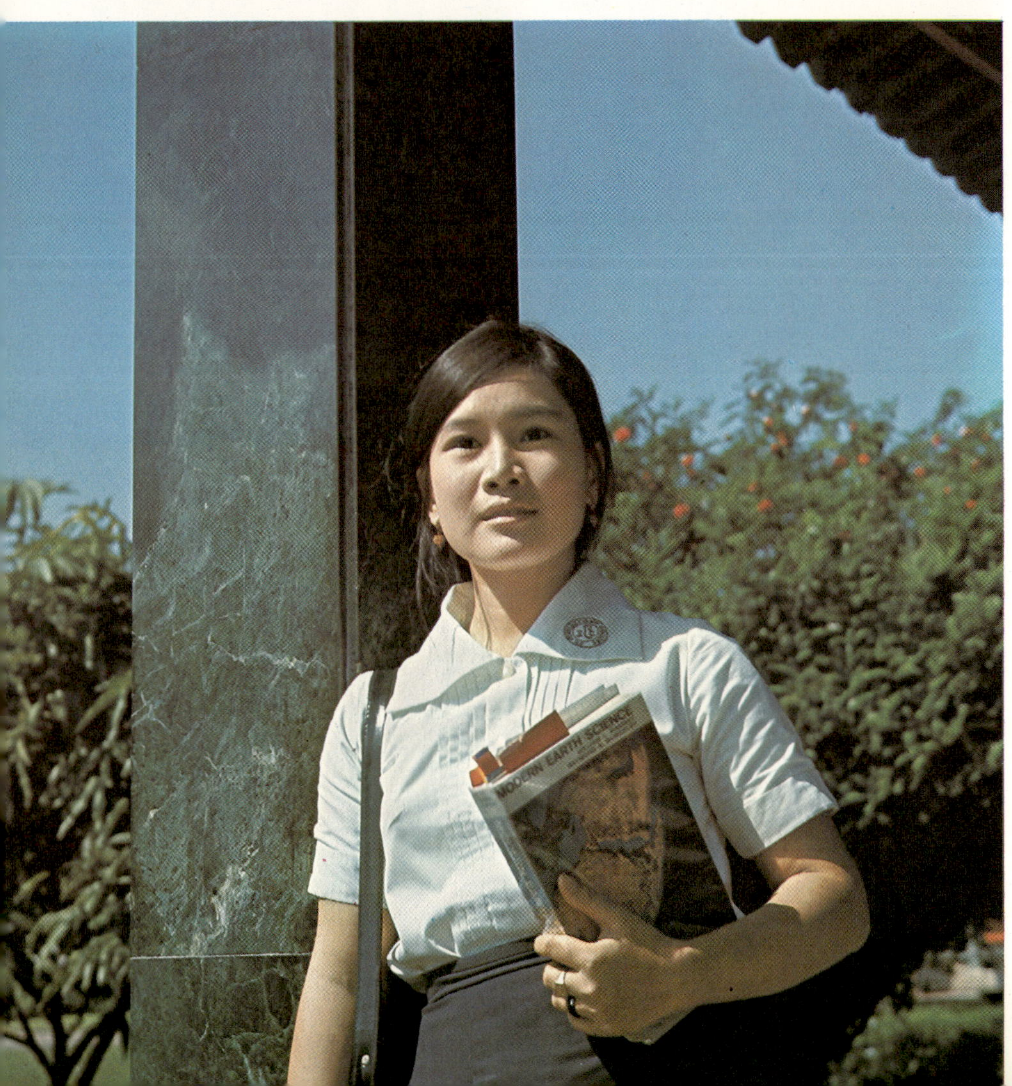

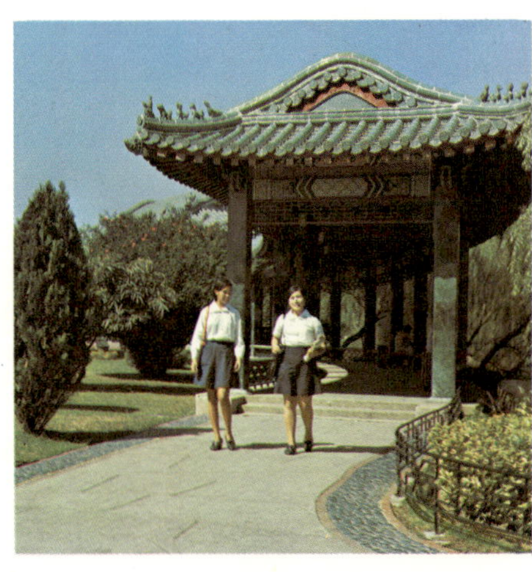

The Chinese Gardens are a favourite place
for tourists and locals alike.
*Page 88/bottom:* Many school children
come to study in the solitude.
*Below—left to right:* A gardener, to protect
himself from the sun, wears strange garb.
*Bottom—left to right:* Hibiscus blooms;
more gardeners, but dressed convention-
ally; a Siamese spirit house (text page 67).

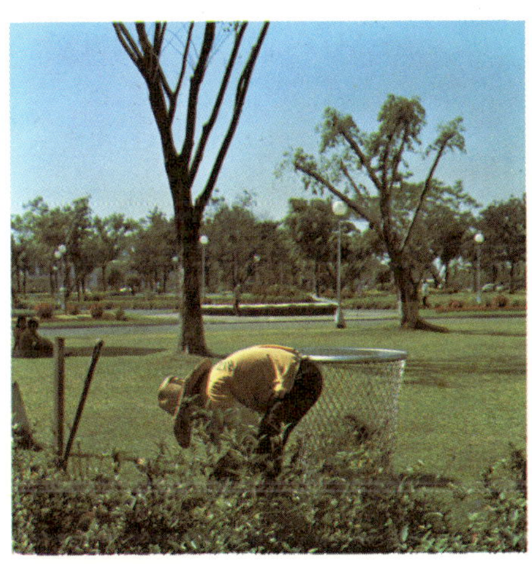
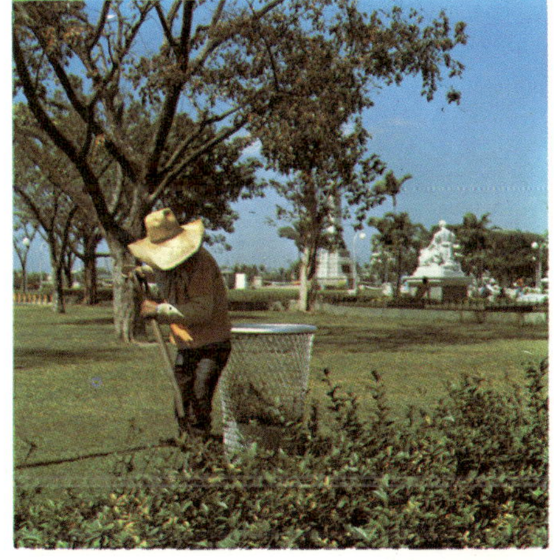
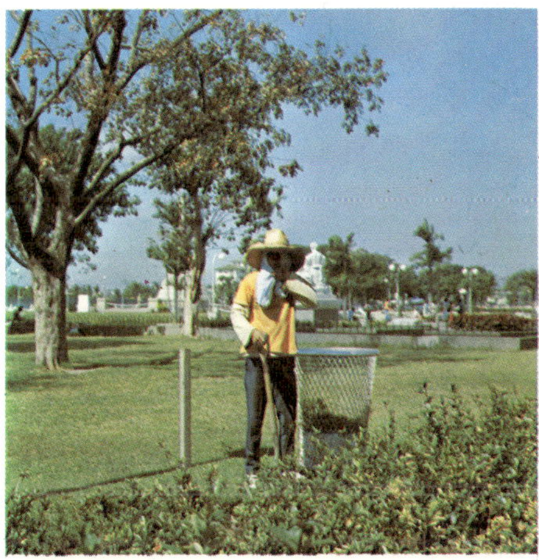
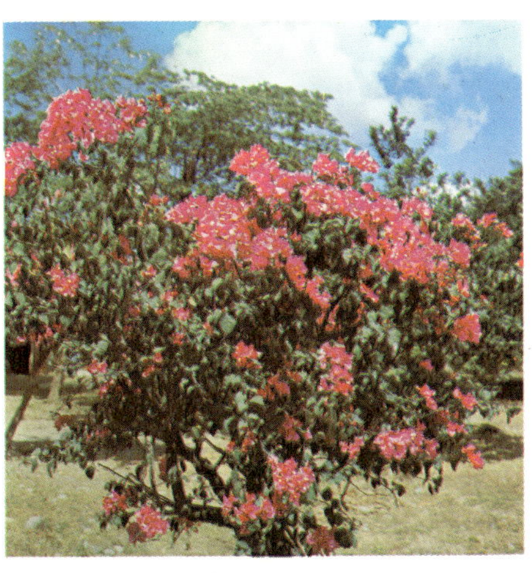
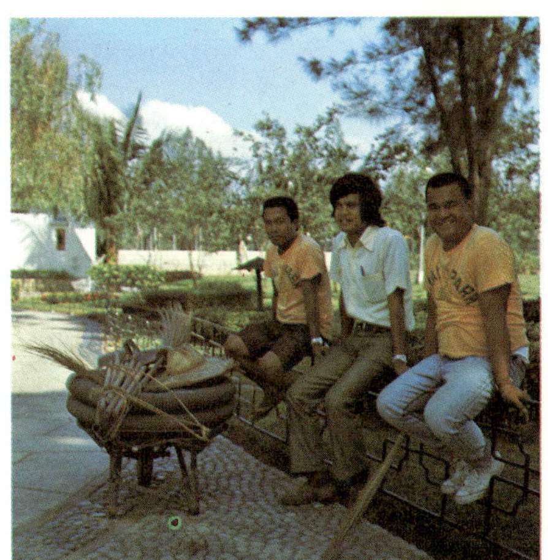
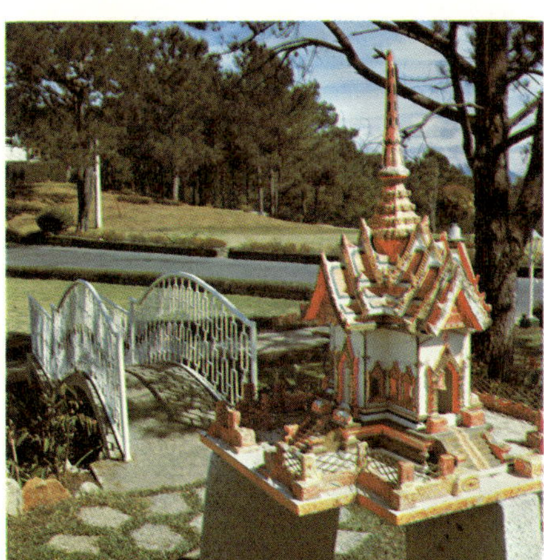

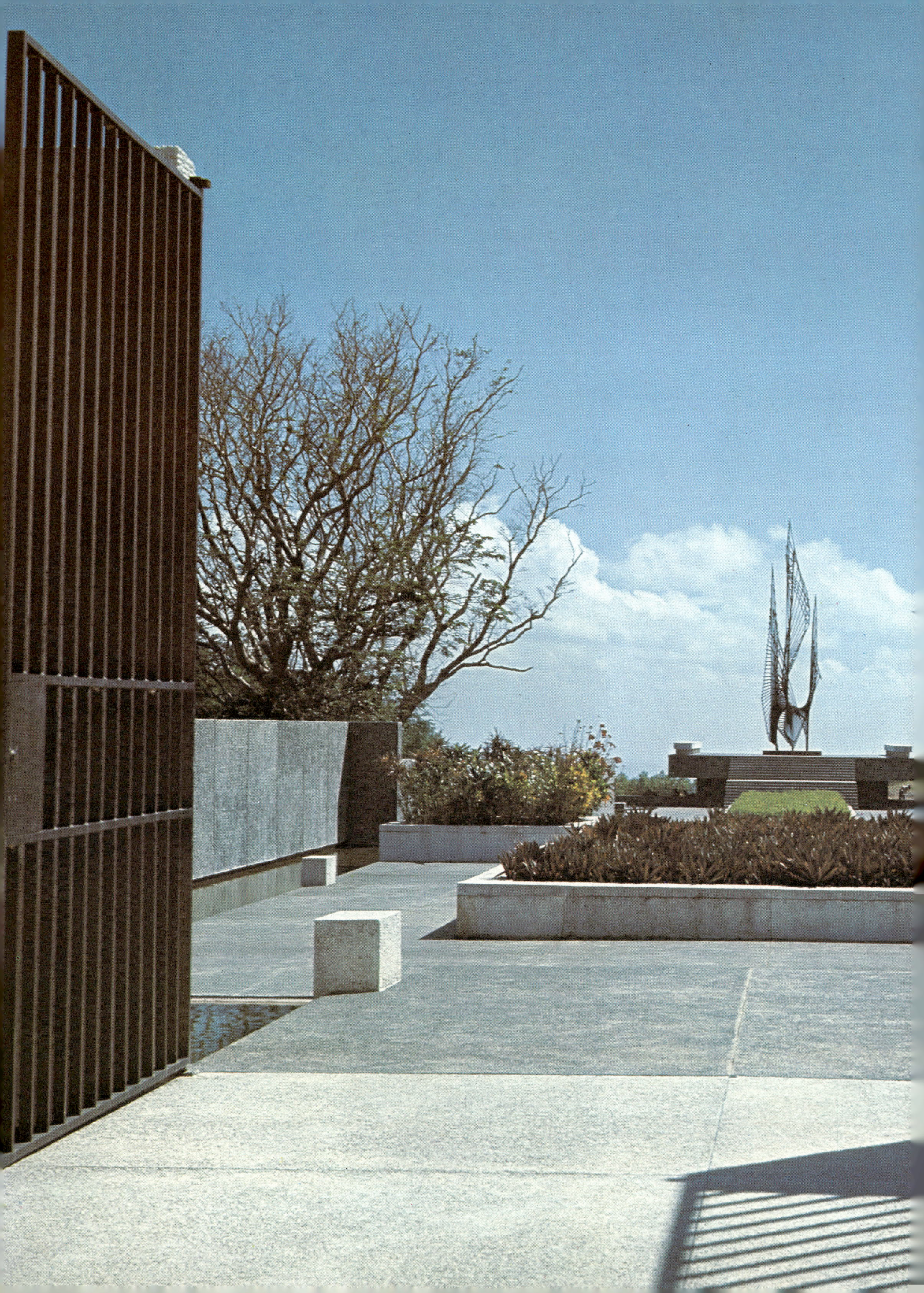

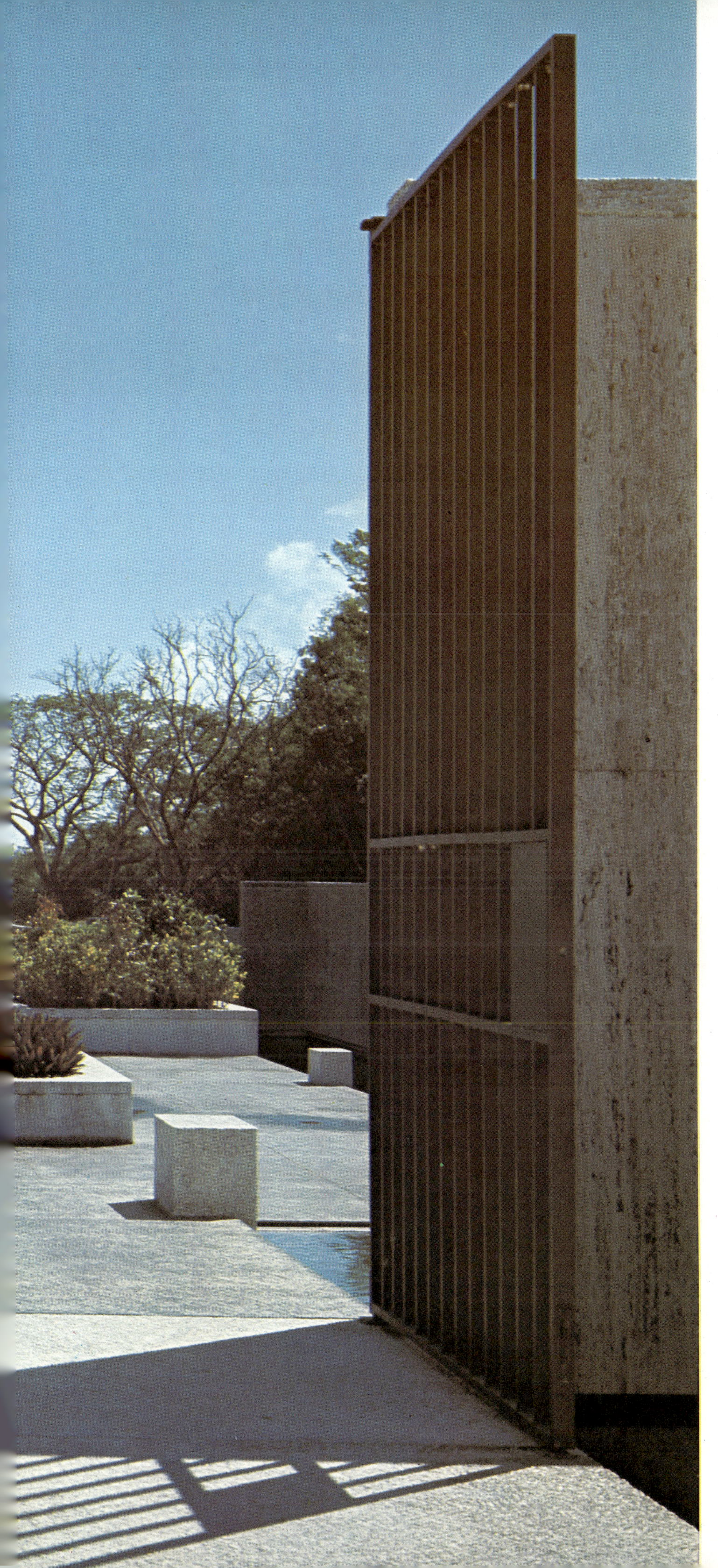

"It is my earnest hope and indeed the hope of all mankind that a better world shall emerge out of the blood and carnage of the past: a world founded upon faith and understanding; a world dedicated to the dignity of man and the fulfilment of his most cherished wish— for freedom, tolerance and justice."

**GENERAL DOUGLAS MACARTHUR**

*(From his address delivered at the signing of the surrender of Japan.)*

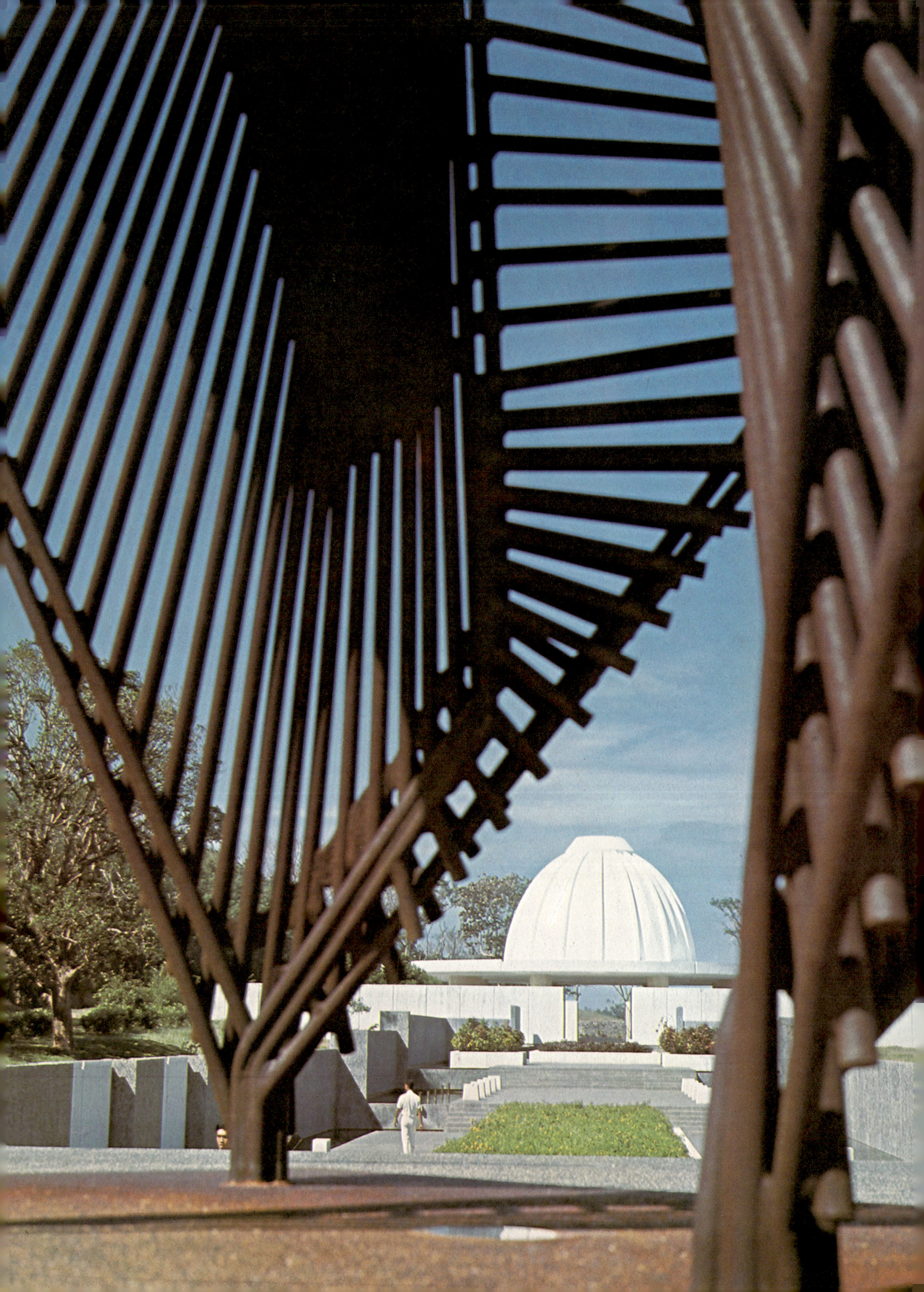

# Corregidor Island



Lying at the entrance to Manila Bay, three miles off Bataan, Corregidor is shaped like a tadpole with its head facing the China Sea and its tail curving towards Manila. But approached by ship the island is formless; low and green.

Bataan and Corregidor are names deeply thrust into Philippine history and synonymous with heroism. After the devastating air attack and invasion by the Japanese Imperial Army, the forces defending the Philippines were overwhelmed until the only resistance was on the Bataan Peninsula and Corregidor.

Corregidor was heavily fortified with 56 coastal guns and mortars, 76 anti-aircraft guns, 10 searchlights and an 8-inch rail mounted gun east of Malinta Hill. The two outstanding batteries were "Geary" and "Way," both consisting of 12-inch, 10-ton mortars capable of traversing 360 degrees. Batteries "Hearn" and "Smith," also with a 360-degree coverage, were coastal guns having a horizontal range of almost 6 miles.

The island was divided into four strategic areas. In the northwest were two rocky plateaus at different heights which were named Topside and Bottomside. At Topside the army located its headquarters, hospitals, shops, the main gun fortifications, and barracks that were four stories high and one mile long. At Bottomside were the wharves, the army dock and a fortified L-shaped pier operated by the Navy. South of Bottomside, the town of San Jose, which had been the seat of the island's government during Spanish rule, evolved into an army community. To the southeast were the Malinta Hills where the famed Malinta Tunnel was built and used as General MacArthur's headquarters from late December 1941, to March 1942. The principal tunnel was 925 feet long and 25 feet wide with 24 laterals each averaging 160 feet long and 15 feet wide. A further group of 12 laterals housed 1200 beds and served as a hospital. The hospital is empty now, but a sign reads:

> PLEASE MAINTAIN SILENCE AND YOU
> WILL HEAR THE WAILING OF THE
> WOUNDED AND THE WHISPER OF DEATH

Twelve days after the Japanese simultaneously attacked Pearl Harbour, Baguio City and Davao, Corregidor was bombarded for the first time on 29 December 1941. The attack lasted 30 minutes when 18 twin-engined planes dropped 50 tons of bombs. Less than one hour later a second wave continued the attack, unloading hundreds of bombs. It was the heaviest pounding that Corregidor sustained during the war. No important installation was destroyed but the Japanese lost seventeen aircraft.

In the afternoon of December 30, always celebrated throughout the Philippines as José P. Rizal Day to commemorate when this national hero was executed by the Spaniards, a small group gathered in Malinta Tunnel to witness the ceremonies inaugurating the second term of Quezon as President and Sergio Osmena as Vice-President of the Philippine Commonwealth.

President Quezon delivered his second inaugural address:

Below: The parade ground on Topside where, on 6 May 1942, the Japanese flag was raised and continued to fly until 22 February 1945 when the Americans regained possession of Corregidor. Topside's shelled, burned-out barracks are stark reminders of those bitter days.


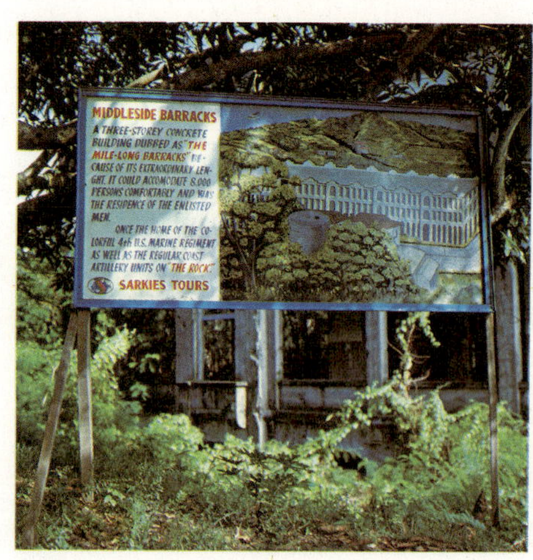

MIDDLESIDE BARRACKS
A THREE-STOREY CONCRETE BUILDING DUBBED AS "THE MILE-LONG BARRACKS" BECAUSE OF ITS EXTRAORDINARY LENGHT. IT COULD ACCOMODATE 8.000 PERSONS COMFORTABLY AND WAS THE RESIDENCE OF THE ENLISTED MEN.
ONCE THE HOME OF THE COLORFUL 4th U.S. MARINE REGIMENT AS WELL AS THE REGULAR COAST ARTILLERY UNITS ON "THE ROCK".
SARKIES TOURS

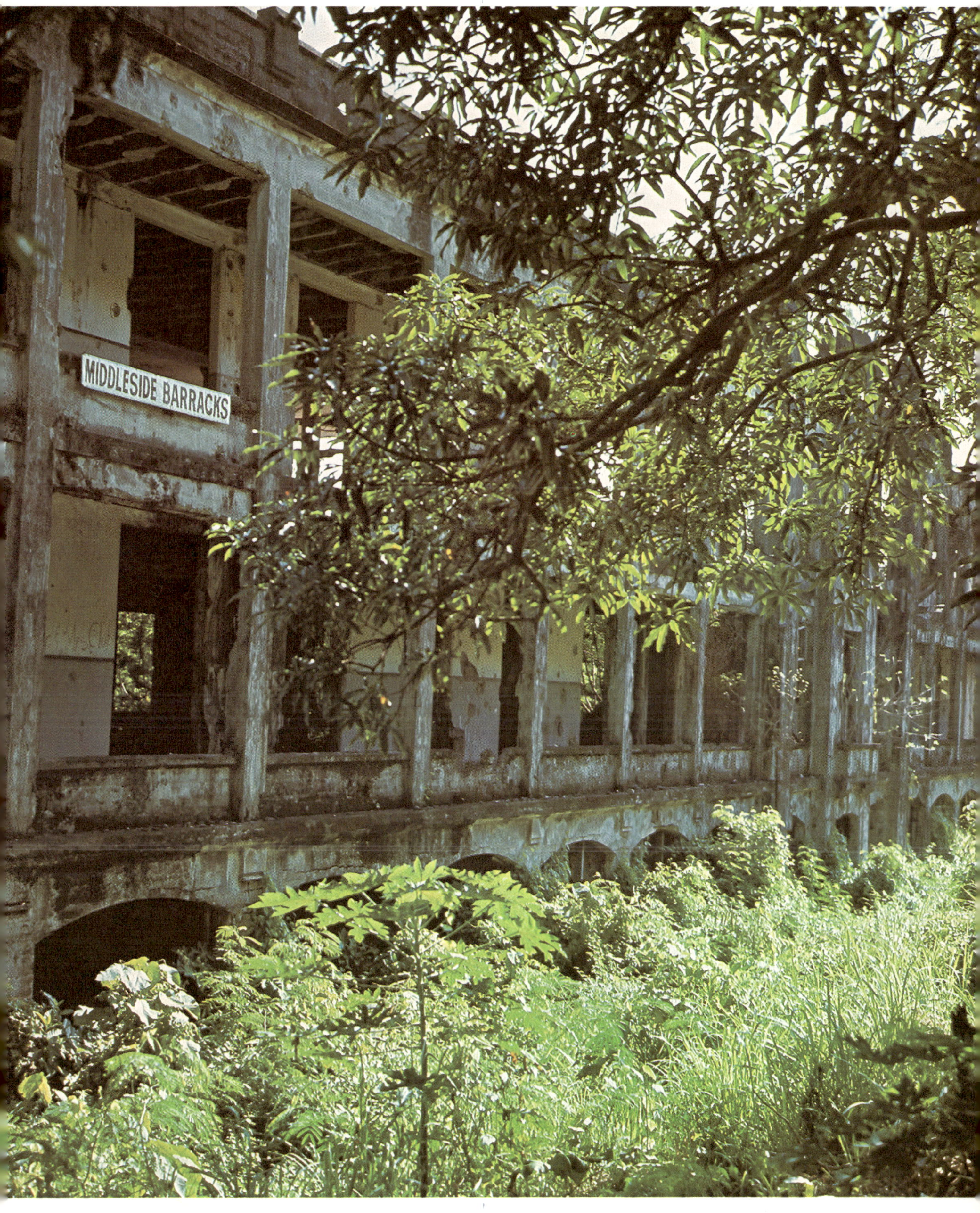
MIDDLESIDE BARRACKS

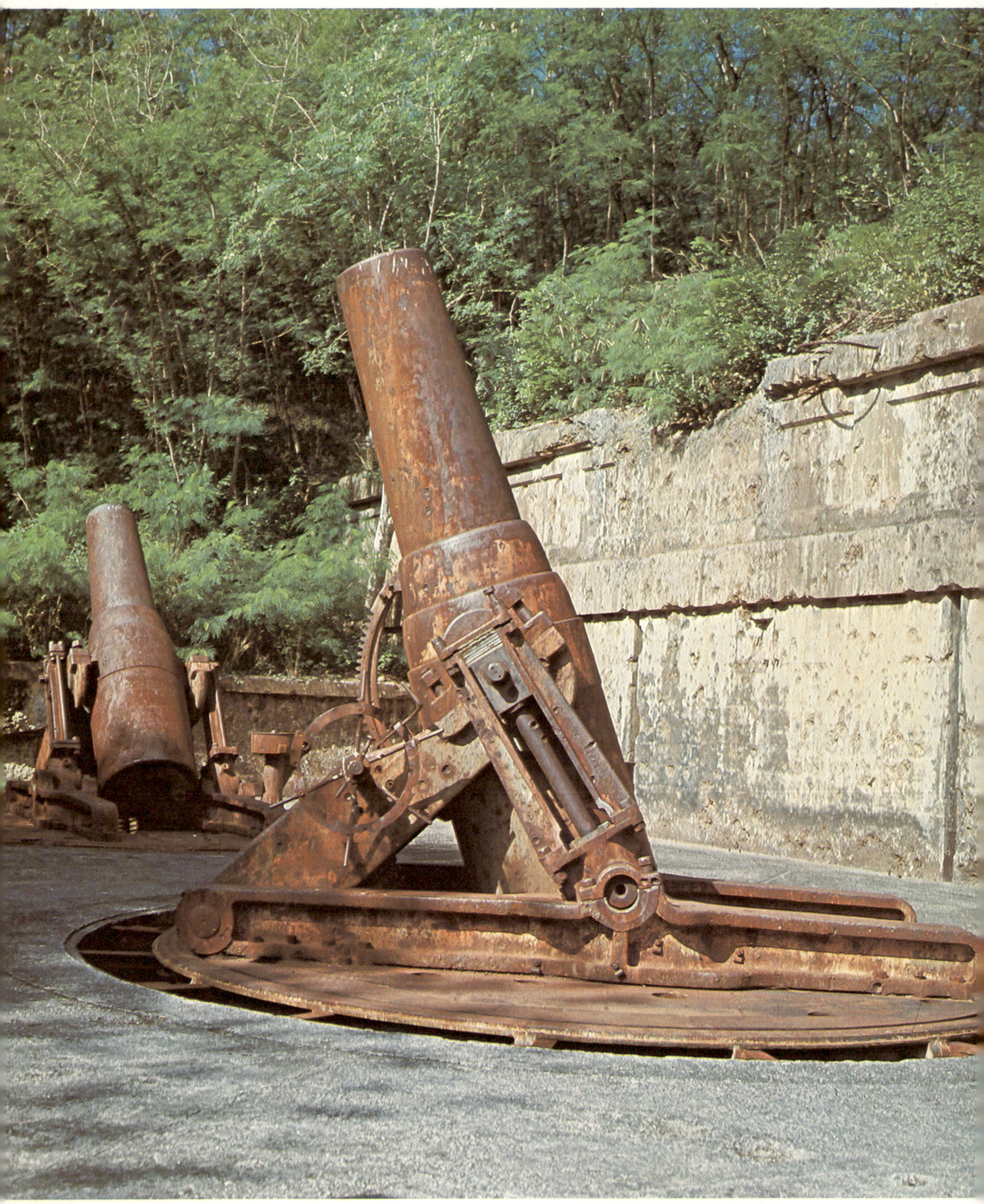

> ... as we face the grim realities of war, let us rededicate ourselves to the
> great principles of freedom and democracy for which our forefathers
> fought and died. The present war is being fought for those same principles.
> It demands from us courage, determination and unity of action.
> In taking my oath of office, I make the pledge for myself, my government,
> and my people, to stand by America and fight with her until victory is won.
> I am resolved, whatever the consequences to myself, faithfully to fulfil the
> pledge.

When General MacArthur spoke, his words assumed dramatic meaning:

> The thunder of death and destruction, dropped from the skies, can be
> heard in the distance. Our ears catch the roar of battle as our soldiers close
> on the firing line. The horizon is blackened by the smoke of destructive fire.
> The air reverberates with the roar of exploding bombs.
> Such is the bed of birth of this new government, of this nation. For four
> hundred years the Philippines have struggled upward toward self-government.
> Just at the end of its tuitionary period, just on the threshold of independence,
> came the great hour of decision. There was no hesitation, no vacillation,
> no moment of doubt. The whole country followed its great leader in choosing
> the side of freedom against the side of slavery.
> We have inaugurated him, we have just thereby confirmed his momentous
> decision. Hand in hand with the United States and the other free nations
> of the world, this basic and fundamental issue will be fought through to
> victory. Come what may, ultimate triumph will be its reward.

On the evening of New Year's Day 1942, Japanese forces declared their
intention to overthrow Manila the next day. January 2 saw the army of the
Rising Sun sweep through the ancient city which was formally surrendered to the
conquerors by Jorge S. Vargas, the acting Mayor.

But for months, the heroic men and women of Corregidor held out in a
battle they knew was impossible to win. From 5 February 1942 Corregidor
was bombarded daily for five weeks and from 15 March heavier artillery began a
further barrage that continued until 12 February; on the first day alone,
Fort Frank received five hundred direct hits.

With the Japanese on all sides, no source of help available, and Bataan
overthrown on 9 April, Corregidor was isolated. General Wainwright took an
inventory of stocks and calculated that by rationing food to 40 ounces daily
for the 11,000 troops and 80 ounces for the 1,500 wounded, supplies, including
petrol, would last until 30 June. The most critical item was water. The
reservoirs held only 3 million gallons and the pumping equipment was beyond
repair.

On 26 April a message reached the defenders of Corregidor from another
group of defenders, perhaps the only people in the world capable of
understanding the feelings of the trapped men on Corregidor.

"People of Malta send their warm greetings to the gallant defenders of
Corregidor," General Sir William George Shedden, Deputy Governor of Malta,
said in his wire.

On Emperor Hirohito's birthday, 29 April, the 206th air alarm sounded.

For the first time the Malinta Tunnel was a target; General Mikami had
launched the final phase of action against the island.

Day after day the bombardment continued. On 2 May, Battery "Geary"
received a direct hit which detonated several tons of its ammunition; the
explosion shook the island. The huge mortars were thrown around like
matchsticks, one of them landing on the golf course 150 yards away.
Twenty-seven of "Geary's" artillery crew died instantly.

The pounding intensified and during the 24 hours of 4 May, 16,000 shells
exploded on Corregidor. Men collapsed from fatigue. Whole companies were
often killed in a barrage of fire. The Malinta Tunnel hospital was overcrowded.

On the evenings of 5 and 6 May, the Japanese launched five hundred invasion
troops who were defeated when Corregidor mustered every available man, gun
and mortar in a mighty final effort to keep the enemy from its shores.
Practically all the invasion boats were destroyed and the Japanese losses reached
a staggering 75 per cent for their 2nd Battalion.

Finally, Battery Denver, about one mile east of Malinta, fell into Japanese
hands. Shortly afterwards, General Wainwright received a radio message from
President Roosevelt:

> During recent weeks we have been following with growing admiration
> the day-by-day accounts of your heroic stand against the mounting intensity
> of bombardment by enemy planes and heavy siege guns.
>
> In spite of all the handicaps of complete isolation, lack of food and
> ammunition you have given the world a shining example of patriotic
> fortitude and self-sacrifice.
>
> The American people ask no finer example of tenacity, resourcefulness
> and steadfast courage. The calm determination of your personal leadership
> in a desperate situation sets a standard of duty for our soldiers throughout
> the world.
>
> In every camp and on every naval vessel, soldiers, sailors and marines
> are inspired by the gallant struggle of their comrades in the Philippines.
> The workmen in our shipyards and munition plants redouble their efforts
> because of your example.
>
> You and your devoted followers have become the living symbols of
> our war aims and the guarantee of victory.

General Wainwright replied:

> Your gracious and generous message of May 4 has reached me. I am
> without words to express to you, Mr. President, my gratitude for the deep
> appreciation of your kindness. . . . As I write this at 3.30 A.M. our patrols are
> attempting to locate the enemy positions and I will counter attack at dawn
> to drive him into the sea or destroy him. Thank you again, Mr. President,
> for your wonderful message which I will publish to my entire command.

Seven hours later the General transmitted his final message from Corregidor:

> With broken heart and head bowed in sadness but not in shame I report
> to Your Excellency that today I must arrange terms for the surrender of the
> fortified islands of Manila Bay. . . .

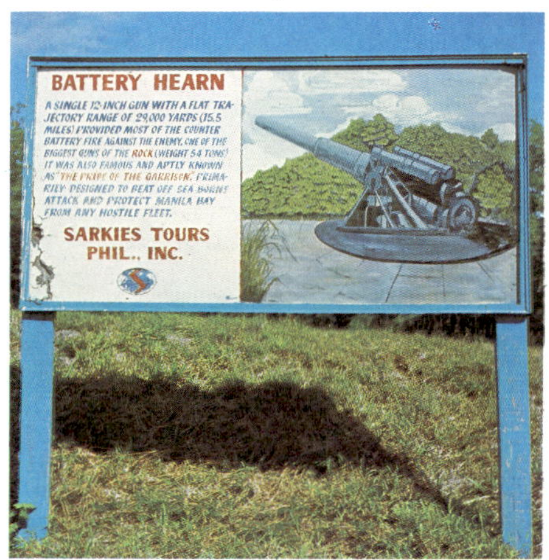

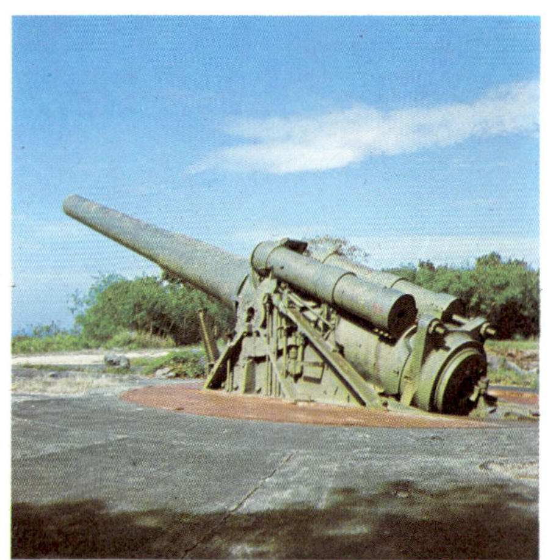

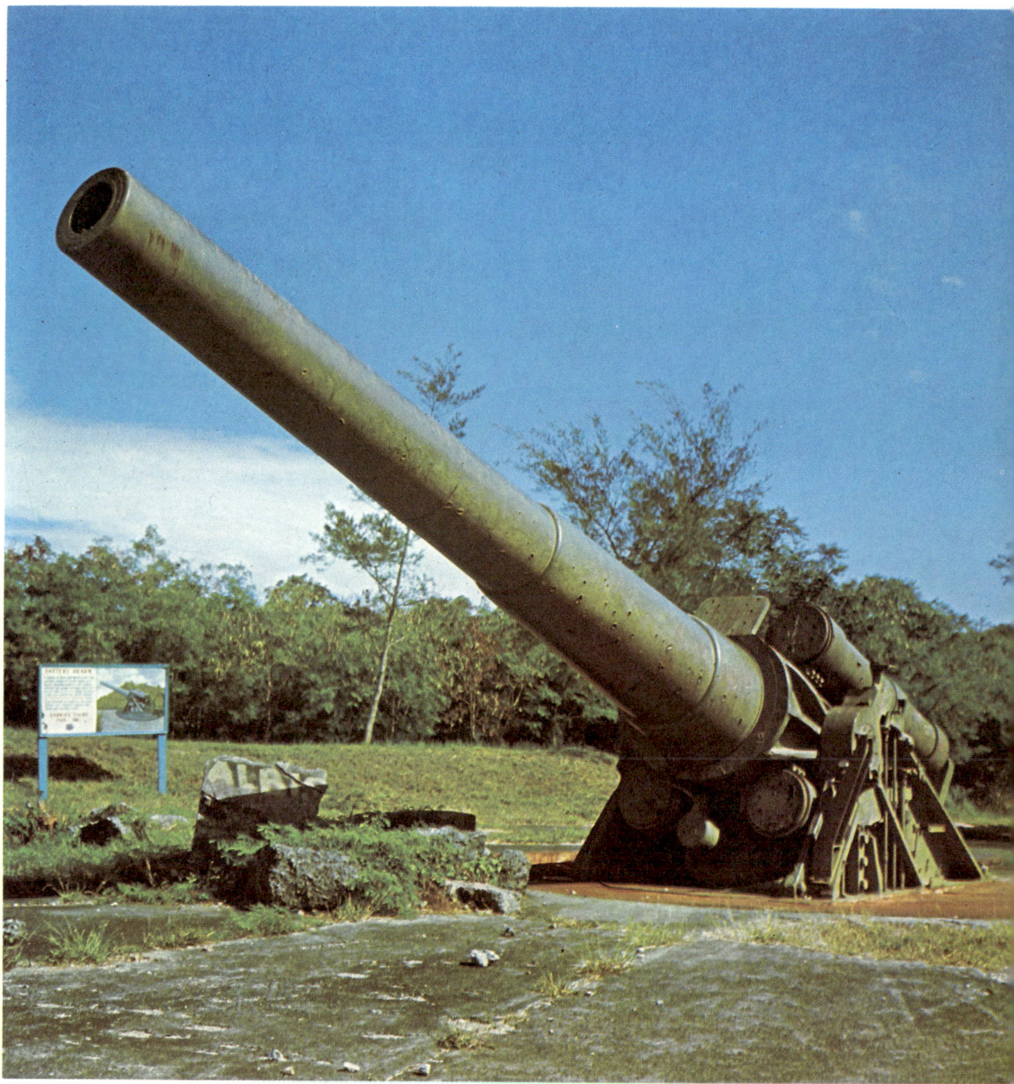

*Above:* Battery "Hearn", the longest range (29,000 yards) coastal gun on Corregidor. *Below left and right:* Shell-pocked fortifications surround the ruins of a mortar emplacement being reclaimed by jungle.

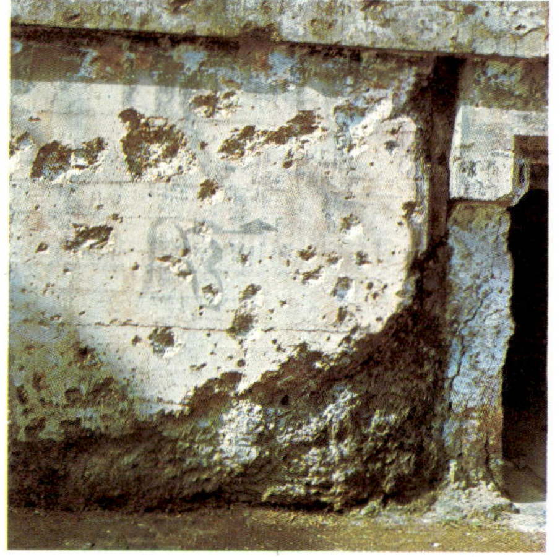

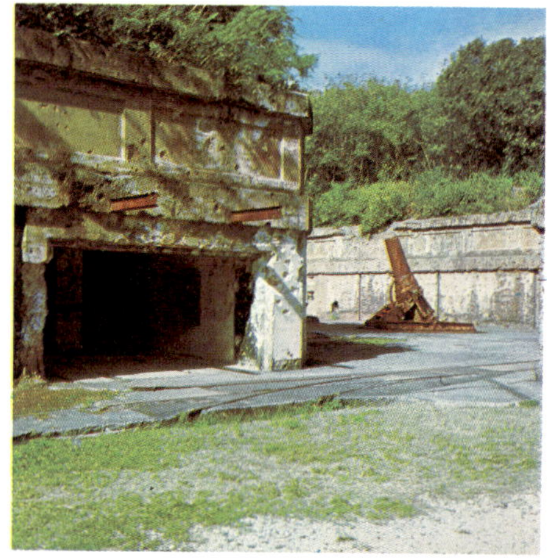

There is a limit of human endurance and that limit has long since been past. Without prospect of relief I feel it is my duty to my country and to my gallant troops to end this useless effusion of blood and human sacrifice. If you agree, Mr. President, please say to the nation that my troops and I have accomplished all that is humanly possible and that we have upheld the best tradition of the United States and its army. May God bless and preserve you and guide you and the nation in the effort to ultimate victory. With profound regret and with continued pride in my gallant troops I go to meet the Japanese. Goodbye, Mr. President.

Corregidor fell, but its defenders had not fought in vain. The hopeless, bloody stand had effectively blocked the Japanese military timetable, thereby enabling the Allies to gain precious months for organizing the defence of Australia and the Southwest Pacific. The sweep of the Japanese over the Pacific had been stopped by an island with an area of only three square miles!

Today, the crumbling "Mile-Long Barracks" are almost covered by trees. Nothing remains but shell-pocked concrete, with fire blackened stairs that lead nowhere and empty windows like the eyes of dead men. Topside is empty. Three mortars that defended Corregidor to the last remain in position with their barrels pointing skywards. Trees and flowers cover other bloody relics. Like the calm after the storm there is a deep silence that makes the spine tingle. "Please maintain silence, and you will hear the wailing of the wounded and the whisper of the dead."

# To Baguio and Banaue



Baguio City is set amidst pine trees and tropical gardens at an altitude of 5,000 feet in what the locals call "big sky country." It is the summer capital of the Philippines and home of the Igorot woodcarvers.

Although less than 160 miles from Manila, the journey to Baguio took about six hours on the winding roads; for the earlier part we drove through a flat landscape with fields of sugar cane on either side. It was several hours before a panorama of mountain peaks was silhouetted immediately ahead. Later, some miles beyond the boundary lines of Pengasinan, La Union and Benguet provinces, these silhouettes became steep mountain slopes covered with deep rain forest. Mighty trees soared to dizzy heights. There were bamboo shoots thicker than a man's leg, the bright green of wild banana fronds, giant ferns, and orchids which clung in the hollow of vine-covered trees, glowing vividly against the bark. After a series of hairpin bends, the forest thinned and we emerged onto a cool plateau far above the dense vegetation. The valley fell away steeply, its wooded flower-strewn sides a maze of interlocking ridges roofed with inscrutable green—here was Baguio.

There are many tourist attractions around the City: Mansion House, summerhome of the President; Baguio Cathedral; the zoological and botanical gardens; Asin Hot Springs; Mummy caves; Bridal Veil Falls; La Trinidad Valley, where all kinds of vegetables are grown; Lovers' Park and the Igorot woodcarvers' village. Some twenty-five miles to the northeast is Ambuklao Dam, the source of electric power to many industrial plants on Luzon; the drive to Ambuklao offers spectacular mountain scenery and there is a man-made lake big enough for boating and fishing.

About an hour's drive away in La Union Province are the beaches Malaysia, Bali-Hai, Mar-Pil, Cresta Ola, Long Beach and Nalinac. These are some of the finest sea resorts in Luzon.

★     ★     ★

It was on the road to Ambuklao Dam where I watched my first cockfight. Just as the English have fox-hunts and the Spaniards have bullfights, so the Filipinos have cockfighting, a legal sport which was popular long before the Europeans arrived and still has an enormous following. The only regulation stipulates that fights must be held away from general business areas. With bets often reaching $20,000 U.S. and more, fortunes are won and lost on this sport.

★     ★     ★

The road to Banaue is rough and unsealed; after storms it is often impassable. Even at the best of times the valley is lashed by rain and wind that sweep across almost vertical hills where, 3,000 years ago, the Ifugaos constructed rock walls to hold their paddy fields. Generally accepted as the "Eighth Wonder of the World," these incredible terraces—often called *stairways to heaven*—have produced more than 100,000 acres of level ground! The journey from Baguio to Banaue takes a whole day and necessitates an overnight stay.

*Below:* Manila is famous for spectacular, fiery sunsets over the Bay. And for its bright moonlight *(left )*.

# Round and About

Like Pagsanjan Falls, the following recommended resorts and places of interest to visitors are all accessible from Manila by road in less than two hours:

BULACAN PROVINCE

*Bustos and Ipo Dams.* Ideal for swimming and very popular at weekends. With easy access to Manila Bay, Bulacan provides large quantities of sea foods; along the shoreline, snipes are also prevalent. Much of the land is used for growing rice.

*Pandi Spring.* Mineral water swimming pools with cabanas for overnight stays. Boating and fishing. Other sporting facilities include a new bowling green.

BATAAN PROVINCE

*Cabcaben Beach.* Sited on Manila Bay and often called Villa Carmen Beach Resort. Excellent facilities for boating, fishing, water-skiing and skin-diving. The duck season attracts many sportsmen. At Limay there is a golf course set in hilly terrain. Other nearby beach resorts are Pulong Bato and Villa Leonar. In fine weather, these beaches can be reached from Manila by ferry which is much quicker than by car.

BATANGAS PROVINCE

*Matabungkay Beach.* Batangas is one of the most picturesque and most progressive provinces. There is a first-class road to this beach. Close to Fortune Island the water is abundant with fish. All resort facilities are available.

*Tulisay Beach.* A new beach resort still under development by the Board of Travel and Tourist Industry. A fine swimming beach fronts Taal volcano.

CAVITE PROVINCE

*Kawit.* Cavite Province is historical and may be compared with Virginia in America. Many of the worst battles between the Spaniards and the Filipinos took place in this province. Here, Filipinos also fought the Americans and it was off the Cavite coast that America defeated the Spanish navy prior to their occupation of the Philippines for more than fifty years. At Kawit is the home of General Emilio Aguinaldo, President of the first Republic of the Philippines under Spanish rule; the home is now a national shrine.

*Dalahican Beach.* More famous for sunsets than anything else; not a resort beach for the tourist.

*Tagaytay City.* Situated at an altitude of 2,500 feet. Mountainous countryside abundant with fruit trees. Tagaytay Ridge overlooks Taal volcano.

*Left:* Ambuklao Dam, about 200 miles from Manila and some 30 miles north-east of La Trinidad Valley, supplies electricity to many industrial plants on Luzon.  When this photograph was taken there had been several months of drought.

*Right:* Salt evaporation beds in Las Piñas; seen on the way to Taal Volcano and Cavite. Blazing sun sucks water from shallow, dammed ponds which are flooded with sea water. Men roll and rake each square to collect the salt as a crystallized residue. During the rainy season these beds are used to breed fish.

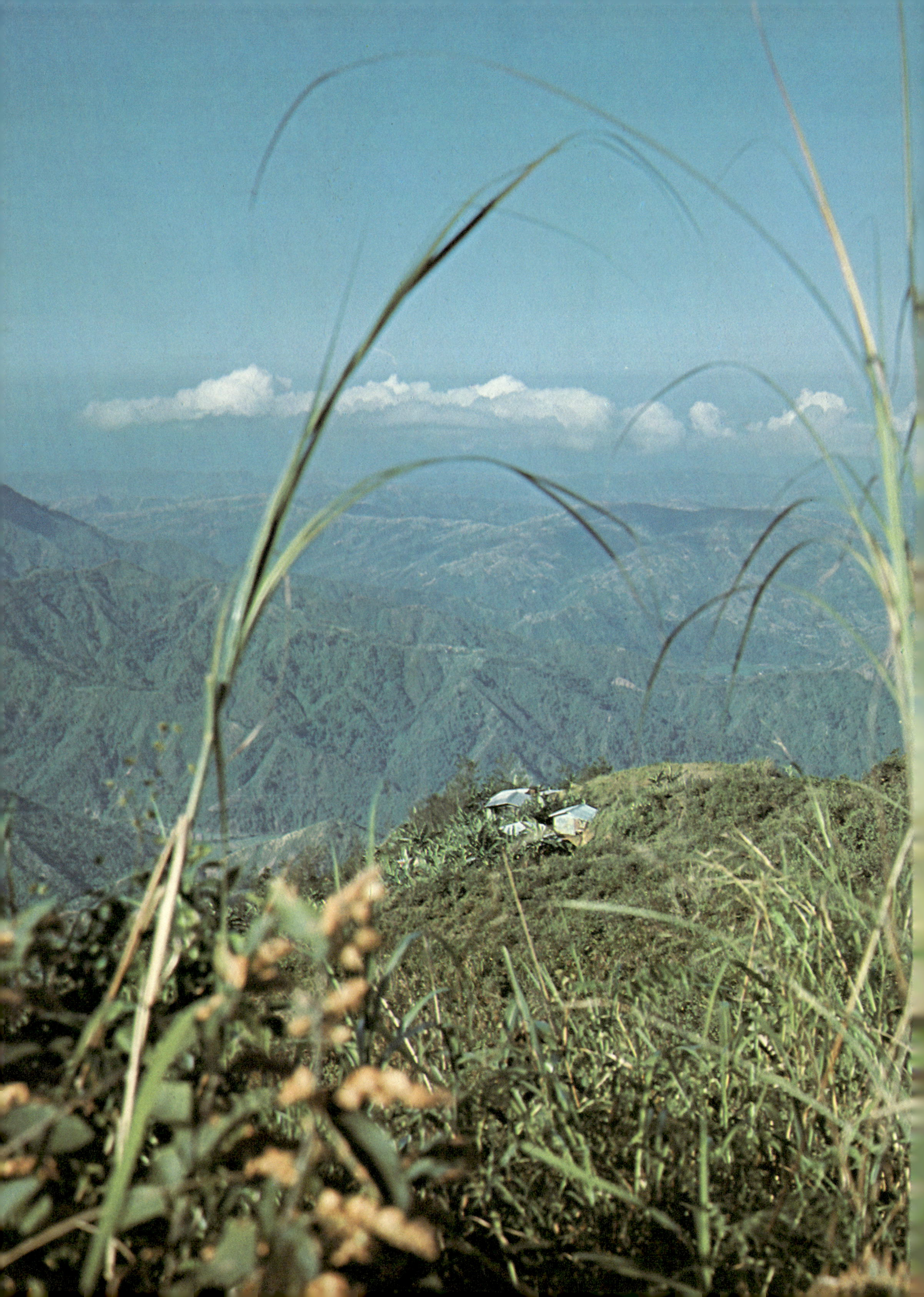

LAGUNA PROVINCE

*Mount Makiling.* A national park with natural hot springs and more than three
thousand species of flora. There is a road to the Philippines College of
Agriculture and Forestry; also to the International Rice Research Institute
built from funds of the Rockefeller and Ford Foundations.

*Calamba.* See page 83.

*Holiday Hills.* Beautiful picnic grounds and a playground for children.
Horse-riding trails and a golf course.

*Los Baños.* A resort town situated on Laguna Lake at the foot of Mount
Makiling. Mineral water swimming pools.

*Forestry Bureau.* Located inside the School of Forestry grounds at the College of
Agriculture. A fine swimming pool under a canopy of enormous tropical trees.
Facilities for dancing as well as for indoor and outdoor sports.

*Pagsanjan Falls.* Pages 85 to 86.

*Sampaloc Lake.* Majestic scenery with Mount San Cristobal as a backcloth.
There is a trail around the Lake and the boating facilities are excellent. The
Franklin Baker desiccated coconut plant is the world's largest installation of
its kind.

QUEZON CITY and RIZAL PROVINCE

*Quezon City.* The national capital. It is difficult for the visitor to define where
Manila ends and the capital begins. Indeed, the areas immediately outside
Manila's city limits were previously referred to as "Greater Manila." Now,
beyond Manila's northern city limit are the towns of Caloocan, Malabon and
Navotas. Quezon City, together with San Juan and Mandaluyong, lies in the east.
Pasay City is to the south. The cities of Caloocan, Pasay and Quezon are all
part of Rizal Province which has a total population exceeding that of Manila;
the international airport is sited in Pasay City.

Quezon City proper has many places of interest: the *University of the
Philippines; Balara Filters* (a magnificent swimming pool, picnic grounds and a
dance pavilion); *Fort Aguinaldo* (headquarters of the Philippines Armed
Forces); *Capitol Hills Golf Club* (claimed to be the finest in the Orient with
both day and night facilities); *La Mesa Dam* (boating, fishing, swimming); and
*Araneta Coliseum.*

*Rizal.* Practically everything of interest that is loosely credited to Manila is
found in Rizal. *Makati* (text pages 43 to 44), *Roxas Boulevard* with its countless
nightclubs, the finest golf courses (page 134), Las Piñas Church with the bamboo
organ; and the popular resorts on the rim of Manila Bay are all here, plus a
thousand other attractions.

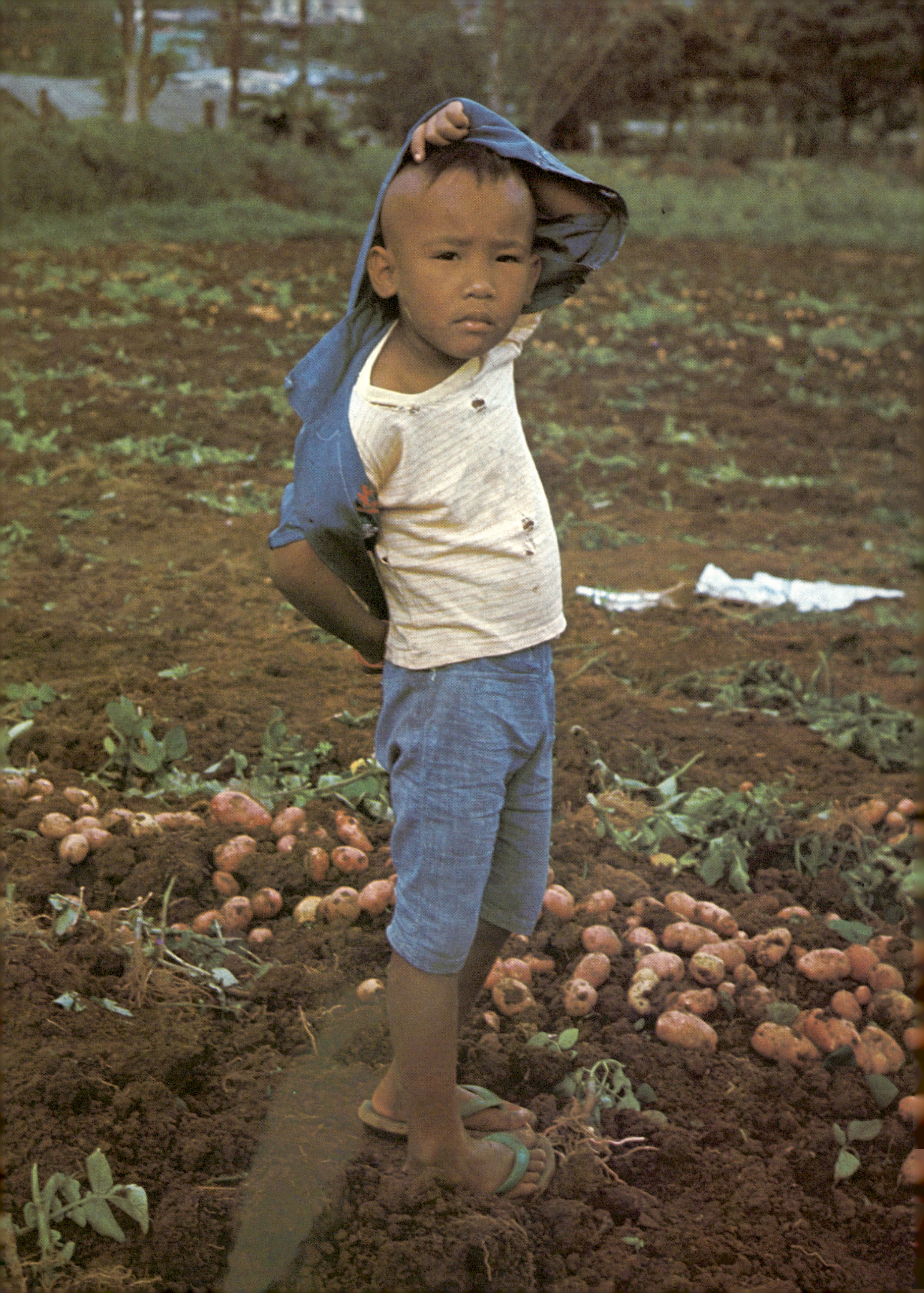

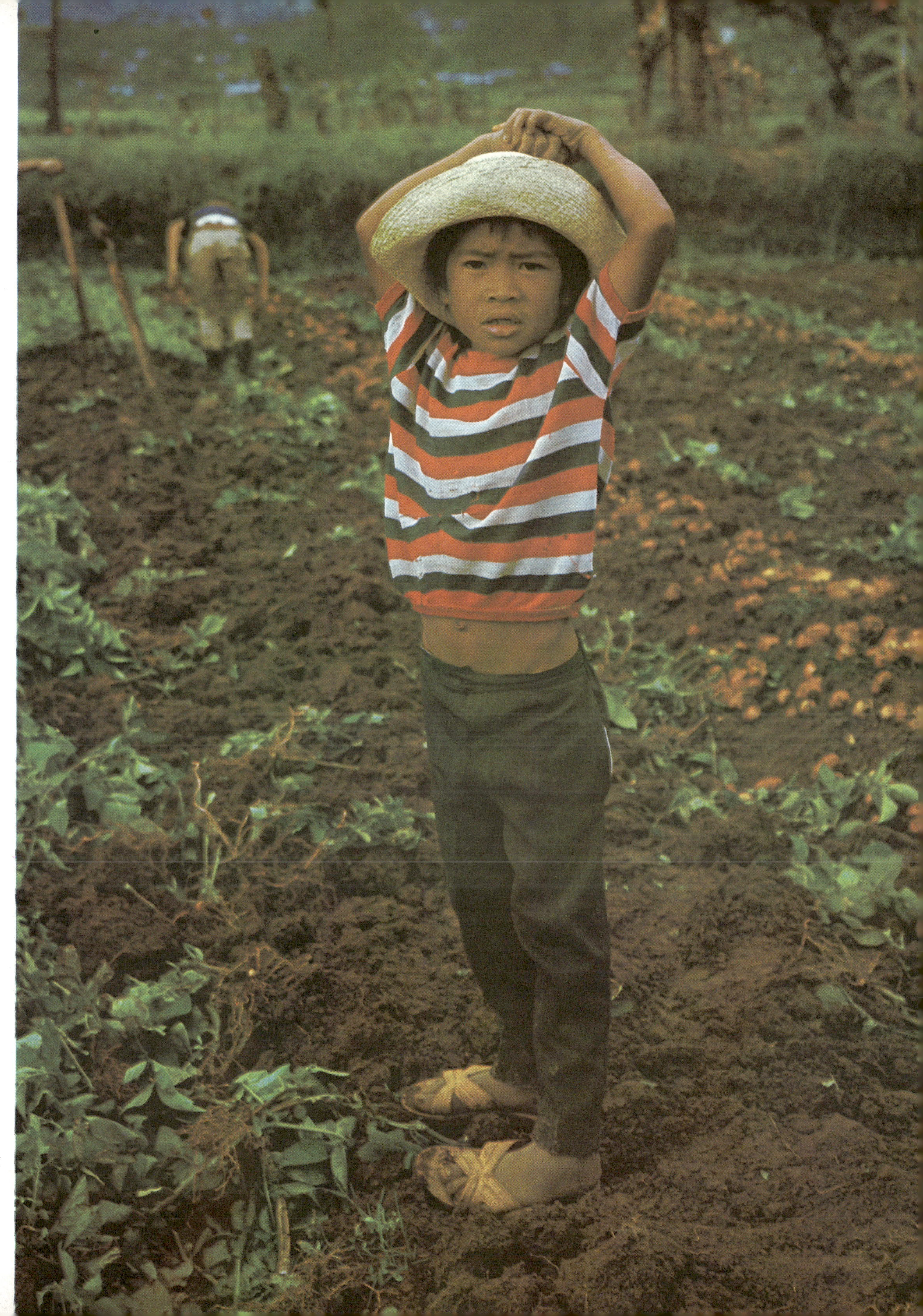

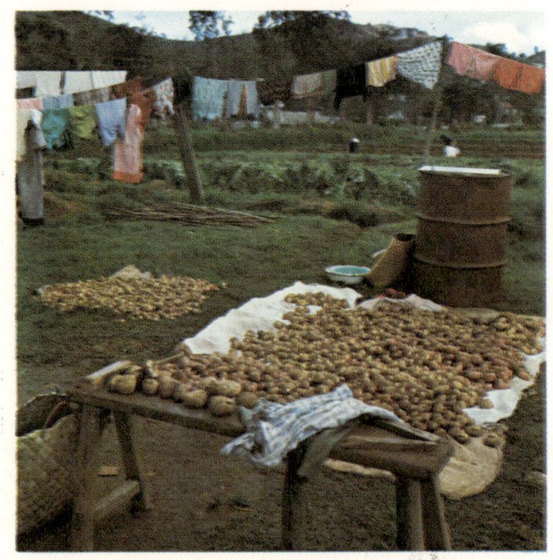

*Above:* Guarding the potato crop is an important job!
*Page 113:* La Trinidad Valley is the Salad Bowl of the Philippines. With rich soil in a sunny, wind protected valley, all kinds of fruit and vegetables are grown. Every field is cultivated, and an entire family will labour on its plot of land.

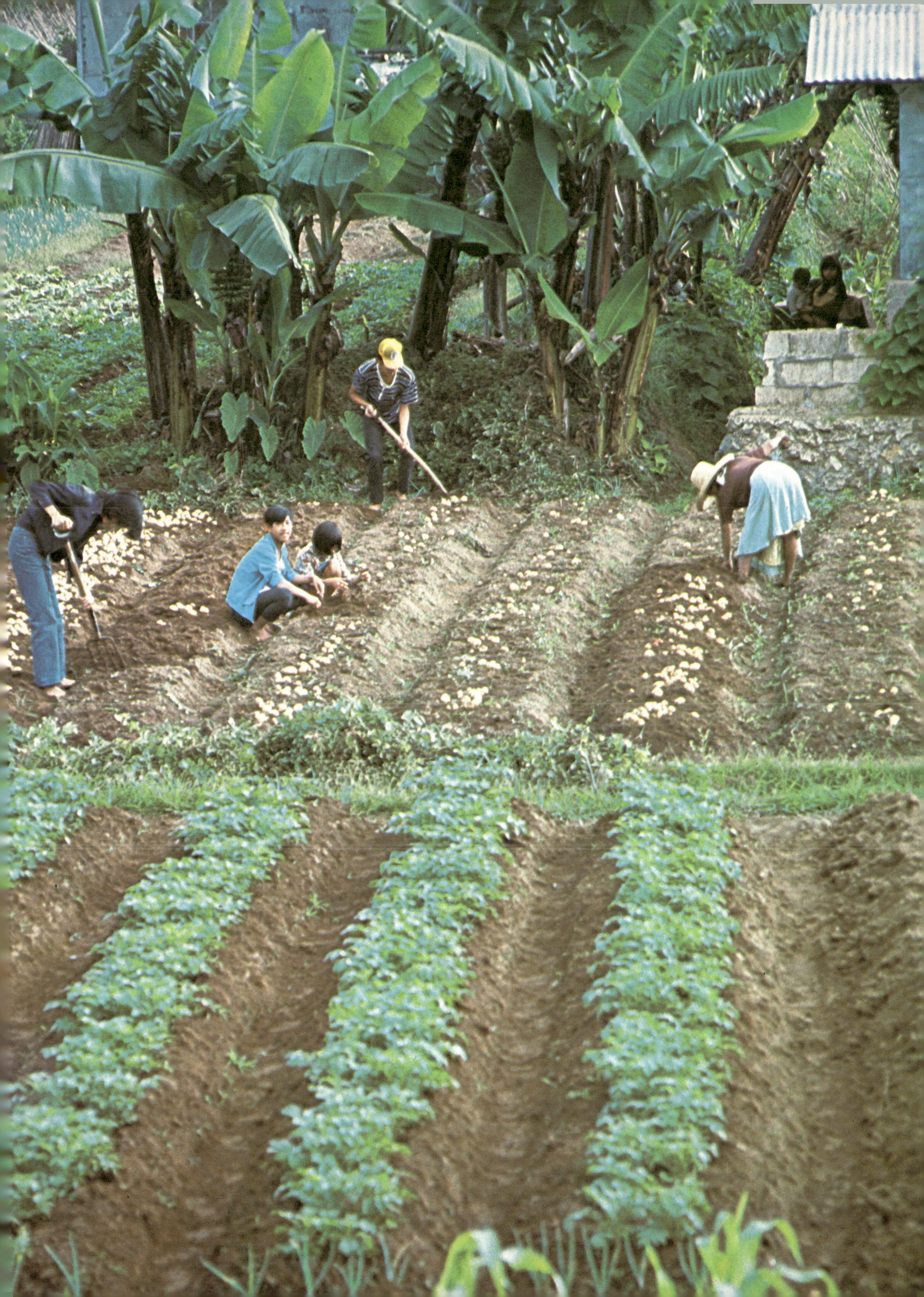

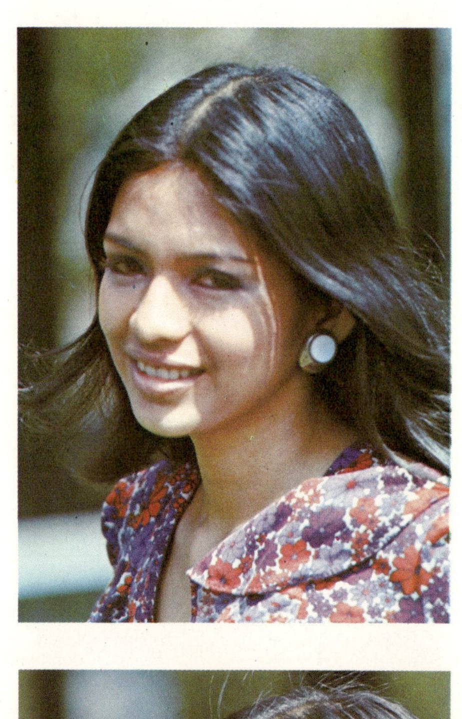
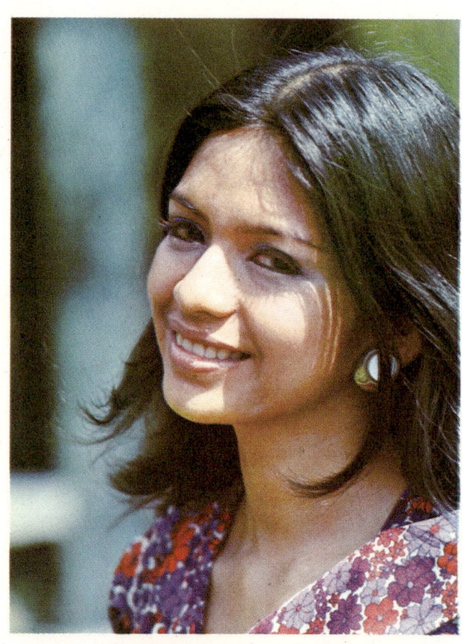
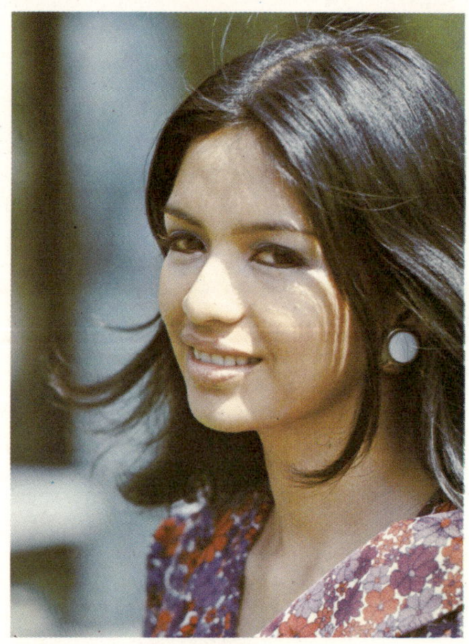
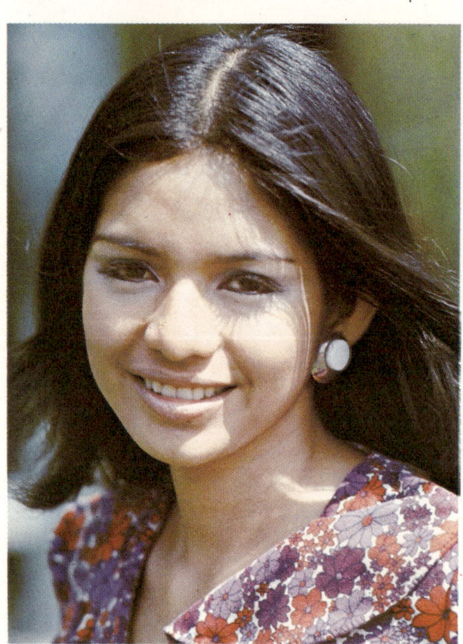

*Above and page 115.* Nelia Sancho—a
beautiful Filipino who was crowned
Queen of the Pacific.

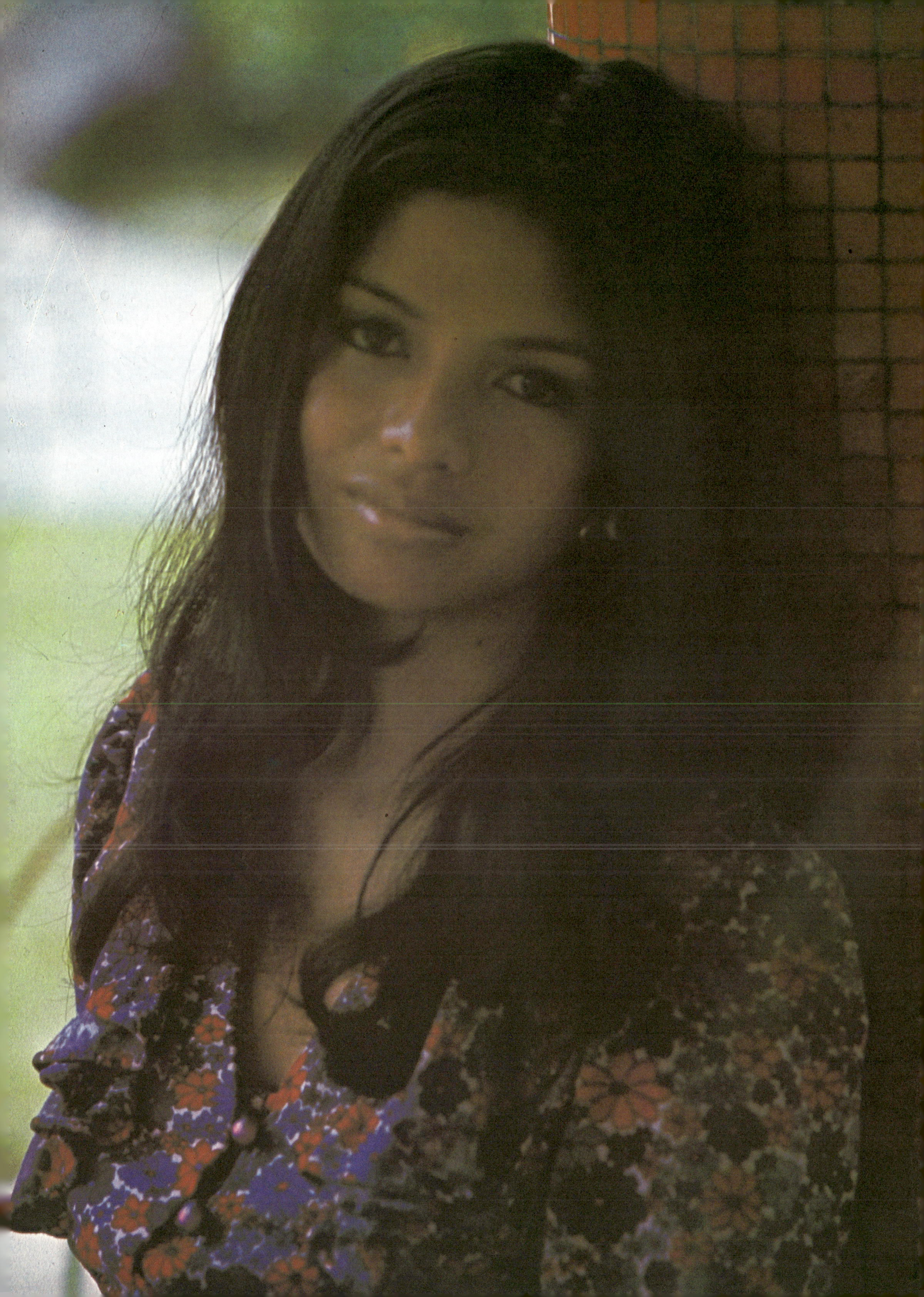

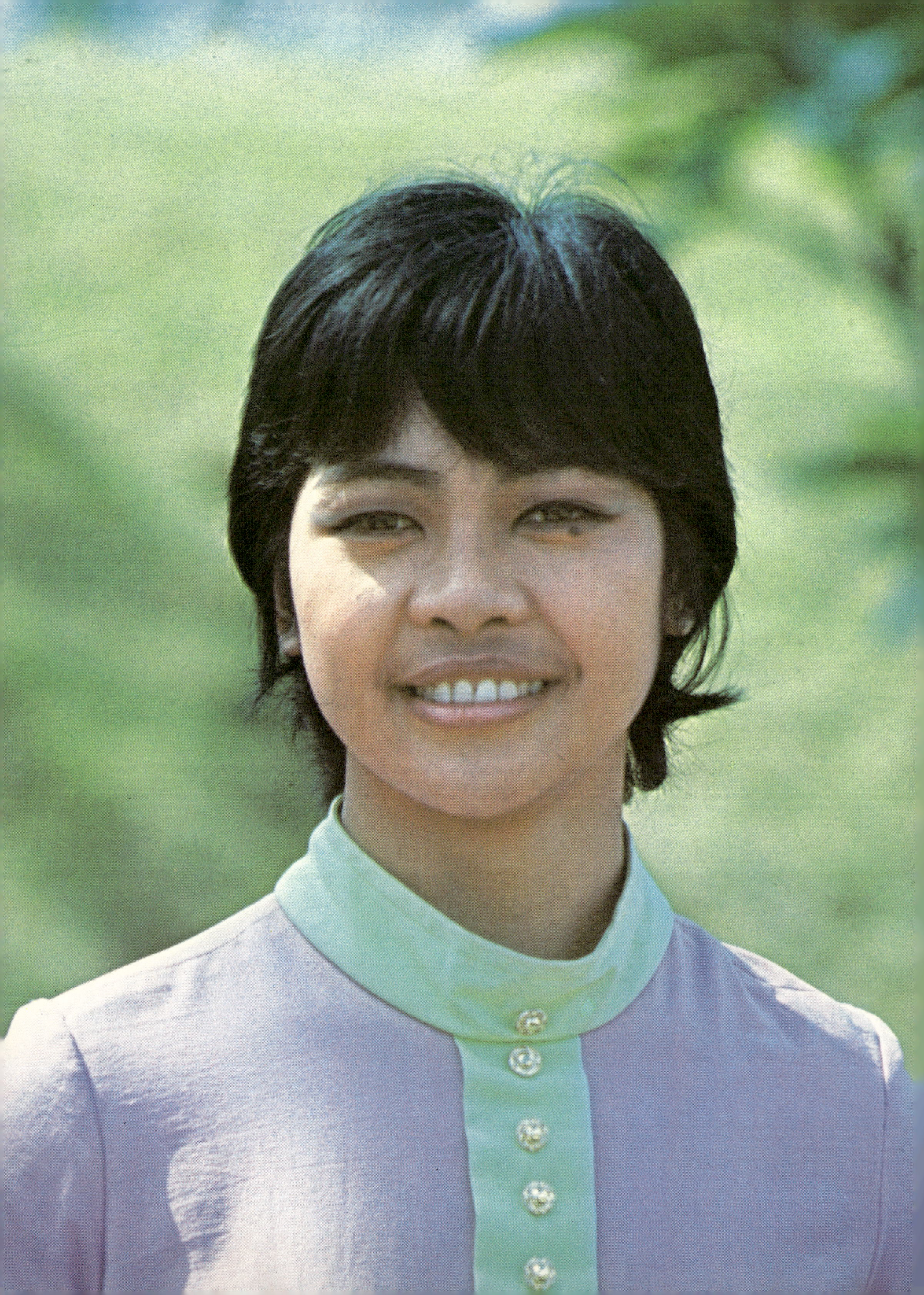

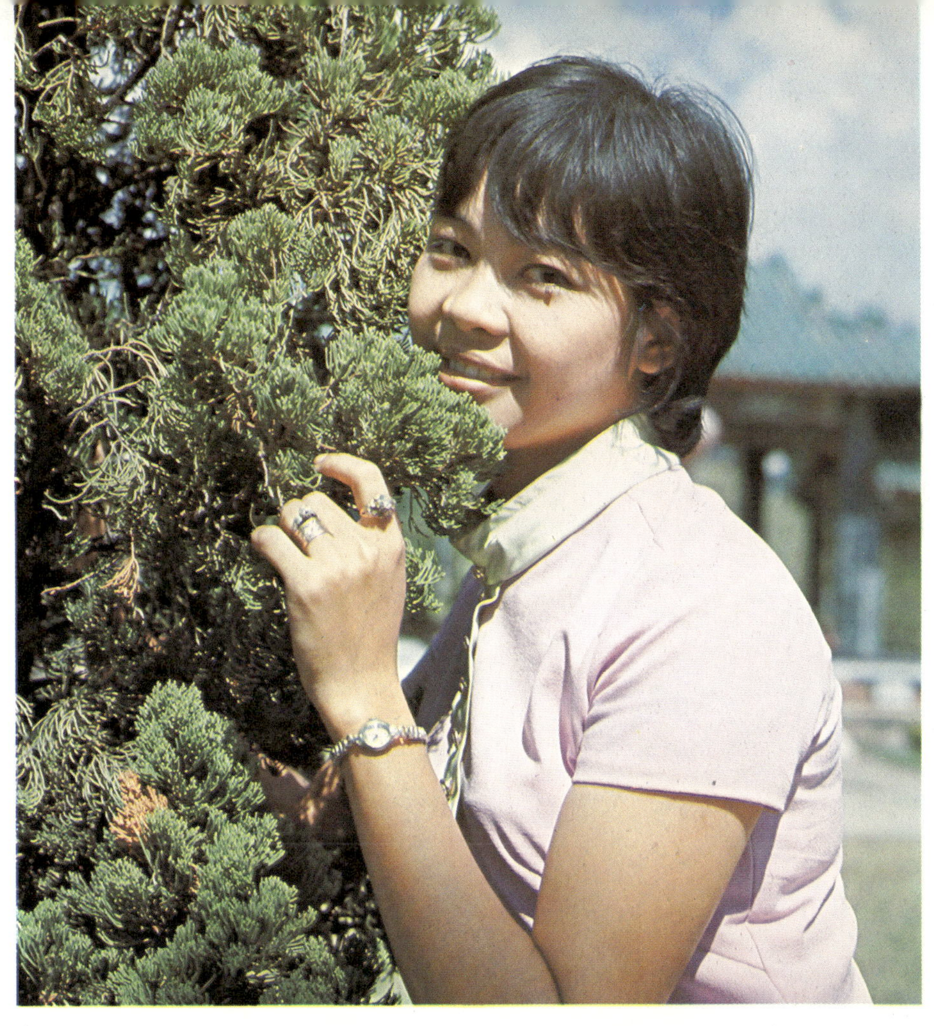

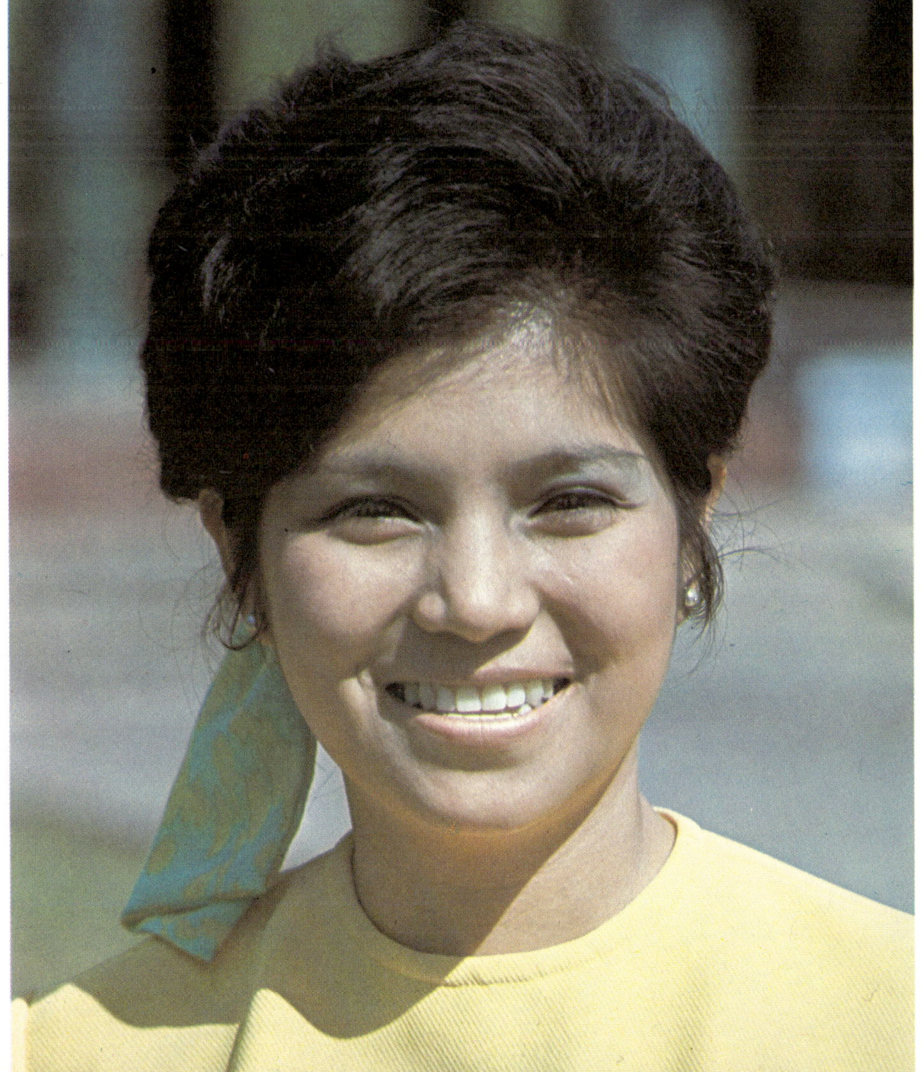

Some girls of the Philippines—*Left/above:*
Yvonne Macatangay.
*Left below:* Ampy Balitbit.

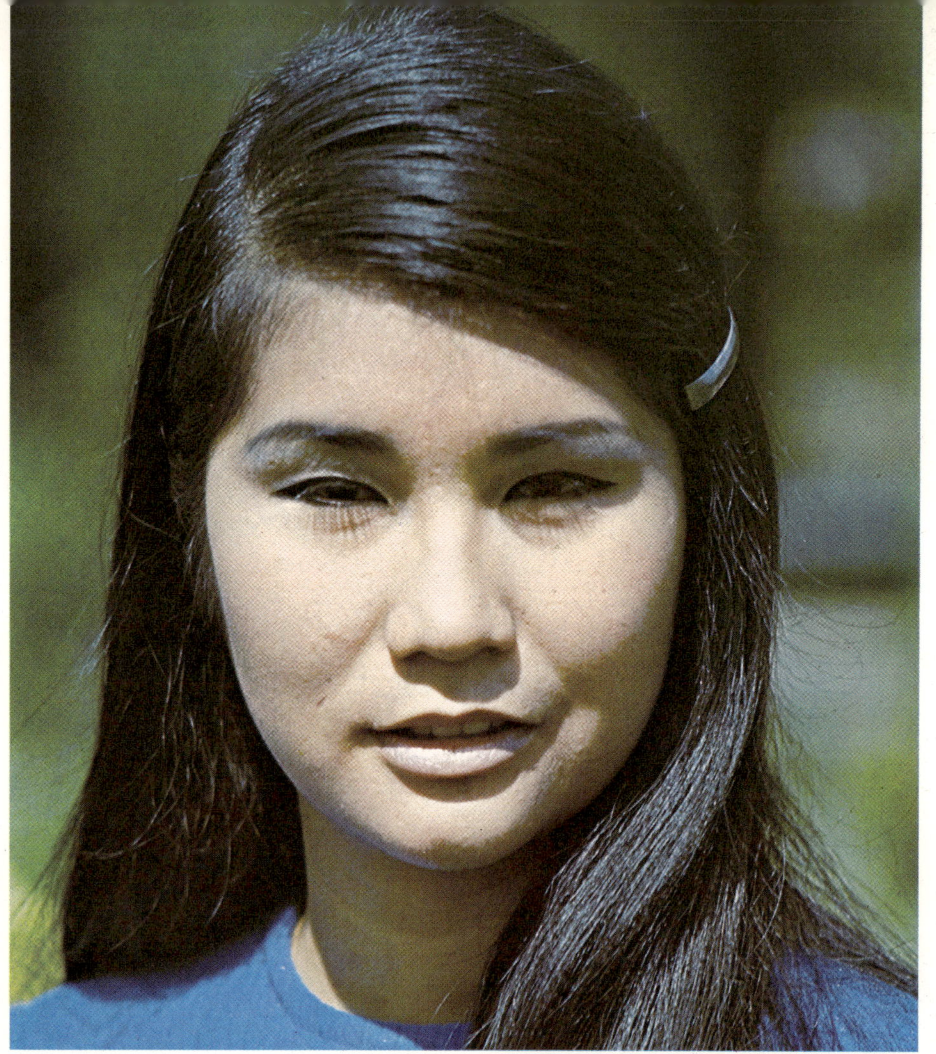

Above: Vicky Bautista

Right: Theresita Pangilinan

118

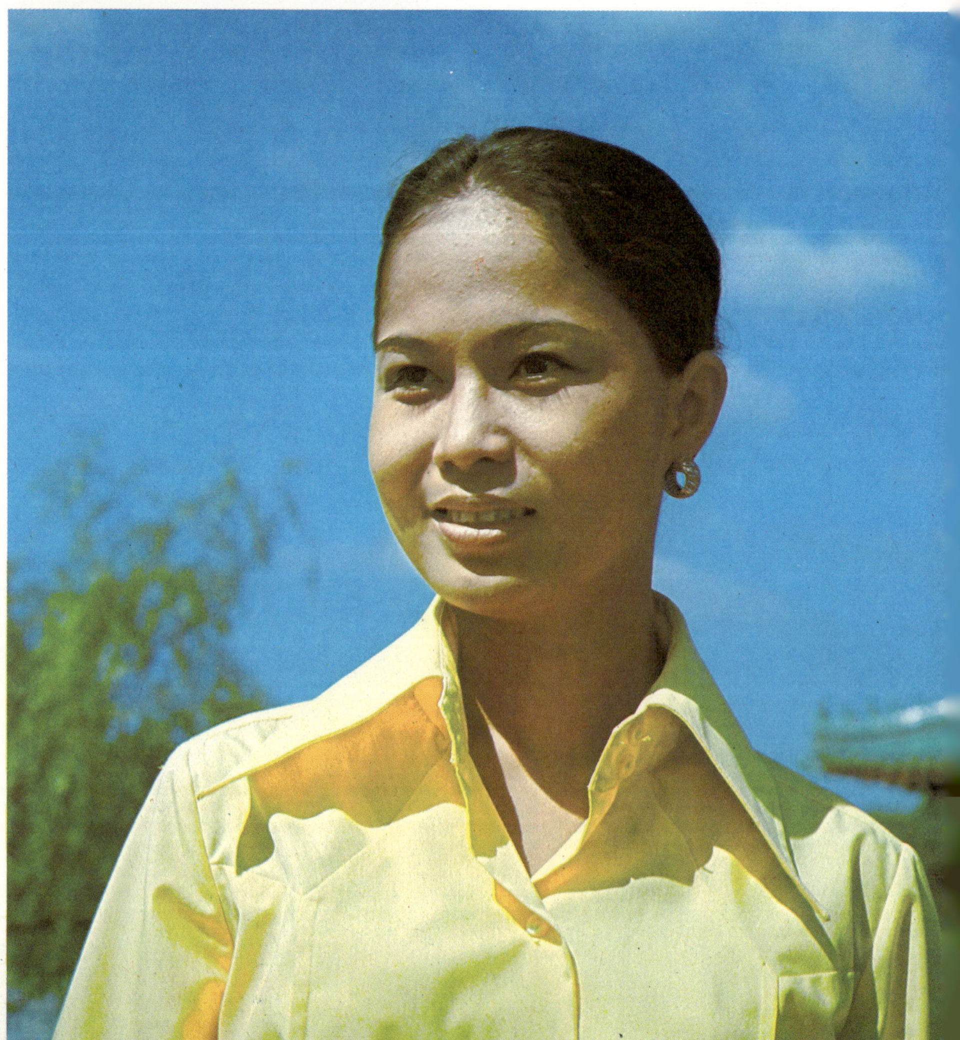

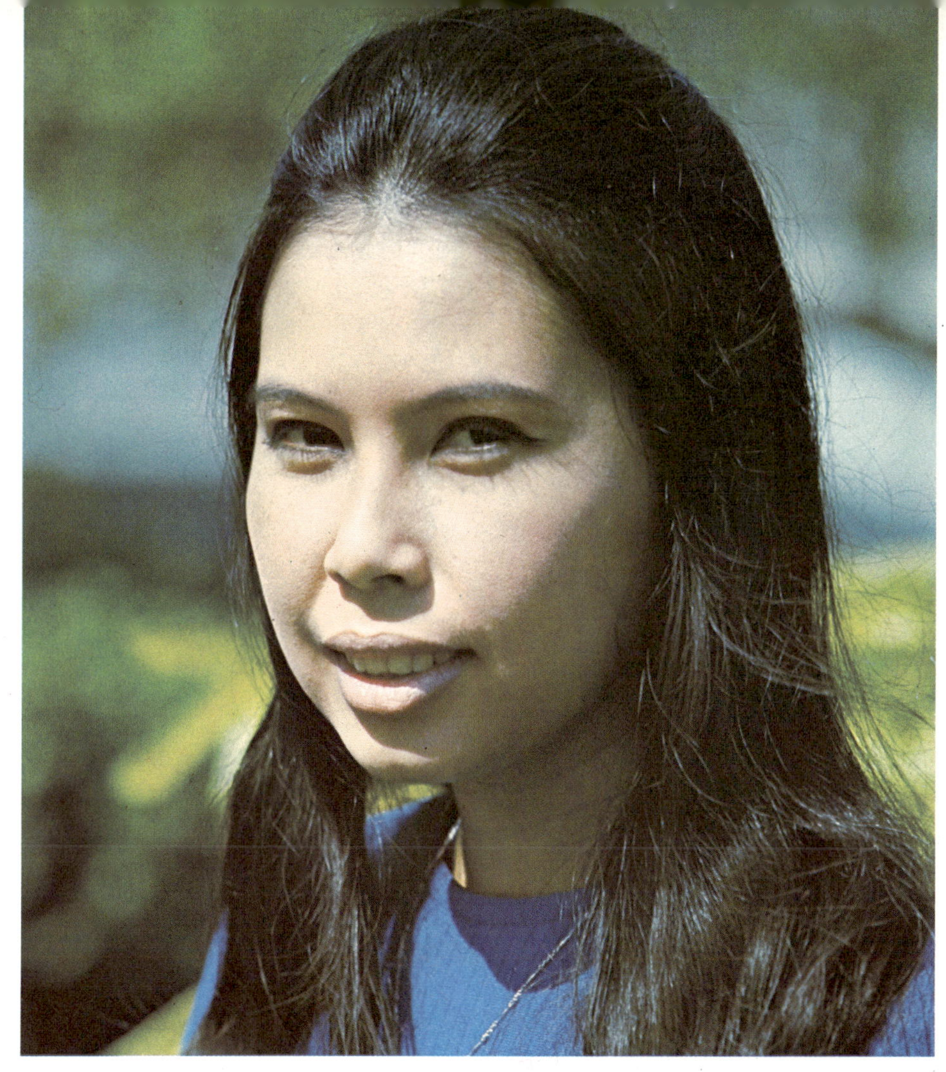

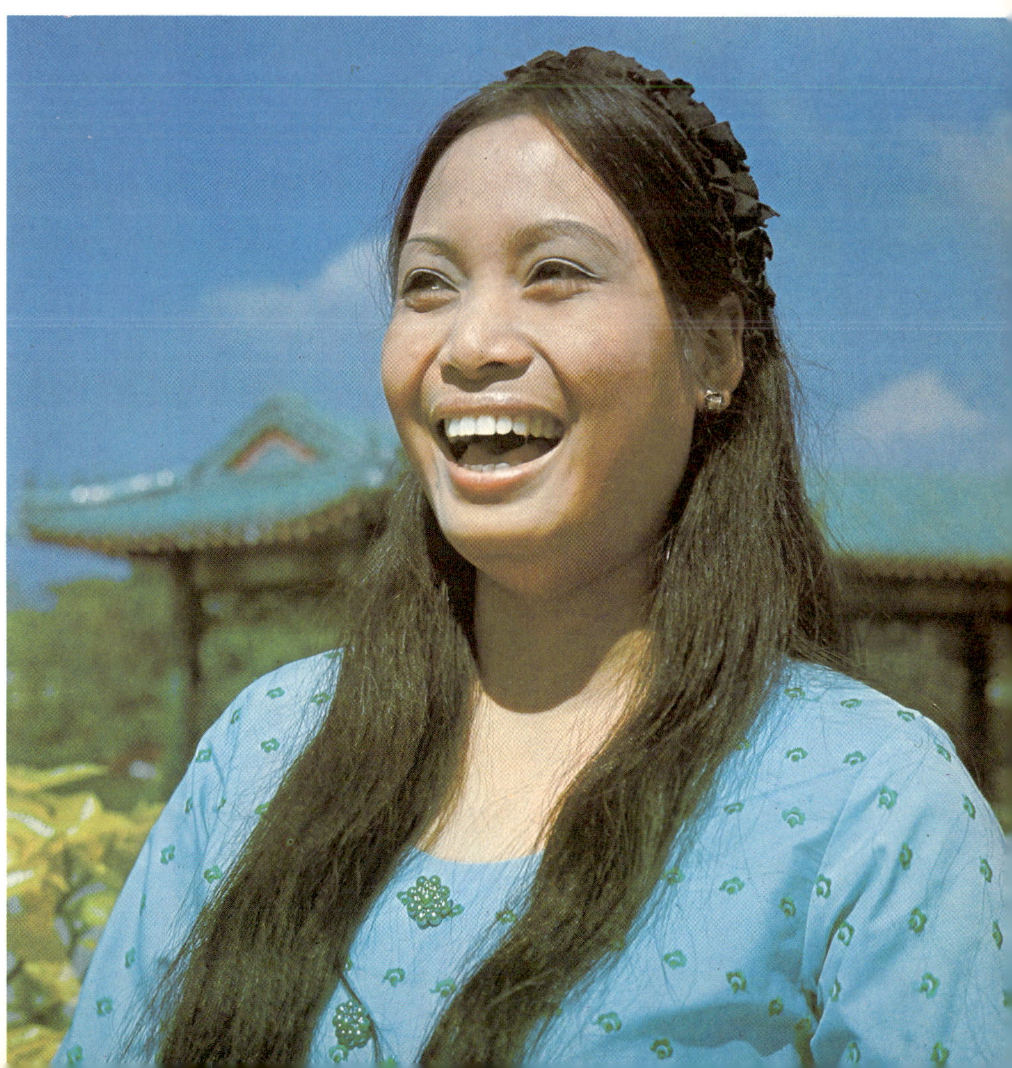

*Left:* Theresa Valero

*Below:* Irene Tobias

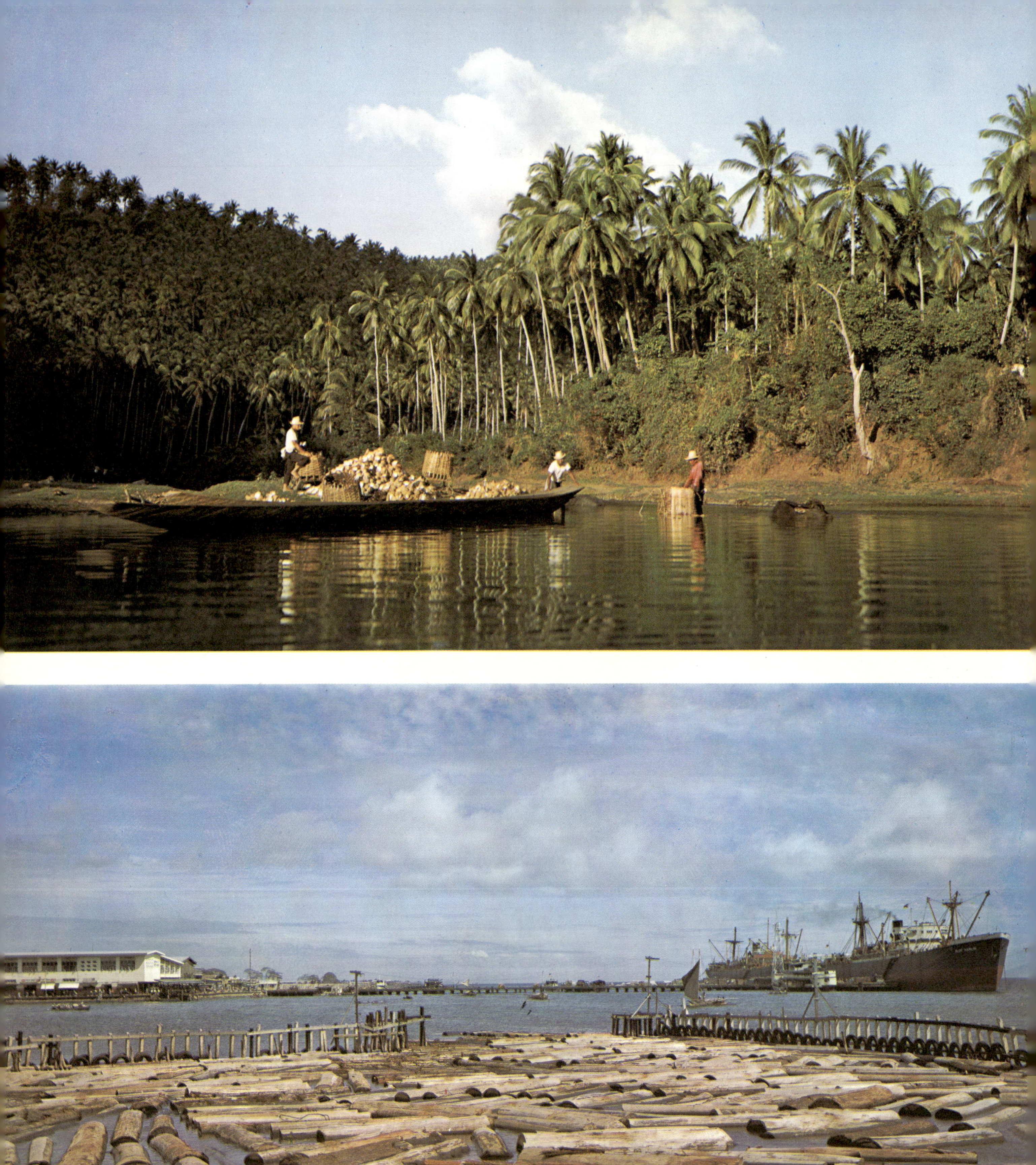

*Further Afield*

*Bacolod City.* Situated on the northern end of Negros Island, this City is the centre for the main sugar-growing area of the Philippines. Visitors can tour the sugar plantations.

*Cebu City.* On the island of Cebu in the Visayas is the oldest City in the Philippines where Magellan erected a cross—now called Magellan's Cross—in 1521. This cross is housed in a waterfront building. A statue of the patron saint of Cebu, the Holy Child, stands in San Agustin Church. Those who are adventurous can take a boat to Bantayan island.

*Cagayan de Oro.* The Del Monte pineapple plantations and cannery are open to sightseers. The Xavier University Museum is also worth visiting.

*Corregidor.* See pages 93 to 100.

*Davao.* The largest city on Mindanao island which is famed for its abacá, coconuts and bananas. Visitors are welcome at the banana plantations at Tagum. A few miles to the southwest of Davao, Mount Apo rises to 9,610 feet and is a backcloth to the Mount Apo National Park where there are waterfalls and hot springs. During the season, Davao Gulf offers excellent tuna fishing. Guided tours can be arranged to the Aguinaldo Pearl Farm situated on Samal Island, a one-hour boat ride from Davao.

*Hundred Islands.* The most famous of these islands are located along the coast of Lucap, Alaminos and Pangasinan. Quezon Island is very popular because of its wide swimming beach.

*Iloilo.* An attractive island famous for its *piña* and *jusi* fabrics. The *barong Tagalog* shirts cost much less than in Manila. In Iloilo and the neighbouring towns, religious art is prominent. The museum exhibits artifacts gathered from the entire province.

*Lake Lanao.* This lake, 2,300 feet above sea level, is the site of Marawi City, the "show window" of Mohammedanism in the Philippines. There are many imposing mosques and the area is famous for its Muslim handicrafts—silk and brassware.

*Legaspi (and Mount Mayon).* Situated in the province of Albay some 350 miles from Manila. This part of Southern Luzon offers spectacular mountain and lake scenery. The biggest attraction is Mount Mayon, a volcano with a perfect cone that rises to 7,943 feet above sea level. Mayon has erupted several times but the worst devastation occurred in 1814 when the town of Cagsawa was destroyed. Except for overgrown ruins there is little to remind visitors of this disaster. The lava-enriched soil has made everything particularly green and fertile. Farmers live around the base of the volcano, cultivating the rich slopes of this sleeping giant which is both enemy and friend. Places to visit are the Tiwi hot springs and boiling lakes, Kalayukaii beach and Tabaco where rope is made. Kawilihan

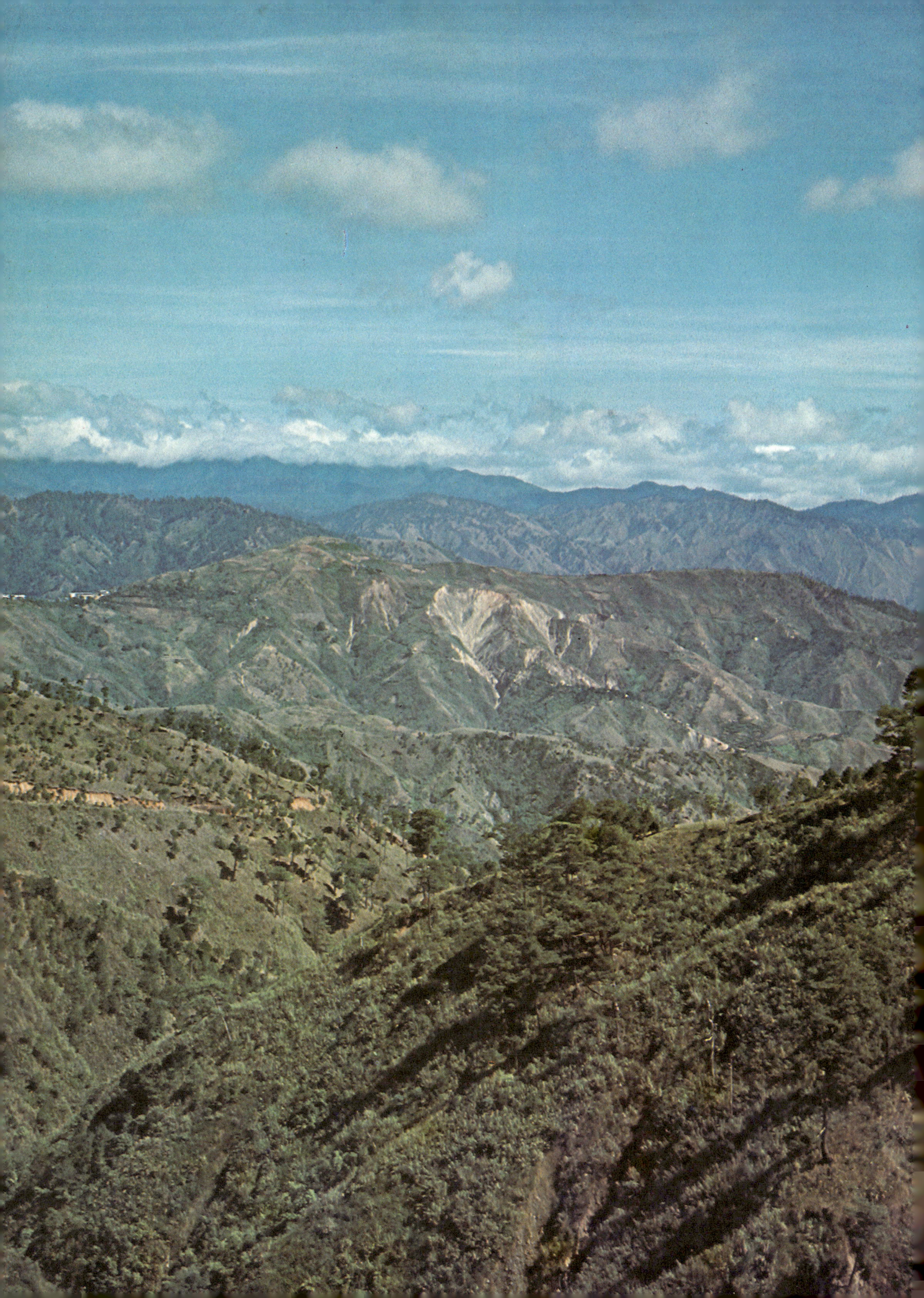

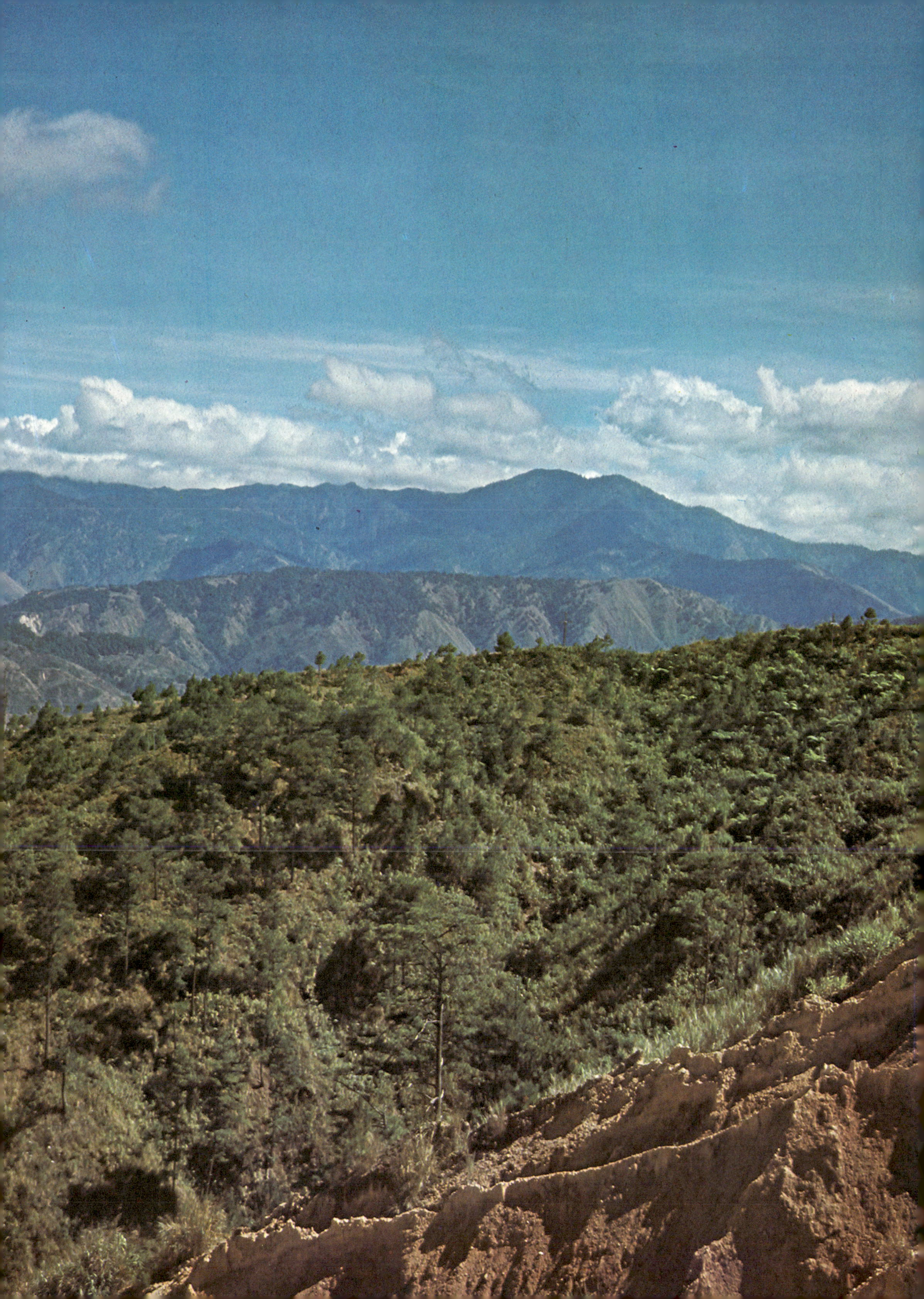

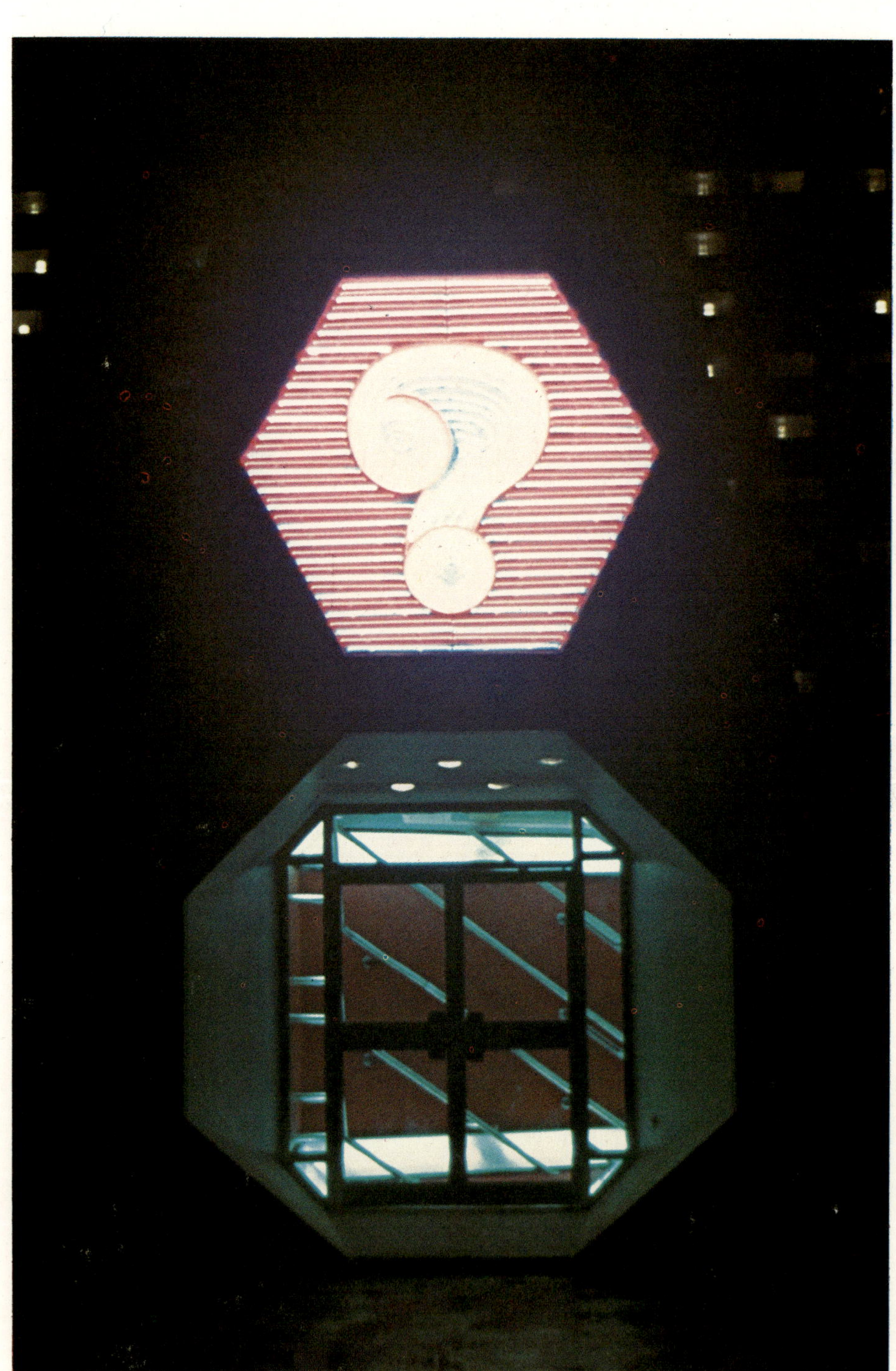

*Right:* Outside—Entrance with a question mark; the Where Else? disco at the Hotel Inter-continental.

*Pages 126 and 127:* Inside—the plushy Where Else?  The decor answers its own question.

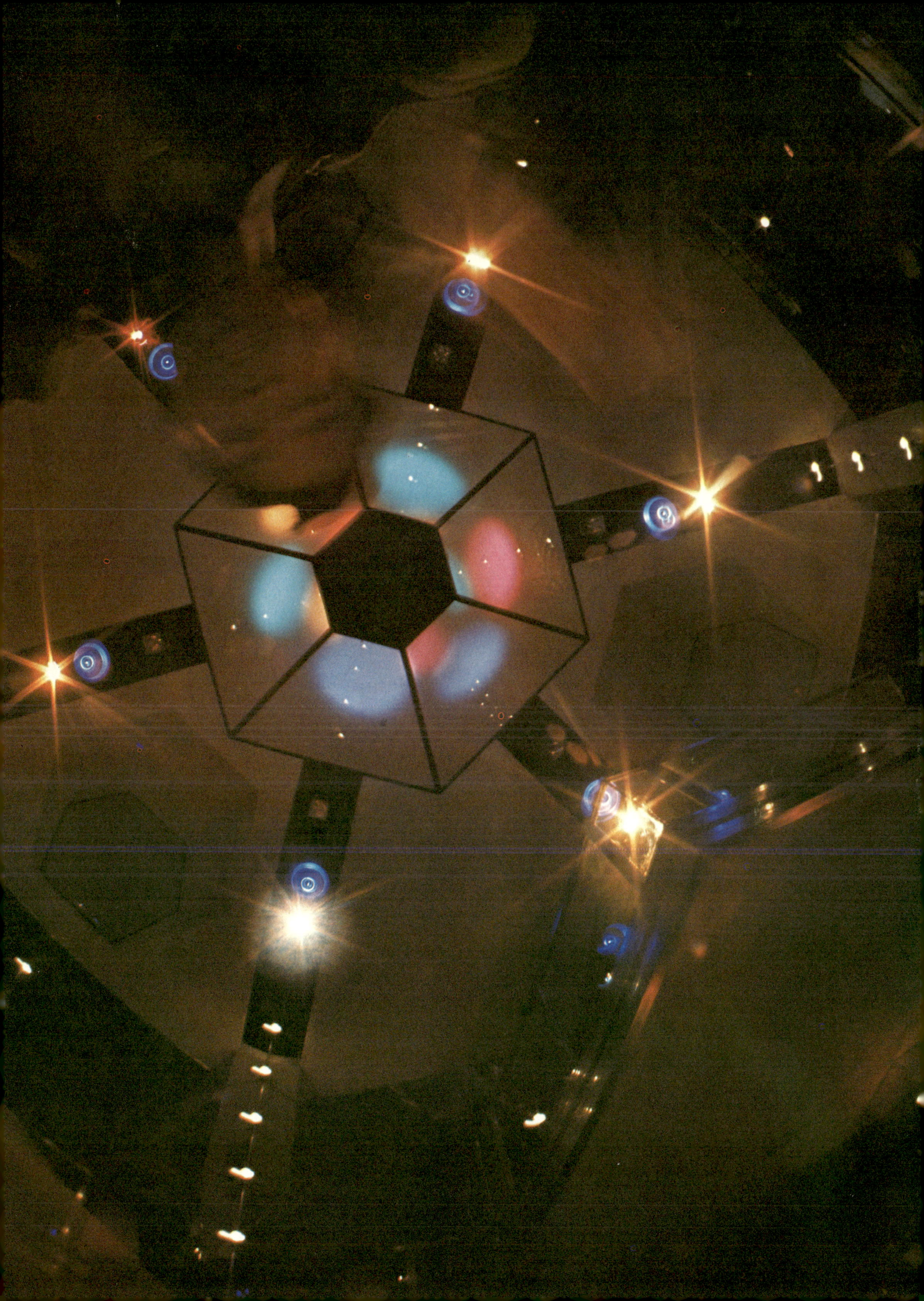

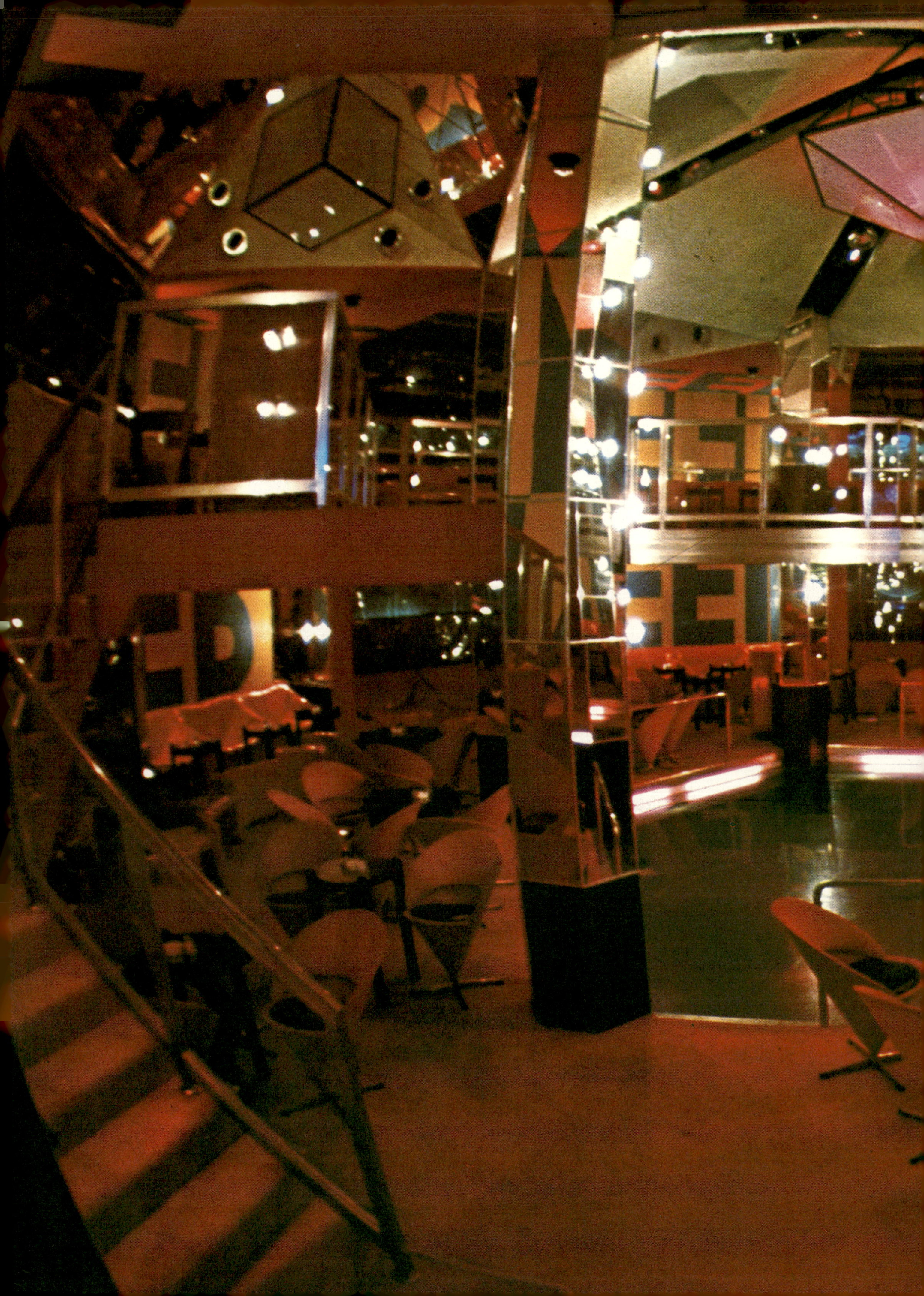

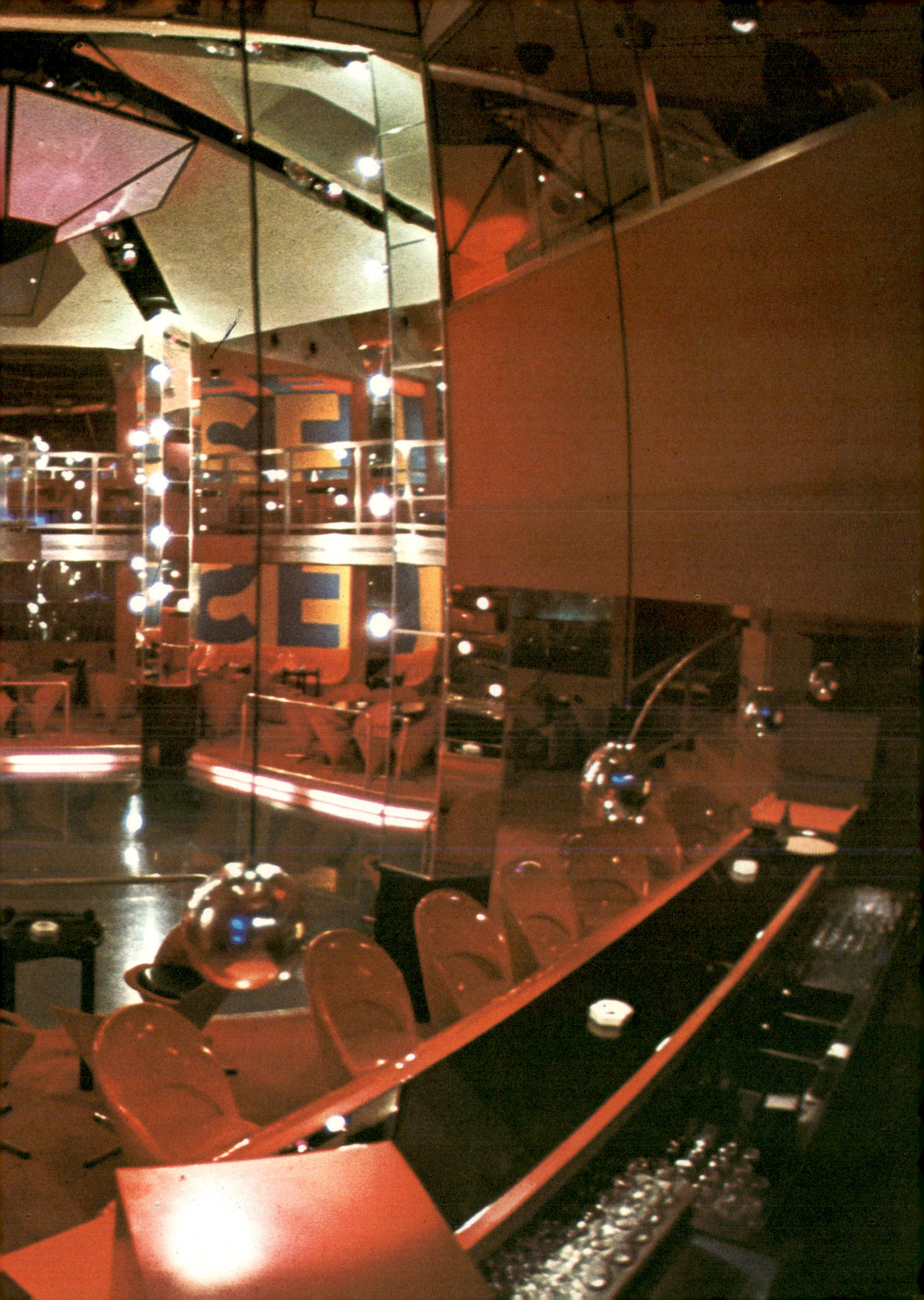

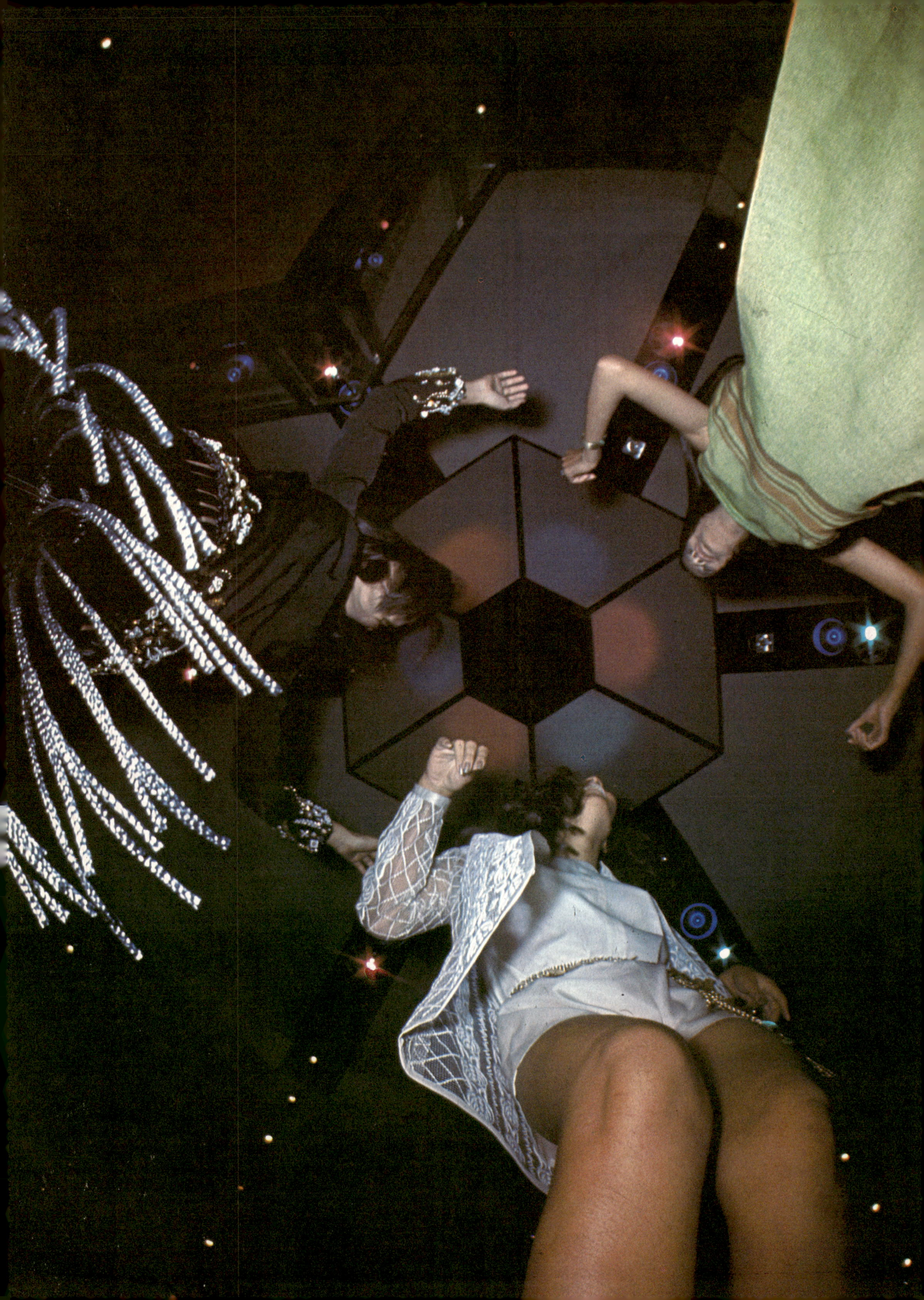

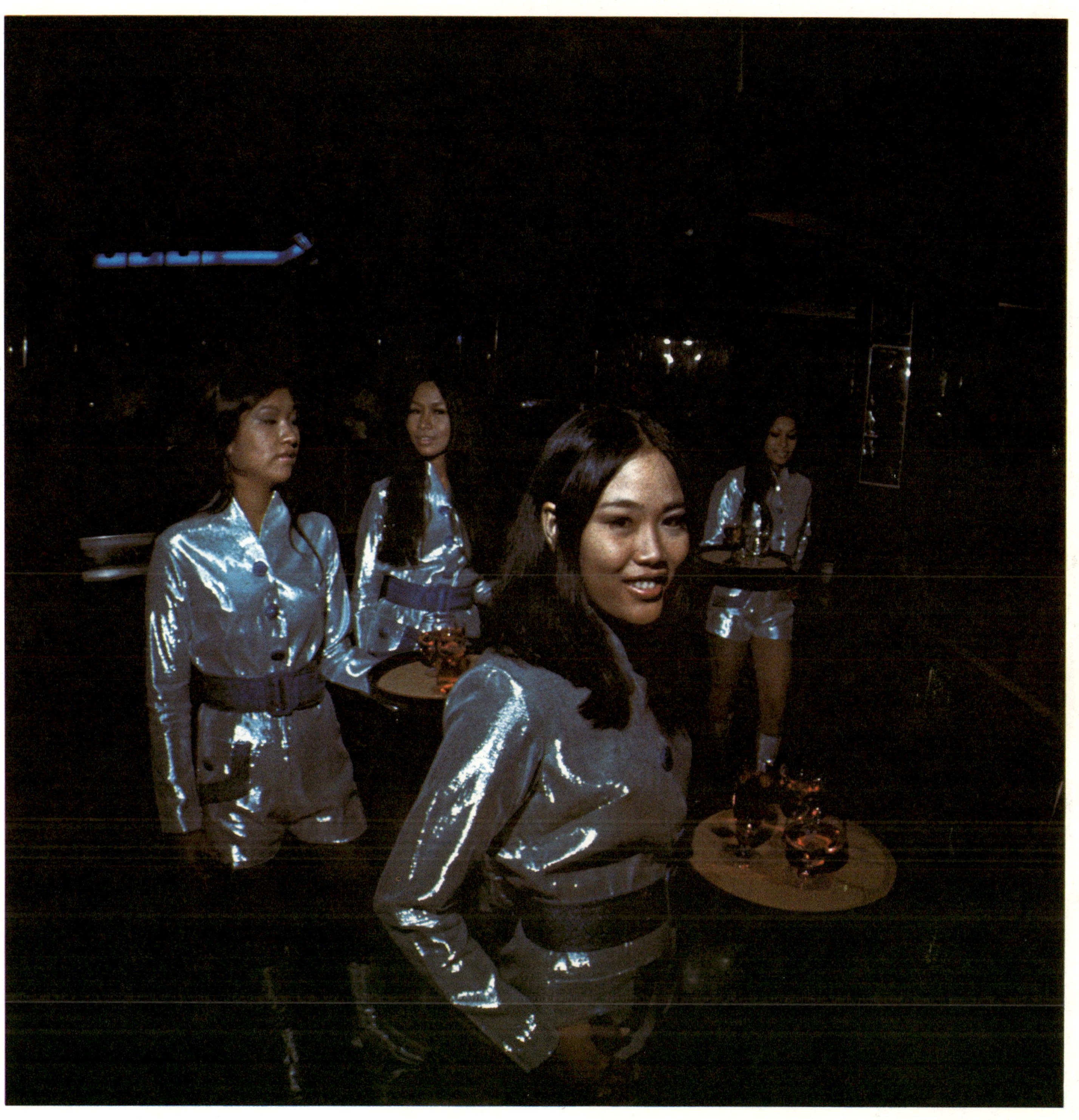

To quote an official guide: ''Night-life can
be legit or illegit, nice or naughty, chic
or cheek, breezy or bawdy, wild or weird.''
(Text pages 69 and 79.)

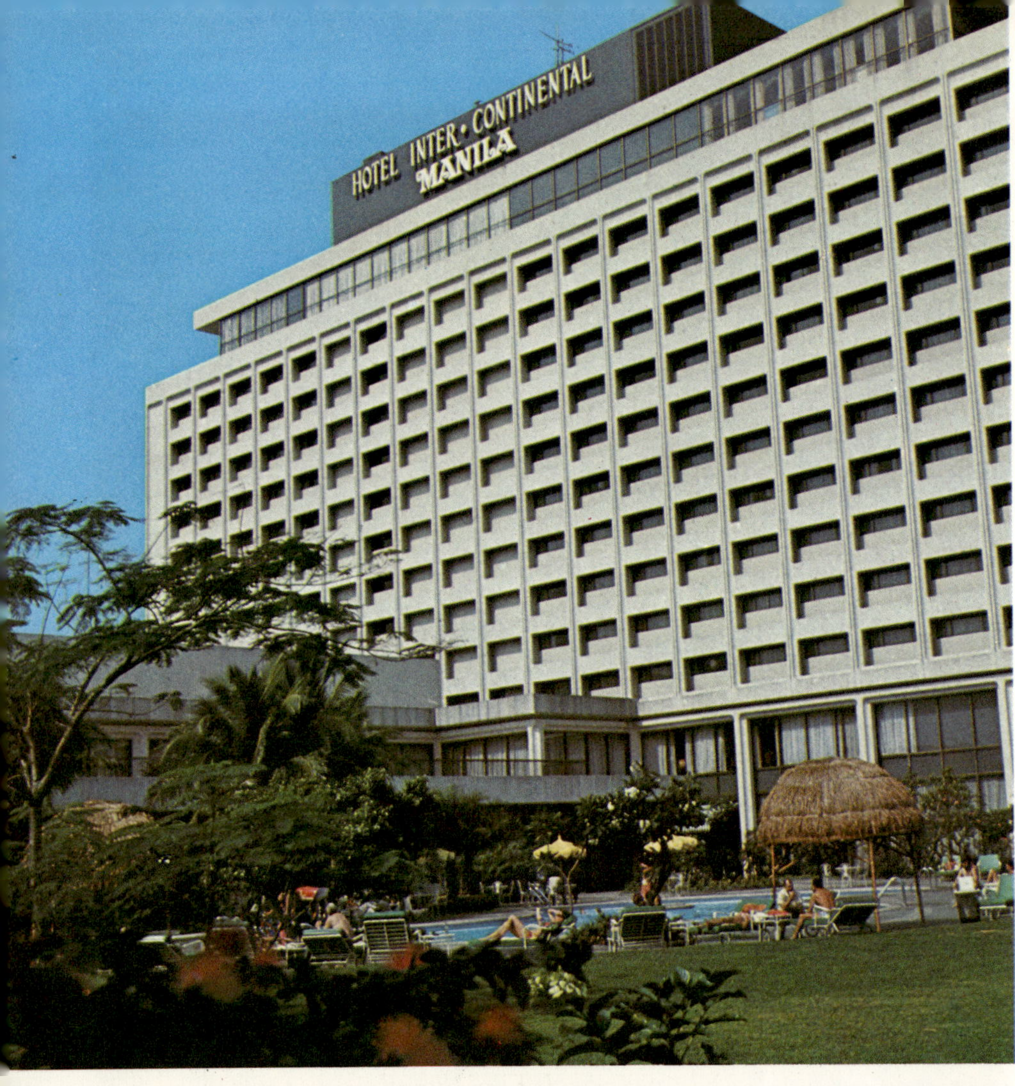

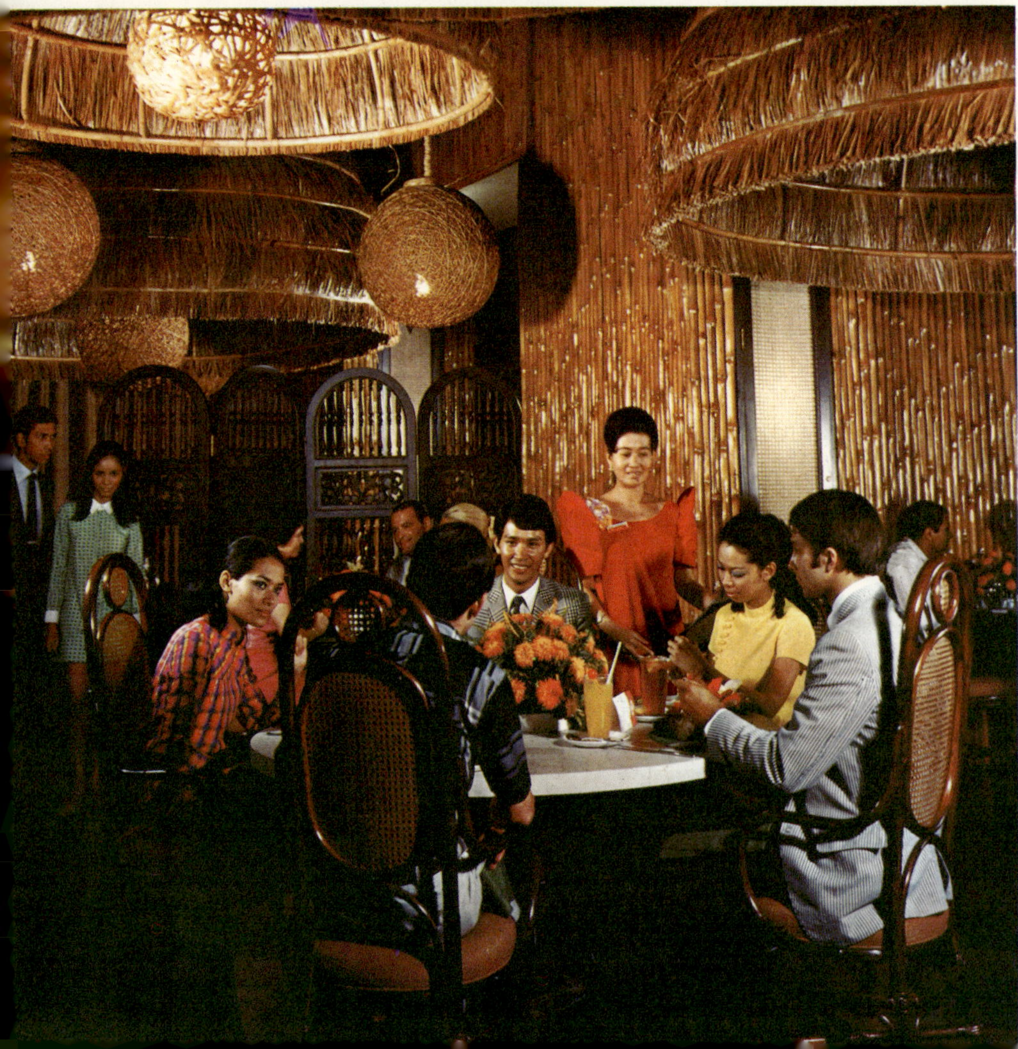

*Left and below:* In the best hotels—like the Inter-continental—there are supper clubs of international standard; excellent floor shows featuring leading artists; groovy disco pads for the young; and a variety of restaurants with opportunities to dance quietly or listen to progressive jazz. Whatever the visitor wants can be found.

resort is half an hour away by boat and offers facilities for boating and water-skiing. Under construction is a swimming pool that will be the largest in Asia.

*Palawan.* The province of Palawan consists mainly of virgin countryside. During April and May, everywhere is vivid with the blooms of cherry trees. Two major attractions are the underground river in Saint Paul Bay and the Tabon Caves where the Tabon man's remains were found. Near Tabon Caves are magnificent beaches; Isla de Canyon and Canigaran beaches are quite unspoiled. In the surrounding mountains, rare butterflies and animals can be found. Birds breed on the islands of El Nido and Ursula. One of the Philippines' richest fishing grounds is in Palawan's Malampaya Sound.

*Zamboanga City (and Basilan).* The capital city of Mindanao Island, Zamboanga is a delightful blend of Spanish, Muslim and American influences. Places worth visiting are: the wharf from where Zamboanga's "sea gypsies" ply back and forth on smuggling missions between Borneo, Indonesia and the neighbouring islands; the market where Muslim handicrafts, especially those from interior tribes, are sold; Fort Pilar; Pasonanca Park and the Muslim village that is in Taluksañgay and reached by a *vinta* or *pumboat.* The nearby twin Sta. Cruz islands have beaches of pink sand, and a wide variety of shells and coral can be found. Four times a day, ferry boats leave Zamboanga to negotiate the strait to Basilan where visitors can see plantations of rubber, coffee, date-palm, pepper and coconut—a landscape that combines the characteristics of Brazil, Malaysia and Africa. Sunday is market day and the Muslim Yakan tribe, in colourful costumes, comes down from its mountain villages.

# National Parks

National Parks in the Philippines cover a total area of 246,344 hectares. Here is a complete list chronologically arranged.

**MT. MAKILING**

Located at Los Baños (Laguna) and Sto. Tomas (Batangas). Special Features: hot springs and flora of three thousand species.

**ROOSEVELT**

Located at Hermosa (Bataan). Special Features: rock formations, natural hot springs and game refuge.

**MT. ARAYAT**

Located at Arayat (Pampanga). Special Features: panoramic and recreational.

**LIBMANAN CAVES**

Located at Libmanan (Camarines Sur). Special Features: series of crystal caverns and beautiful cataracts.

**BICOL**

Located at Basud and Daet (Camarines Norte) and Lupi and Sipocot (Camarines Sur). Special Features: panoramic, virgin forest and game refuge.

**MT. CANLAON**

Located at Bago, La Carlota, La Castellana, Murcia, Canlaon and San Carlos (Negros Occidental), and Vallehermoso (Negros Oriental). Special Features: famous crater, waterfalls, hot springs, gorges and peculiar rock formations.

**QUEZON**

Located at Atimonan, Padre Burgos and Pagbilao (Quezon). Special Features: recreational and panoramic.

**MT. BULUSAN VOLCANO**

Located at Casiguran, Barcelona, Bulusan, Irosin and Juban (Sorsogon). Special Features: famous crater, mineral hot springs, peculiar rock formations and panoramic. Lake resort.

**CALLAO CAVES**

Located at Penablanca (Cagayan). Special Features: inspiring caves, deep canyon and beautiful streams.

**SOHOTON NATURAL BRIDGE**

Located at Basey (Samar). Special Features: natural stone bridge, waterfalls, historical and recreational.

**SUDLON**

Located at Cebu City. Special Features: historical and scientific; waterfalls and natural swimming pools.

**MT. APO**

Located at Kidapawan (Cotabato) and Sta. Cruz and Guianga (Davao). Special Features: medicinal hot springs, waterfalls, and highest mountain in the Philippines.

**MT. DATA**

Located at Atok, Bokod, Tudlay, Kabayan, Kibungan, Mankayan, Impasugan, Benguet; Kaingan and Hunduan (Ifugao) and Bauko, Ennaso, Kayan and Sabangan (Mt. Province). Special Features: waterfalls, numerous springs, towering rocks, bottomless ravines, zig-zag road, temperate climate and pine forest.

**KUAPNIT-BALINSASAYAO**

Located at Baybay and Abuyog (Leyte). Special Features: panoramic and scientific.

**TONGONAN HOT SPRING**

Located at Ormoc (Leyte). Special Features: medicinal hot spring, recreational, and scientific.

**MAHAGNAO VOLCANO**

Located at Burauen and La Paz (Leyte). Special Features: medicinal hot spring, recreational, panoramic and scientific.

**CENTRAL CEBU**

Located at Balamban, Toledo and Cebu City. Special Features: scientific; only remaining forest in Cebu.

**AURORA MEMORIAL PARK**

Located at Bongabon, Nueva Ecija and Baler (Quezon). Special Features: swimming pools, spring, invigorating climate, scientific and game refuge.

**BIAK-NA-BATO**

Located at San Miguel (Bulacan). Special Features: historical, geological, panoramic and recreational.

**MT. DAJO**

Located at Patikul, Talipau, Jolo. Special Features: historical and game refuge.

**CARAMOAN**

Located at Caramoan (Camarines Sur). Special Features: caves, subterranean river and panoramic hills.

**MAYON VOLCANO**

Located at Albay, Camalig, Guinobatan, Sto. Domingo, Ligao, Manlilipot, Tabaco (Albay). Special Features: panoramic, scientific and recreational.

**MT. ISAROG**

Located at Naga, Calabanga, Tinambac, Goa, Tigaon and Pili (Camarines Sur). Special Features: health resort, wonderful canyons, gorges, ravines, waterfalls and game refuge.

**TIRAD PASS**

Located at Angaki, Concepcion, Bigay, Cervantes and Cuyo (Ilocos Sur). Special Feature: historical.

Located at Ilagan (Isabela). Special Features: caves, educational and recreational.

PAGSANJAN GORGE

Located at Cavinti and Lumban (Laguna). Special Features: waterfalls, gorges, natural swimming pools, panoramic and recreational.

BASILAN

Located at Lamitan (Basilan City). Special Features: waterfalls, natural swimming pools, virgin forest and game refuge.

MADO HOT SPRING

Located at Awang (Cotabato). Special Features: medicinal hot spring, recreational and health resort.

MANLALAUAG SPRING

Located at Mangatarem (Pangasinan). Special Features: medicinal hot spring, recreational and health resort.

RIZAL

Located at Dapitan (Zamboanga). Special Features: historical and panoramic.

HUNDRED ISLANDS

Located at Alaminos (Pangasinan). Special Features: unique physical composition of islands, recreational and scientific.

MTS. BANAHAW AND SAN CRISTOBAL

Located at San Pablo, Lilio, Nagcarlan, Rizal, Majayjay (Laguna); Sariaya, Candelaria and Dolores (Quezon). Special Features: panoramic and recreational.

BATAAN

Located at Hermosa, Orani, Samat, Abucay, Balanga, Pilar, Bagac and Moron (Bataan). Special Feature: historical.

QUEZON MEMORIAL PARK

Located at Diliman (Quezon City). Special Feature: recreational.

MANILA BAY BEACH RESORT

Located at Manila and Paranaque (Rizal). Special Features: recreational, scientific and health resort.

TIWI HOT SPRINGS

Located at Tiwi (Albay). Special Features: recreational, scientific and health resort.

BESSANG PASS

Located at Cervantes (Ilocos Sur). Special Feature: historical.

LAKE NAUJAN

Located at Naujan, Pola and Victoria (Oriental Mindoro). Special Features: scientific; breeding place for marsh birds.

MAINIT SPRINGS

Located at Compostela (Davao). Special Feature: medicinal hot spring.

LUNETA, MANILA

Located at the City of Manila. The largest open space in the heart of Manila, ideal for recreation. Includes site of Rizal monument and Quirino Stadium.

INITAO

Located at Initao (Misamis Oriental). Virgin forest, beautiful sandy beaches; recreational.

NORTHERN LUZON HEROES HILL

Located at B. Sulvec, Santa and Narvacan (Ilocos Sur). Special Features: lagoon, waterfalls, rock formations, Spanish tower, and historical.

# Golf Courses

| Clubs | Location |
| --- | --- |
| LUZON | |
| Baguio | Baguio City |
| Basa | Floridablanca, Pampanga |
| Binictican | Olongapo, Zambales |
| Caltex Refinery | Bauan, Batangas |
| Canlubang | Canlubang, Laguna |
| Capitol Hills | Quezon City |
| Clark | Clark Air Base, Pampanga |
| Dagupan | Dagupan City |
| Del Carmen | Floridablanca, Pampanga |
| Fernando Air Base | Lipa City, Batangas |
| Fort Aguinaldo | Quezon City |
| Fort Bonifacio | Makati, Rizal |
| Fort Del Pilar | Baguio City |
| Holiday Hills | San Pedro, Laguna |
| Isabela | Ilagan, Isabela |
| John Hay Air Base | Baguio City |
| Laguna | Santa Cruz, Laguna |
| Lepanto Divot Diggers | Lepanto, Mt. Province |
| Luisita | San Miguel, Tarlac |
| Malacañang | Malacañang Palace Grounds Manila |
| Mani | Porac, Pampanga |
| Manila | Makati, Rizal |
| Mansion House | Baguio City |
| Muni Golf Links | Manila |
| Muntinlupa | Muntinlupa, Rizal |
| Nichols | Pasay City |
| Nueva Eciji | Cabanatuan City |
| Princess Urduja | Lingayen, Pangasinan |
| Peninsula | Limay, Bataan |
| Paradise | Cutcut, Angeles, Pampanga |
| Sta. Ana Park | Makati, Rizal |
| Silvertown | Marikina, Rizal |
| Sunnyside | Laoag, Ilocos Norte |
| Taclobo | Tabangao, Batangas |
| U.P. | Quezon City |
| Valley | Antipolo, Rizal |
| Veterans | Quezon City |
| Wack Wack | Mandaluyong, Rizal |
| Pasumil | Del Carmen, Floridablanca Pampanga |
| VISAYAS | |
| Bacolod | Bacolod City |
| Cebu | Cebu City |
| Club Filipino de Cebu | Cebu City |
| Damaguete | Sibulan, Negros Oriental |
| Guinhalaran | Silay City, Negros Occidental |
| Iloilo | Sta. Barbara |
| Marapara | Bacolod City |
| Victorias Milling | Victorias, Negros Occidental |

| Clubs | Location |
| --- | --- |
| MINDANAO | |
| Apo Golf | Bago, Davao City |
| Cagayan de Oro | Cagayan de Oro City |
| Cotabato Golf | Nuling, Cotabato |
| New Davao | Matina, Davao City |
| Del Monte | Bukidnon |
| Zamboanga | Zamboanga City |
| Mt. Malindang | Ozamis City |

The sun has set over the Bay and a thousand clubs, theatres, restaurants and discos are advertised in an extravaganza of coloured, flashing lights. The day has ended. The night is just beginning. This is Manila! This is the Philippines!

# Notes on Photographic Equipment

For those interested in the technical aspects of photography the following equipment was used.

*Equipment:*

(a) Rolleiflex Models "T" (f/3.5 75mm Carl Zeiss Tessar); the f/2.8 (80mm Carl Zeiss Planar); and the f/3.5 (100mm Carl Zeiss).
These are $2\frac{1}{4}$" square, twin-lens reflex cameras produced by Franke & Heidecke in Braunschweig, Western Germany. I realise there *are* $2\frac{1}{4}$" square cameras made with interchangeable lenses but after long experience in practically every part of the world I have found that only a Rolleiflex is tough enough to withstand tremendous rough usage and continue to function accurately in all climates. Rolleiflexes are the most expensive cameras of their type but they will give a lifetime of service.

(b) The Canon QLFT with the following lens/shutter assemblies, all with lens hoods:
　f/3.5　19mm Canon FL
　f/2.5　35mm Canon FL
　f/1.4　50mm Canon FL
　f/2.5 135mm Canon FL
　f/3.5 200mm Canon FL (This is about the maximum focal length that can be hand-held without utilizing a shutter speed of about 1/1000 second and/or a tripod.)

*Exposure Meter:*
A Weston Master V with invercone for incident light readings; particularly useful for colour work.

*Filters:*
A standard range of colour correction filters used only in light conditions of extremely high or low colour temperature; an ultraviolet filter and a "pola" screen for selective control over (1) reflections from non-metallic objects and (2) light from a clear blue sky when at right-angles to the direction of the sun; a "pola" screen is the only means of darkening a blue sky without distorting the colour reproduction of other objects.

*Film:*
All photographs were made on Kodak Ektachrome-X, daylight type, and exposed for the recommended ASA rating of 64. Film was processed by Kodak in Manila.
No artificial light sources of any kind were employed.